What If?

Alternative Views of Twentieth-Century Ireland

Diarmaid Ferriter

Gill & Macmillan

Published by Gill & Macmillan Ltd
Hume Avenue, Park West, Dublin 12
with associated companies throughout the world
www.gillmacmillan.ie

© Diarmaid Ferriter 2006
ISBN–13: 978 07171 3990 3
ISBN–10: 0 7171 3990 5

Type design: Make Communication
Typesetting and print origination: Carrigboy Typesetting Services, County Cork
Printed by ColourBooks Ltd., Dublin

This book is typeset in Linotype Minion and Neue Helvetica.

The paper used in this book comes from the wood pulp of managed forests.
For every tree felled, at least one tree is planted, thereby renewing natural resources.

A CIP catalogue record for this book is available from the British Library.

5 4 3 2

What If?

Alternative Views of Twentieth-Century Ireland

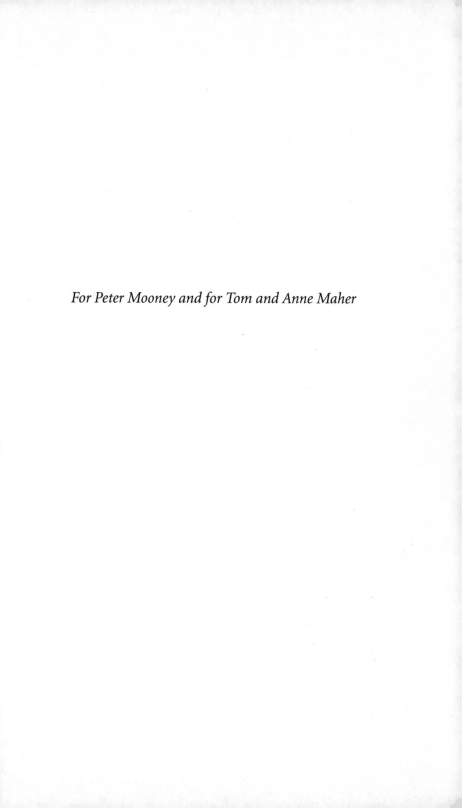

For Peter Mooney and for Tom and Anne Maher

Contents

Acknowledgements

RTÉ Radio One Producer Peter Mooney came up with the idea for the programme on which this book is based and deserves my gratitude for his production of the shows, which involved hard work, good humour in and outside of the studio, originality, professionalism, generosity, and attention to detail. I am also grateful to Lorelei Harris, the editor of Features and Arts on Radio One; Joe Taylor for doing the voice recordings when needed; Robert Canning, Ian Murray, Paula Maher and Brian Rice from the RTÉ sound archives, and Gavin Burke in the RTÉ television archives, who were invaluable in finding the archival clips for the programmes. Thanks also to the RTÉ technical staff whose patience and perseverance got the programme on air every week. I am also grateful for the insightful contributions of the guests who appeared on the show: Margaret O'Callaghan, Mary Daly, Margaret MacCurtain, John Cooney, Eunan O'Halpin, Tom Garvin, Sam Smyth, Pat Leahy, Alex White, Ann Marie Hourihane, Pauric Travers, Ultan Cowley, Martin Mansergh, Michael Kennedy, Catriona Crowe, Eoghan Corry, Ronan Furlong, Ivana Bacik, Colm Tóibín, June Levine, Mark O'Connell, Stephen O'Byrnes, Barry Desmond, Maurice Manning, Brian Hanley, Mary O'Rourke, Joe O'Toole, Terry Dolan, Éilís Ní Dhuibhne, Liam O'Dowd, John Coakley, David McCullagh, Fintan O'Toole, John Waters, Alan Titley, Caoilfhionn Nic Pháidín, Dave Fanning, Barry Devlin, Mark O'Brien, Míchéal Foley, Richard Sinnott, Frank Flannery, David Andrews, Brian Trench, Sinéad McCoole, John Regan, David Neligan, Ruth Barrington, John FitzGerald, Tom Stack, Val Mulkearns, Finola Kennedy, Mags O'Brien, Marie Mulholland, Peter Ward, Míchéal MacGréil, Bernard McGuckian, Martin Breheny, Liz Howard, Michael Laffan, Marnie Hay; and to all who listened and responded to the programmes. Thanks also to Catriona Crowe, Paul Rouse and Greg Prendergast for suggestions and advice, and Anne Maher and Nollaig Feirtéir for their skill and expertise.

I am grateful to Fergal Tobin for the invitation to write this book and to the staff of Gill & Macmillan for their help and professionalism.

Once again, my thanks to the staff of St Patrick's College, especially James Kelly and my other colleagues in the History Department.

As usual, I am indebted to all the Ferriters and Mahers, most especially to Sheila and Enya, who make these things possible with their love, support, humour and humanity, and who are the centre of my world.

Introduction

'An extravagance of the imagination?'

In the autumn of 2003, I presented a new RTÉ radio series called *What If?* in which some of the key events, personalities and milestones of the twentieth century were assessed by means of looking at possible alternative endings. Over the course of the following eighteen months, 35 such programmes were broadcast, covering social, political, economic, cultural and sporting matters.

It was a concept some academics may have baulked at. Professional historians can sometimes be distinctly uncomfortable, if not utterly cynical, about the notion of speculating on alternatives, or 'counterfactual history' as it is formally described. A typical response to those intent on speculating is 'why bother?' as nobody knows what would have happened, and the possibilities are endless. Another angle on this is that there are very sound reasons for not exploring 'what ifs'; historians have enough to be doing finding out what actually did happen, and need to concentrate their energies and research skills on locating sources and information that will shed light on the facts; that even with events that we believe have been well documented, there will always be more information to be uncovered to relay adequately what actually did happen.

It is an understandable scepticism that has been articulated quite fiercely by some well-known historians. In 1997, a book edited by Niall Ferguson was published, entitled *Virtual History: Alternatives and Counterfactuals*, in which leading historians speculated on, amongst other things, England without Cromwell, the First World War without British involvement, the enactment of Home Rule in Ireland in 1912, a German invasion of Britain in May 1940, 1989 without Gorbachev, and no assassination of John F. Kennedy in 1963.[1]

In his introduction, Ferguson detailed some criticisms that had been made about forays into counterfactual history. He quoted E. H. Carr who maintained that it was a mere 'parlour game' and 'a red herring'; that 'history is a record of what people did, not what they failed to do'. The assessment of the English philosopher, Michael Oakeshott, was also cited:

> The distinction . . . between essential and incidental events does not belong to historical thought at all; it is a monstrous incursion of science into the world of history . . . a pure myth, an extravagance of the imagination.

The historian E. P. Thompson was more succinct, but certainly no less damning. The whole counterfactual exercise, he suggested, was 'unhistorical shit'.[2] For the purists, perhaps it is, but for many more, it can be enormously entertaining and illuminating, particularly when the speculations of the radio programme are based not on wild flights of fancy, but on very real possibilities, or documentary evidence from an archive, and when the programme's guests are not just from academic history departments, but include journalists, novelists, economists, politicians, musicians, priests and community activists. History, after all, is far too important to be left to historians. The great R. B. McDowell of the history department at Trinity College Dublin, still striding about Dublin city as a nonagenarian at the beginning of the twenty-first century, warned some years ago that 'there can be the danger of getting into a closed room in which the experts chat to and fro and impinge very little on the outside world. I do not want to see history in that room'.[3] Neither did those involved in this programme.

It also seemed to me that the programme was an effective way of 'humanising' history—reflecting on the achievements and failures of Irish independence, the progress made and the lost opportunities, and the manner in which individuals related history to their own lives and experiences. It is surely one of the functions of historians to keep asking questions as well as attempting to answer them; to continue to question their own assumptions.

Put the guests into a studio for a live discussion on a Sunday morning and the results can be very satisfying for both participants and listeners. Some were solemn, some whimsical or satirical and some facetious; but what they all had in common was a willingness to explore, speculate and discuss the significance of what actually had happened. One of the added advantages was that many of the guests had been active participants in the events and controversies under discussion and were able to give a good insight into how past and present intersect.

Often, the 'what if' question was simply used as a starting point or a springboard for a general discussion of seminal moments in twentieth-century Irish history; some programmes were based on a single 'what if'; others threw out a whole host of them. The producer of this series, Peter Mooney, spent many hours in the RTÉ archives, sourcing the archival clips that punctuated the shows, in order to give listeners a sense of times past, and to illuminate the discussions between the two guests and myself each week. We could have had more, but felt that to allow a free-flowing discussion, two would suffice.

Despite the scepticism documented by Ferguson and others, many leading Irish historians have indulged in the counterfactual exercise, either implicitly or explicitly; indeed, one of the main features of the 'revisionist' debate that influenced the writing of Irish history from the 1970s onwards was the contention that the Irish revolution in the 1916–21 period was unnecessary; that independence could have been achieved by constitutional means and without the bloodshed of the War of Independence. Even when not writing an essay in counterfactual history, historians and political scientists have often found it necessary to speculate in order to fine-tune their assessment of what actually did happen. In 1991, in a publication to mark the 75th anniversary of the 1916 Rising, Tom Garvin, Professor of Politics at University College Dublin, and a regular guest on the programme, wrote the following:

> There is a common argument to the effect that the violent birth of modern Independent Ireland was in some way foolish and unnecessary, because the democratic politics of consensus, reasoning and bargaining would have achieved independence

more easily and without bloodshed. Let me speculate briefly on what might have happened had the Rising not taken place. With the arrival home of the veterans in 1919, and with the discredited Redmondites still holding on in Westminster, armed nationalism (which would have returned from the trenches with rather pronounced opinions about the British establishment and its right to rule anybody) would have been alienated fatally from constitutional nationalism. An incoherent but vicious sectarian war between North and South, with no new generation of political leaders in place, could easily have occurred. The Rising redefined the quarrel as one between two vaguely defined entities, England and Ireland, rather than one between Catholics and Protestants.[4]

The renowned historian of Ulster unionism, Alvin Jackson, contributed an essay of over 50 pages to the Ferguson book, speculating on what would have happened if home rule had been imposed on Ireland in 1912, noting that 'the 1912 Bill, suitably presented, had a greater chance of success than its predecessors [in 1886 and 1893], and is therefore an intellectually more valuable focus for counterfactual speculation.' He concluded that 'the price paid by all the Irish for a unitary state might well have been higher than the price paid for partition; an unstable thirty-two county Ireland, as opposed to an unstable six-county Northern Ireland . . . had Ulster Unionists been eased into a home rule Ireland, then it is just conceivable that a stable pluralist democracy might have swiftly emerged. But it would have been a high risk strategy, with every possibility that a short-term political triumph for Liberal statesmanship might have been bought at the price of a delayed apocalypse.'[5]

The pioneer of women's history in Ireland, Margaret MacCurtain, another guest on the series, co-edited in 1978 a seminal collection of essays on the historical dimension of women in Irish society, and she, too, found herself wondering about alternatives when assessing the contribution of women to one of the most important parliamentary debates and votes in twentieth-century Ireland, at the time of the Anglo-Irish Treaty of December 1921. Referring to the five women in the Dáil at that time, she wrote:

The unanimity and powerful rhetoric of the women's speeches in the Treaty debate where one and all took the republican side has not yet received an explanation fully satisfying . . . what is clear from their speeches was their inflexible and doctrinaire republicanism. Their political ideology had not kept pace with the change in atmosphere after World War I. Had they been more constitutionally agile in the Treaty debate they might well have held the balance of power between the two sides. Five of the six women in the First Dáil were relatives of men executed in 1916, or killed in the Anglo-Irish War. Mrs Pearse, Mrs Clarke, Mary Mac Swiney, Mrs O'Callaghan, Dr Ada English, all suffered loss of their men folk, and Markievicz had been through the rebellion. This electoral mechanism rapidly became a criterion for selection of women to the Dáil and to this day has been carried into the party system of the southern state. Irish women in post revolutionary Ireland did not make the political traditions; they inherited them from fathers, husbands and brothers.[6]

These words were written in a book that, even nearly twenty years later, MacCurtain saw as an expression of the vitality of the intellectual and creative energy of the 1970s, when those from a generation who grew to adulthood after the tumultuous events of the Irish revolution were not afraid to question what had happened, and what they believed could or perhaps should have happened.

Another great excavator of twentieth-century Ireland, Joe Lee, also seemed to suggest that counterfactual ideas went to the heart of all historical discussion, and should be encouraged as a means of getting historians to be more adventurous in pursuing lines of inquiry. He offered this definition of history:

History is not merely what happened. That is mere chronology. History is what happened in the light of what might have happened and to understand what might have happened one has to have a historical sense about potential alternatives over a longer period.[7]

It is that definition of history that went to the heart of the *What If?* programme, but it also served to fulfil other important functions, by drawing attention to neglected themes and personalities, and rescuing from obscurity individuals who had made profound contributions to the development of modern Ireland; by introducing the research of a new generation to test the old theories and hypotheses, and asking representatives of two generations to assess the same event.

The programmes revealed an enduring interest in trying to answer the following questions: When did the transition from a 'traditional' to a 'modern' Irish society occur? How important were the views and policies of the post-Civil War generation? Has the impact and legacy of the de Valera generation been exaggerated? How corrupt is Irish politics? How effective have Irish journalists and Irish television and radio been? Was Ireland a cultural wasteland for much of the twentieth century? Do we need to reassess the icons of Irish independence? Could Ireland have been richer sooner? How do those who reached adulthood during that decade now view the 1980s? Has the impact of the rise and decline of Irish Catholicism been adequately analysed? In the course of attempting to answer these questions, the guests, and the clips from the archives, offered many fascinating vignettes of modern Irish history.

Key players in the events discussed often found themselves posing the what if question in the midst of their participation in various dramas, or even the workings of government. In 1983, Ann Marie Hourihane, a passionate member of the anti-amendment side during the pro-life amendment referendum campaign in 1983, was just one of many activists who believed that the 'what if' question went to the heart of the abortion issue—'What if a girl became pregnant as a result of rape? What if there was a danger of a pregnant woman dying?'[8]

At a more general, and perhaps trivial, level, there will undoubtedly always be much interest in alternative scenarios/ endings, because we all reflect on the what ifs of our lives almost every day of the week. Who has not drifted into a daydream that centres around the possible alternative routes a life could have taken? And what, in any case, is wrong with 'an extravagance of the imagination'? Life would be a lot duller without such extravagance.

Chapter 1

What if there had been no *Late Late Show*?

On New Year's Eve 1961, the first broadcast of Ireland's domestic television service featured addresses by the President of Ireland, Eamon de Valera, and the primate of all Ireland, Cardinal D'Alton. The Cardinal blessed the station with the following words:

> On this New Year's morning, I ask you all to join with me in praying that God may abundantly bless Telefís Éireann, may the Holy Spirit guide the directors in their work, so that this new and important venture in our national life [may] become an asset and an ornament to our country.

Both men issued warnings about the potential negative effects of television, indicative of an apprehension felt by many. Modern media, they seemed to suggest, had the potential to disturb an isolated nation on the fringe of Europe. D'Alton mentioned the possibility of addiction to the new medium, while de Valera, then aged 79, had the following to say:

> I must admit that sometimes when I think of television and radio and their immense power, I feel somewhat afraid. Like atomic energy, it can be used for incalculable good, but it can also do irreparable harm. Never before was there in the hands of men an instrument so powerful to influence the thoughts and actions of

the multitude. The persistent policy pursued over radio and television, apart from imparting knowledge, can build up the character of the whole people, inducing a sturdiness and vigour and confidence. On the other hand, it can lead to demoralisation and decadence and disillusion.[1]

Initially, the television service was largely confined to Leinster, but growth throughout all of Ireland followed rapidly, and by the end of 1965, it was estimated that there were 350,000 homes in the country with televisions, representing more than half the households nationwide. There were a few television programmes that seemed to encourage the ventilation of problems that had long gone unmentioned, in public at least. So animated did one politician—the redoubtable Fine Gael TD, Oliver J. Flanagan—become, that he famously complained, 'there was no sex in Ireland before television'.[2]

The *Late Late Show* will forever be associated with encouraging more frank and open discussion in this regard. What began in 1962 as a summer-filler show, hosted by Gay Byrne, went on to become the longest-running chat show in the world. Prior to the *Late Late*, Byrne had worked at Granada Television and presented *Open House* on BBC; he was utterly professional, did not indulge in the drinking that was common in media circles, and preferred to stay, in the words of Michael Parkinson, 'on the fringe of everything', when it came to socialising.

Byrne himself recalled that the first four *Late Late* programmes were 'utterly detested and hated';[3] after its initial run, Byrne was replaced by Frank Hall, who proved a disappointment, and Byrne agreed to return, on the condition that he could also produce the show.

Various, often extravagant, claims have been made about its impact. There is much truth in Byrne's own simple contention, that 'we looked at new ways of entertaining and that was it',[4] and he certainly did not see himself as remotely socially radical. One of the strengths of the show was its format, to which Irish audiences responded very well; they could watch discussions and debates in a free-flowing manner, much as they might observe at home or in the pub. Essentially what Byrne was doing was experimenting, by redeploying the American chat-show format, but with a native twist, or an element of seeming 'adhoc-ery', in which all three elements were crucial: the presenter, the panel and the audience. But the seeming casualness belied the careful planning and co-ordination that went into the show. This was ultimately about show business, with the row or heated discussion coming at the end; it was also risky, in the sense that it was always a gamble to have an unedited live show, a risk few twenty-first-century hosts will take or, indeed, be allowed to take.

Was it really the great moderniser of Irish society? What if there had been no *Late Late Show*? Would we still be in the dark?

The two guests on this programme, which opened with a clip that enlivened many people's weekend ('Ladies and gentlemen, to whom it concerns. . .') were novelist Colm Tóibín, who had previously written about the show and Byrne's impact in the 1980s, suggesting, 'he is like the priest who manages the affairs of the parish. Behind the mystery of the mass lies cold hard work. He is generally quiet spoken, but he is also ruthless; he wants things done',[5] and feminist June Levine, author of the acclaimed *Sisters*, the story of the personal voyage of an Irish feminist, who had worked as a researcher on the *Late Late Show* in the early years.

I was anxious that this show would not become a fawning *Late Late* love-in, and would address both the strengths and weaknesses of the show, and, indeed, of its host, though using the word 'weaknesses' in relation to Gay Byrne is still regarded as slightly blasphemous by many. It is a measure of his iconic status that few will utter a bad word about him, and, to his credit, his broadcasting skills have not been bettered. Even his critics would acknowledge that, despite what they may have thought of him, he always had the trump card of being able to present them with the biggest publicity coup they could get—to be featured as a guest. In 1984, for example, Tony Gregory, Mick Rafferty and Fergus McCabe of the North City Centre Community Action Project criticised Byrne for constantly emphasising on his radio programme the negative side of parts of the inner city, but Gregory acknowledged, 'he also presented us with the *Late Late Show* which was the biggest thing we'd had.'[6]

There was also a certain insecurity that pervaded Byrne's relationship with RTÉ; for most of the time, he was on three-month contracts, was refused significant pay rises, lived a very regimented life, and, in his own words, until a very late stage in his career, when competition opened up in Irish television, he 'never felt secure in an industry that was run as a monopoly . . . if you took a break, someone could come in and be better than you'.[7]

In the midst of debate about the impact of his show, Byrne had consistently maintained that he was facilitator rather than innovator; that he could not impose a discussion on a society that was not ready for it. On the face of it, this seems to suggest generous modesty on Byrne's part; but it could also have been defensive— Byrne always had to protect his various, often vast, viewing constituencies, so the idea of him as 'host' and not 'instigator' was important, and rarely did his mask or his professionalism slip. As early as 1972, he had suggested that his success was a result not of his own vision, but of observing the skills of others: 'I think it could be said that Eamonn Andrews is responsible for most of it'.[8] Most people born in Ireland from the 1950s on will remember their first opportunity to watch the *Late Late*. Tóibín remembered that, growing up in Wexford in the 1960s, the children of the house

were banned from watching it. I was born in 1955 and it was the one thing you were not allowed to see and it was the one thing you kept asking about. Despite all the cartoons, all the other things that were on, it was the thing you wanted most to see, because I think all the adults watched it in a very serious way. The door was closed and the children were sent to bed and as you got to a certain age, you'd say, 'When I'm what age will I be able to watch the *Late Late Show*?' which was a sort of rite of passage. The first time I was brought down from my bed to watch it was not when an enormous sort of cataclysm took place in Irish society, but when Lieutenant Gerard from *The Fugitive*, who'd been searching for the one-armed man all the time, when he appeared on the *Late Late Show*, it was felt he would be suitable for me. But once it was over, you never knew, because they never announced in advance who was coming on next and it could be a nun who didn't believe in being a nun or it could be someone talking about sex and there had never been talk about sex in our house. I remember sometime,

I must have been let watch it from the age of 11 or 12, but I remember one night when Conor Cruise O'Brien and Máire Mhac an tSaoi came on together and Máire said that there were couples who had been married for many years who had never seen one another naked and, I can tell you, the silence . . . now I'm talking about an extended family, not the nuclear family, but aunts, uncles, maybe even a visitor, 12-year-olds, 13-year-olds, all of us watched— 'Máire Mhac an tSaoi said "naked" on the *Late Late Show*!' There weren't headlines the next day, but it was that sort of silence that caused people really to worry. You couldn't turn it off—no one had a zapper—you could have run over to turn it off but that would have been considered square. So it began for me by being forbidden, and then became immensely interesting with great moments of pure embarrassment and, as I say, a great amount of Hollywood in it—any actor who was passing through town would be on it as well, so the show business and whatever things that were unsayable in Irish life were mixed together.

Any discussion of sex was, of course, as mesmerising to the audience as it was uncomfortable. There was a simple reason for this, maintained Tóibín: there were so many people 'who had never heard about sex'; indeed, he went so far as to suggest that there was a whole generation of people who would have lived and died in twentieth-century Ireland without ever having heard any discussion about sex if there had been no *Late Late Show*. To that extent, at least, Oliver J. Flanagan was absolutely right. But Tóibín also remembered programmes on issues such as compulsory Irish, and the emergence of young intellectuals like Garret FitzGerald, who, perhaps, in contrast to the previous generation of public intellectuals and politicians, were only delighted to hot foot it down to RTÉ to get a slice of the action, particularly because there 'was nothing that wasn't up for grabs'.

I asked June Levine about comments she had made in her autobiography concerning Gay Byrne's attitude to women. She conceded that he was a chauvinist:

He was never a pig, but he was a bit chauvinistic in those days and he improved as time went on. He was the first person to give us feminists a serious platform and he gave us the whole show, and

Senator Mary Robinson came in to chair it and it went very well. Every issue was aired, and I think the wonderful thing about the *Late Late Show* was that the people of Ireland could participate— it was their first platform, if you like, because no matter what show came after that, the magic of the show, for me, was always the unexpected. You had panellists, you had extended panels in the audience and you never knew what these ordinary people of Ireland, who'd come in from wherever, were going to say about any subject. On the subject of the women's movement, it got to every woman in Ireland, so that later, a couple of weeks later, when we all met in the Mansion House for our very first public meeting, not everyone could get in, it was so jammed.

But was it the case that, with the research team, there was an element of hostility towards radicals?

If the item was going to be interesting, if it was going to get people talking, I don't think Gay would have given a hoot what we were going to talk about. For instance, I did a show on an unmarried mother—the first unmarried mother on Irish television, and she told her whole story from start to finish and people were absolutely amazed at this, and I'm sure Colm would have been sent to bed! It was an amazing thing in Ireland at that time, and we're talking now about the 1970s, when, you know, so many Irish women had gone to England pregnant to return 'virgins' once again. And, yet, the unmarried-mother programme raised a huge fuss.

Aside from sex, and women's liberation, what were the other issues that Tóibín remembered?

Well, there were figures like Fergal O'Connor who were, I suppose, liberal priests, who were constantly on the show. And there was great debate at the time—it seems like a crazy debate now—about compulsory Irish; figures like John B. Keane on the show and, oddly enough, somebody like Garret FitzGerald, really making his name on the *Late Late Show*, coming on constantly, talking about various issues [Levine intervened to remind that 'he ran in from his fireside when the women were on']. Yes, and of course, you'd always have members of your family who wouldn't like one of them. Fergal O'Connor would come on—'Oh, that fella's on again'

or 'Look at him!'—you know, the people of Ireland developed a
relationship with the show and, of course, at the beginning, there
was an amazing number run by Ulick O'Connor and Denis
Franks. Franks had a more English accent, Ulick a more Dublin
one, and they went at each other, and of course people had never
heard that level of (a) eloquence and (b) of every issue being up
for grabs. There were people, incidentally, who never came on.
Charles Haughey sidled on once on a programme about the
Dubliners, to shake hands with Ronnie Drew, but he never sat in
the chair to be asked the questions. In other words, there were
certain people who wouldn't do it because it was unpredictable. I
remember when Des O'Malley went to do it, and thought he could
launch the Progressive Democrats on it, and it didn't quite work
for him. You could never judge it.

Did Levine believe politicians were scared of it?

They weren't as scared as they would be now. I think that was the
wonderful thing about the *Late Late*. People were innocent. We
didn't have multi-channel television. People hadn't travelled a lot,
air travel wasn't cheap. So, people, including politicians, were quite
innocent. It was amazing after you were on the *Late Late* to walk
down Grafton Street the next day, and be stopped every ten
minutes and people arguing with you or disagreeing with you.
They didn't know that was going to happen to them. But nowadays
they do, and I would think that people are much more careful now.

But in terms of arguments and combativeness, did Byrne have the
instincts of a Rottweiler? Levine put it simply: 'When he was cross,
like most of us, he could be pretty cross'
Tóibín elaborated:

He did an amazing attack on John Feeney, for example, who came
on as a sort of left-wing student who had been picketing churches.
He had long hair, sitting on the panel, and Gay Byrne went for
him. And he went for him in a way which was unusual for him. In
other words, he started a tirade of his own.

Levine counteracted with the suggestion that:

I think he had this magical way of being able to pick up what the ordinary person at their fireside was thinking. You can be sure that if he attacked Feeney, then people in your family were ready to do the same and were cheering him on. Because that was the wonderful thing about the show. He did speak for the people of Ireland. And he gave them a voice. There were many, many issues and we had to know about them. I really firmly believe that the *Late Late* did Ireland a service. We hadn't talked about anything important to each other. We hadn't discussed any of the important things in life to each other or with each other. You couldn't talk about sex; you couldn't talk seriously about spirituality. You couldn't talk about changes in the church. I remember interviewing Hans Küng, who was probably my favourite interviewee of all time, and he was like a breath of fresh air and he was on the *Late Late*, and the wonderful part about any show was that the audience could put a hand up and be heard and these were drawn from the plain people of Ireland. It wasn't rehearsed or scripted. I remember absolutely and clearly it wasn't rehearsed. What happened was that I went and interviewed somebody and talked to Gay about it and wrote down cogent points on a card and then he took that, and then the next thing I saw was when he had the guest on the show and he spoke to the guest and referred to the cards. Now, he very seldom departed from the cards. He had these bits of information there and we had what we called an extended panel. Some people called them plants—they weren't plants; they were people who were interested in the subject or educated about the subject and they were invited to come along and then the rest of the audience were just people who had tickets, and you never knew what was going to come out.

Tóibín observed, 'His written-down questions were only the beginning—the first ten minutes. The rest was what was unpredictable.'

But what of the times his mask slipped? To get a flavour of some of the more controversial aspects of Byrne's interview style, and, indeed, his own personal preferences, an archival clip of Byrne interviewing Annie Murphy, mother of Bishop Eamon Casey's son Peter, was played. Murphy was on to promote the book, *Forbidden Fruit*, which highlighted her affair with Casey. An obviously hostile Byrne was giving her a hard time. ('He would say, Annie, he didn't have faith in your capacity as a mother . . . if

Peter is half the man his father is, he'll be doing well'. Murphy gave him a withering look and replied, 'I'm not so bad myself', and stormed off set as the interview concluded). Tóibín suggested that Byrne on this occasion had let his mask slip, that it was:

> a very strange moment where he seemed almost to lose it . . . there was something about her that he didn't like. He's not somebody with strong opinions and he dislikes strong opinions though he sees the show-business potential of them. He dislikes strident people but he loves a performer. And for him, in all the years, Eamon Casey had been on the *Late Late Show*, a great performer; he'd sing, he'd laugh, he'd talk—he was a great guest on the show and you've got people like that; Gay lit up when he saw them because he knew, 'This guy's going to light up my show', and that's all he cared about. It wasn't that he was pro-Catholic or pro-clerical or anti-clerical or anti-women or pro-women; it was merely that there was somebody like Eamon Casey that for him would have been someone he liked enormously but with something like the Annie Murphy interview—that was a very, very strange moment when he seemed almost to lose it. He seemed to say something quite cruel and unnecessary to her—information he didn't have. Somehow something about her he didn't like and you very seldom got to see that. Terribly interesting.

Levine also noted that Byrne did not like surprises, or losing control and direction. I put it to her that there were issues that the *Late Late* avoided; that there were still taboo subjects such as child abuse and paedophilia not being discussed. She rejected this: 'I lived in Ireland at that time. I did not know the extent of what was going on and I think I was pretty wide awake. I had no idea. It was well covered up and it's emerging now, but I wouldn't have been able to sit quietly if I'd known the way some children were being treated, the way helpless poor orphans were being treated.'

Of course, with the passage of time, and an Irish television audience's exposure to other channels, the show was likely to lose some of its power and novelty, even shock value. Most things that were taboo had been articulated by the early 1980s; the issues that had caused shock on the *Late Late* in the 1960s and 1970s did not register the same impact any longer. For the show to continue to be relevant and interesting, it needed a host who could sense the winds of change, but also what turned people off. In that sense, Byrne and his researchers were quite lucky; they came to prominence at a time when a number of controversial issues were surfacing—contraception, the manning of the barricades in Northern Ireland, the role of the laity in the post-Vatican II Catholic Church, for example.

There were public perceptions about many of these issues; but when people were presented with the reality, as articulated by guests, there was often surprise. Probably the most effective thing it did was to demonstrate that there was a context for these issues, but was it the case that, 20 years later, the show was not the best forum for breaking new ground, and how important did the radio show become? Byrne seemed to become a replacement for the priest, in the sense of him listening to the confessions, live on air, of thousands of Irish women. He commanded 800,000 home listeners; he believed that it was acceptable that the personal views of the presenter should emerge (and he sometimes annoyed his producers, including Alex White, who found his attitude to law and order 'very irritating'. Byrne described his attitude on this subject as 'not quite hang 'em and flog 'em, but something must be done').[9]

Tóibín was adamant:

The power moved from the television programme to the radio programmes sometime in the early 1980s and the number of very, very memorable radio programmes when he had what was basically a housewives' choice programme. It began as that and there was often consumer items—were you getting better value in Dunnes Stores or Superquinn, and so on. But because of that, and because there were breaks for music, if he stopped to do an item, on the death of Ann Lovett, for example, or on areas like abortion, areas in the 1980s which were controversial . . . the two programmes would sort of feed into each other in certain ways. I think that it became more difficult in that show-business environment, with breaks for music and with the need to get somebody on from Hollywood, to do those big tragic things that happened in the 1980s in the same sort of way on television; I felt the show lost its power. People also started to go out a lot more—much more, I think, on a Saturday night. Or maybe I just got older and things wouldn't shock me. But certainly there was nothing you could really say about the church that hadn't been said. A lot of those issues that were aired were sort of over by then and I think the show grew tired, but I think the radio show grew increasingly robust and somehow he fed it in, and the sort of power he got from the *Late Late Show* added enormously to the radio show.

An archival clip was also played of Gay Byrne interviewing Gerry Adams (in which Adams rejected the contention in Byrne's introduction that Adams was 'the most controversial man in Ireland'—Byrne had been told by RTÉ not to shake his hand), and in which Hugh Leonard attacked Adams while Byrne looked on. I posed the question as to whether Byrne was the right person to be interviewing politicians.

Tóibín responded:

I think the most significant thing is that there's no interview with Adams that I've seen or heard that wasn't like what Lloyd George said about de Valera in 1921—like picking up mercury with a fork—and that it simply had to be done in some way—he had to be challenged and the decision was made to do that. The main interest was that the North was back on the agenda—there was a new era in the North and the *Late Late* could start dealing with it again. It was very powerful to watch and what was very interesting about the *Late Late* was how fickle the audience could be. The audience could applaud the person you didn't agree with and the way in which Hugh Leonard, though he seemed to me to be right, lost the plot with Adams and Adams remained calm, Adams remained the peacemaker, Hugh Leonard sounded like the aggressor. In other words, that television itself was the problem rather than the *Late Late Show*. Again, it was one of those moments where you realise, this is a significant change going on, watching Adams present himself in this way, watching him suddenly emerge as being a figure of the centre, and watching Gay allowing that to occur since that was the natural way the programme was going; not intervening, not stopping it—he never stood in the way of history as it were, he merely brought it to you, showed it to you. So, influence is a funny business: he was never influential in the programmes he stopped; perhaps on the programmes he made, but he was influential in the way he represented the flow and allowed the flow to continue and that programme is a significant version of that.

Levine added: 'and they talked about it all week afterwards, didn't they? I remember the programme on death by Colm Hutchinson and there was no entertainment, just the whole time talking about death. I mean, people had been dying in Ireland forever, but nobody ever talked about it.'

So, what, in the final analysis, would Irish society have been like without the *Late Late Show*? (Byrne hosted his last show in May 1999.) Would the silence around the traditionally taboo subjects have been broken anyway? Both Levine and Tóibín felt that this was a show that made a great difference to people. Tóibín addressed a fundamental reality of the show's impact. Despite the traditional thesis on the show—that it was the great moderniser of Irish society—he maintained that it was not about the conservative fear that television would break an intact culture, but about communication at its most important. It was an antidote to loneliness, and, looking back, it can be asserted that were very many lonely people who saw the show as a constant and welcome presence in their lives at the weekend:

Dev's and everyone's worry was that theirs was an intact culture in Ireland that television could suddenly interrupt and destroy. It actually wasn't like that; there was a great deal of loneliness and there was a great deal of very, very intelligent people who had left school at 14, who had no way of hearing what was going on in the outside world and of hearing that challenged. While you could have religious affairs programmes or current affairs programmes, having things challenged in a forum whereby it was unexpected was immensely interesting for very intelligent people. I wrote a novel, *The Blackwater Lightship*, where I have an old woman living in an isolated place and she loved the programme because it brought to her that outside world and she loved more than anything the arguments, the rows, the shouting and the next guest—not knowing who it was going to be—and sitting there, uninterrupted, watching them, hating some of the shows. Not only some of the people, but also there were some very dull nights sometimes—'Oh, the *Late Late Show* last night was just terrible!'

What about an Ireland without the *Late Late Show*? The issues it touched on, suggested Levine, would have emerged—'They'd have had to come to light with multi-channel TV but more slowly and with less fun.'

Tóibín concluded:

I think it picked up a flow and went with the flow rather than created the flow. But it also meant the early days of Irish television were immensely important and powerful in all parts of Ireland and made a great difference to people. In a way, it didn't just entertain them, it did much more for them, but the flow was starting and the genius was to catch it at exactly the right moment as the wave was breaking each time it broke on the issues: feminism, on the North, on all the other issues, even on Hollywood—to get all these things and catch them as they broke and drop them when they dropped too far.

Levine added:

I'm sure that's true. But the fact is that it was Gay Byrne, and he was the first and he was there, and perhaps it could have been somebody else. I personally do not think there would have been somebody else as good as he was and I think it's a sad thing that shows are going on now and they're being compared to Gay. It's like comparing Marilyn Monroe with another person who isn't Marilyn Monroe.

Chapter 2

What if there had been no pro-life amendment referendum in 1983?

O n 7 September 1983, the Irish electorate was asked to decide the fate of the proposed eighth amendment to the Constitution—what was otherwise known as the 'abortion referendum'. At the time of the amendment, each year, approximately 3,600 women who sought abortions in Britain were giving Irish addresses.[1] The text of the amendment, originally introduced by Dr Michael Woods, Fianna Fáil Minister for Health, read:

> The state acknowledges the right to life of the unborn and, with due regard to the equal right to the life of the mother, guarantees in its laws to respect, and, as far as is practicable, by its laws to defend and vindicate that right.

In the event, the amendment was endorsed by 66.45 per cent of those who voted. 'Bitter' and 'divisive' have been the two words most frequently used to describe the referendum campaign. It has also been referred to as a watershed in Irish politics, and 'the second partitioning of Ireland'.[2] It was, according to Nell McCafferty, 'the weight of the pig ignorant slurry of woman-hating that did us temporarily down'. In contrast, William Binchy of the Pro-Life Amendment Campaign insisted that the amendment was 'desperately necessary.'[3] Given the emotiveness of such language, and the obvious passions the campaign engendered, it is surprising that only 55.6 per cent of the electorate actually voted. The archival clip which opened this programme included a contemporary news report to the effect that:

> The country has voted by a majority of two to one in favour of the constitutional amendment in relation to abortion. The Pro-Life Amendment Campaign said the purpose for which it was formed had been achieved. The Anti-Amendment Campaign said it was very gratified at the number of people who voted against the amendment. A statement by the Catholic Press Office recalled that the bishops had said that a constitutional provision couldn't of itself be a full response to the abortion problem. The Church of Ireland Primate, Archbishop Armstrong, has called for the restoration of harmonious relationships following the outcome of the referendum.

Abortion was not a new issue in Irish society in the 1980s. Both Sandra McAvoy and Ray Kavanagh have revealed the extent of the abortion clinics in 1940s Ireland. Several people were convicted of performing abortions during this period, and, after a clampdown in 1943–4, they were dealt with severely by the courts, receiving long sentences of penal servitude. They included Christopher Williams, a prominent chemist, Dr James Ashe, medical examiner to the matrimonial division of the High Court, and Henry Coleman, who ran an extensive abortion practice in Merrion Square.[4]

For a generation, perhaps two, the words 'Nurse Cadden' were regarded as synonymous with evil. She qualified as a midwife in 1926 and later went into business as an abortionist. She performed a number of botched operations and became known nationally in 1956, when she was charged with the murder of Helen O'Reilly, a deserted mother of six who died from an embolism, on Cadden's kitchen table in her squalid bedsit in Hume Street, as a result of the pumping into her body of a mixture of air and disinfectant. Cadden was convicted of her murder and, despite the flimsiness of the evidence against her, was sentenced to death by hanging, commuted to penal servitude for life. The ambiguity associated with the case was interesting—former High Court Judge Kenneth

Deale, who wrote an account of the trial, questioned whether it would have succeeded if Cadden 'had been a respectable midwife of good reputation', which also points to the suppression of a public discourse on abortion.[5] Cadden died in the Central Mental Hospital in 1959.

The reason for the murder charge was that under section 58 of the 1861 Offences Against the Person Act, a person who 'unlawfully' procured the miscarriage of a woman was considered to have committed a felony. A patient dying as a result of such a procedure was not considered to have died during a medical operation, so a murder charge could be brought against the person who carried out the procedure. But this in itself was ambiguous. The act referred to those 'unlawfully' using instruments or administering drugs to procure abortion; did this imply that there were circumstances in which abortion might be lawful? And what was the implication of this legislation for the medical profession? No charges were ever brought against doctors or midwives for performing abortions for medical reasons, so the Irish courts never tested the application of the legislation in such cases. It may have been the case that by the 1980s, there was a fear that the law relating to abortion might be interpreted in a way that legalised abortion, prompting a small group to exert pressure on politicians to give a commitment to a referendum, which both Fianna Fáil and Fine Gael did in the early 1980s.

The current abortion law exemplifies moral and legal ambiguities. In 1992, Judge Niall McCarthy of the Supreme Court, referring to the 1983 constitutional amendment, insisted: 'the failure by the legislature to enact the appropriate legislation is no longer unfortunate, it is inexcusable. What are pregnant women to do? What are the parents of a pregnant girl under age to do? What are the medical profession to do?' Jennifer Spreng, an American academic, suggested in 2004, in a book on divorce and abortion law in Ireland, that the current inertia, 'may arise more from uncertainty about what to do than from any real satisfaction with the current state of the law'.[6] But this was better, she seemed to imply, than the situation in the US, where, because of the liberalisation of the 1960s and the attempt to rescind that, absolutists on both sides are allowed to dominate the debate. The voices of women who have had abortions are rarely heard. In Ireland in 2000, for example, after a Green Paper on abortion had appeared, organisations and individuals were invited to address an all-party Oireachtas committee. The churches and the doctors duly made their submissions, but the views of women with direct experience were not heard. Medb Ruane concluded that 'theological and legal arguments supplant the personal testimony of women.'[7]

Clearly, therefore, the debate surrounding the issue did not end in 1983. Four referenda on the subject followed, over the course of the next 18 years, and thousands of Irish women continued to travel outside the state to have abortions. But what if the referendum had not taken place? What if it had been deemed unnecessary?

Both of the guests on this programme had been involved in the anti-amendment campaign and it seemed timely, twenty years after the referendum, to have a new look at it, removed from the emotive and nasty environment of 1983. A complaint was made to the Broadcasting Complaints Commission after this programme was broadcast, claiming that it was unfair and one-sided, a complaint the BCC rejected. Alex White, a barrister, had formerly been a producer with RTÉ and was elected as a Labour county councillor in Dublin South in 2004. Ann Marie Hourihane, a journalist with the *Sunday Tribune*, also wrote the acclaimed *She Moves Through the Boom*, an account of Celtic Tiger Ireland as seen through the lives and preoccupations of those living through it.

White explained the legal position in relation to abortion:

> Since 1861 it has been illegal to procure or to have an abortion in Ireland. Leaving aside the Constitution and all the referenda for a moment, that's the law that applies. That's the law that applied in 1983 as well. So why did we need to change? Why did we need to have a referendum? Why did people advocate a referendum? Well, what the Pro-Life Amendment Campaign said at the time was that the way the Irish Constitution was being interpreted by the judges, and by the Supreme Court, led them to believe or to suspect or, I suppose, to fear, that in due course or in time, the Constitution would be interpreted in a particular way by the Supreme Court so as to allow abortion. The privacy provisions in the Constitution

would be interpreted in a particular way by the Supreme Court
which would 'allow abortion in' and that was a phrase I remember
very much at the time. That was certainly something that William
Binchy [Trinity College law professor and leading anti-abortion
campaigner] said and his colleagues said, that we would have
abortion, and I also remember the phrase (and I'm not saying
Binchy used it) that we would have 'abortion in the back door',
which was the suggestion it would come through Europe and
all that, so the 1861 act was the act that was the law, but the
PLAC campaign suggested we needed to be sure that (a) the
Supreme Court doesn't change it in some way by interpreting the
Constitution in a particular way or (b) politicians and the
Oireachtas wouldn't introduce legislation or do something inside
in the Dáil or the Senate which would change things that the
people wouldn't have control over. So that's why they said we need
to lock it in to the Constitution—this is the way the argument was
put—a 'pure form ban' in the Constitution that has the effect of
banning for all time, abortion, or any abortion law in Ireland.

It seems that it was also easier for PLAC to put pressure on
politicians because of the political instability of the era, when
every vote was absolutely vital, given that little separated Fianna
Fáil and Fine Gael/Labour under Haughey and FitzGerald and
Spring respectively. Was it the case that if there had been more
political stability it would have been easier for the lobby groups to
be resisted? White suggested:

Clearly there was political instability, three general elections
between 1981 and 1982 and the economy wasn't in good shape.
There were also a lot of things happening in the North—it was
very volatile; we had come out of the H Block period the year or
two before—I think it's fair to suggest that maybe for politicians,
this wasn't something they particularly wanted—they didn't really
want to go there—other people were better organised on the issue
than they were. A lot of politicians felt 'look, well, we're against
abortion, we don't think it's a good thing and here's a well-
organised lobby group who've thought about it more than we have
and they seem to be right and so, yes, we'll go with that; that seems
to make sense'. And sure enough, within months, some of the
leading politicians, including Garret FitzGerald, were regretting

ever having made the promise. He changed his mind on the issue. He had originally given that pledge before the second of the two 1982 elections; he'd gone into government then with Dick Spring on the basis that they would introduce the same wording as Haughey had brought forward, but he subsequently changed his mind.

Looking back, Hourihane was first struck by the huge difference between the climate of the early 1980s and now:

I think it's a very difficult period to explain. I think even as a middle-aged person it is a very different memory from other memories. It seems like another planet, and when I look back on it, it seems an incredibly dark period that I remember partly for the reasons that Alex has explained—the hunger strikes were just over, the North was desperately black. The economy was in tatters and your options as a young person, as I was at that time, were few. Most of your friends had emigrated—that was true pretty well across all classes and backgrounds; unemployment was a really, really serious problem—there was no money. Culturally, U2 were only starting—I try to explain to my younger colleagues by saying that it was pre *The Joshua Tree*—this is actually a date line they have no concept of.

And her perspective of the period, as a young feminist? She was adamant:

It was like living in Franco's Spain . . . I would have been much more involved than most people because I was a member of the women's right-to-choose group and our slogan was 'every bishop a wanted bishop'. But to say that we were in a tiny minority is to understate the case. I worked counselling women who were going to Britain for abortions, so I was much more closely associated with the subject than most people—most of my friends and so forth. But I also worked in family planning clinics and women were in an appalling position at that time. If you think about it—the 1979 family planning act is what was on the books, which said you had to be married and you had to have a prescription in order to obtain condoms. Imagine the patronising result of that to women and men. Now, the abortion issue was not discussed, it really wasn't. Even though women were going in a steady stream to

Britain for abortions, as of course they still are today. But there was no divorce, homosexuality was illegal . . . women came into family planning clinics in secret; it was unusual if their partners came with them, frankly—they travelled enormous distances to come to Dublin, because their doctor or their local pharmacist—they literally didn't want to go there. So that's actually a very difficult thing even to remember with accuracy, let alone to imagine if you haven't personally witnessed it.

Hourihane also recalled the confusion about what was being proposed and about what its implications might be. Clearly, the type of campaign that evolved had not been envisaged by those involved:

The fact of the matter is that nobody knew what they were in for. Alex has emphasised that the politicians didn't know what they were in for; it was a Pandora's box. I think the point should be made that nobody knew how dirty, how vicious, how personal this was going to get on all sides. It was really nasty and I think everybody was surprised—the thing was being put together as we went along on both sides and people were shifting ground and making alliances and so forth that no one had envisaged at the start of the campaign. Now the upshot of that was, I think, that it mobilised opposition to the church on a breadth that they didn't know even existed, but the fact of the matter was nobody knew it existed until it happened. Nobody knew there was going to be a Farmers Against the Amendment, nobody knew that you'd have Protestant clergymen on platforms with radical feminists, nobody knew that lawyers in suits were going to be prepared to go up and down the country. Nobody knew that doctors were going to come out and say, 'Listen, this mightn't be good.' At the same time, nobody knew that doctors would come out on the anti-amendment side either, so there was this feeling of being in a spinning vortex.

White recalled a similar sense of turmoil and unpredictability, but suggested that it was important for different reasons:

I think that's right and I think an awful lot of people cut their teeth politically as well in that period. When you look at events like 1983 and look at them from this vantage point of 20 years later, one doesn't know at the time how something is going to look 20 years later, and it's fascinating to look at the period that follows on from 1983. The period immediately before it, but also what follows on from it. You mention the political situation—for the church also in 1983, things were reasonably comfortable still, it seems to me, looking back at that—you had 1979 and the Pope in Ireland and all the rest of it and it seemed that they were almost beyond challenge in respect of having their way, on the social issues and political issues—issues that politicians were effectively afraid of.

But what of the confusion over the wording, and why was there such a poor turnout?

White responded:

> I think that's curious as well . . . there was a lot of campaigning around the country and certainly the anti-amendment people tried to do that—the anti-amendment campaign tried to do it. I was involved. There was an attempt made to bring the campaign around. But I still think there were two campaigns actually. There was Dublin, with maybe some of the larger urban centres—and there was the rest of Ireland. There really was still a very clear urban/rural division in terms of what happened in 1983 and I think in Dublin you had a debate—quite a vicious debate at times, as Ann Marie has said. You had it on the radio, you had it on television. I know they were available nationwide, but there was a sense when one was outside Dublin at the time, as I remember being, that there was no debate and it was almost as if this was still a taboo subject—it wasn't even mentioned.

According to Hourihane,

> There was a fury from people in rural areas saying, 'Do you expect me to go down and explain this to people down where I live? You don't understand!' There was an absolute fury about how the Dublin anti-amendment campaign completely failed to understand what they were up against, I think. And things happened—for example, there was to be a walkout from mass when the bishops sent around the pastoral. I was talking to a friend of mine today about this time and she was remembering how relatives of hers in a small town in Ireland walked out of mass that Sunday. What an

enormously courageous and controversial thing this was to do. Life was much less suburban and anonymous all over Ireland than it is now. Everyone lived in much smaller communities both in cities and towns, and there was no local radio.

An archival clip was played from the Gay Byrne radio show in 1985, in which he recalled the divisions of 1983, and the fact that the issue had still not been clarified:

> The Constitution guarantees the right to life of the unborn. But despite this, Irish women in large numbers—about 3,500 each year—continue to travel to England to terminate their pregnancies. Officially, we as a nation may find abortion unacceptable but as individuals many of us clearly do not. When you think back to the months before the referendum, you probably remember, as I do, endless, endless debates about when life begins: is a foetus a person? who has rights? who hasn't?—mothers or unborn babies. The whole subject was debated up and down the country for months and months and there arose from that considerable agitation. Well, we're not going to re-open those debates again, but abortion is still part of the way that we live whether we like it or not.

Why was there still such confusion given the clear-cut result of the referendum? And what of the irony of the fact that the amendment actually paved the way to a limited form of legal abortion?

White thought it was fair to argue,

> . . . that the pro-life amendment campaign overplayed their hand in what they did in 1983. Just from their own strategic standpoint as to what they wanted to achieve and they had their own legitimate objectives—that must be said. We didn't all share them, but what they actually brought about, what actually happened, was not what they purported to want to achieve. Because they wanted what I regard as a pure form ban against abortion, but it will never happen and can never happen. But the wording that went into the Constitution, into article 40 subsection 3 which was according an equality between the unborn and the mother—that they would be seen to be equal, acknowledging the right to life of the unborn and with due regard to the *equal* right to life of the mother, and that of course was precisely the phrase that the Supreme Court had to

consider in the X Case in 1992 where the court decided in relation to that particular phrase that there were circumstances, interpreting that precise phrase, in which abortion was to be lawful and could be lawful.

Contemporary news reports were played which captured the drama of the controversy about the lifting of a ban on a 14-year-old girl ('X'), pregnant as a result of rape, travelling outside the country for an abortion in 1992. How did Hourihane feel about the impact of the X case—was it a question of this controversy humanising the issue?

I think it is very interesting that this series is called 'What if?' because the fact of the matter is, the whole argument, the whole amendment argument, was what if? what if? Rape, for example. What if a girl is raped? Then the pro-life people were saying, 'You know that doesn't make it right', and so on, and it is correct to emphasise the sincerity, indeed the goodness, of most of the people who were in the pro-life movement and voted pro-life. But the fact of the matter was—and *both* sides let this slip—that the argument became so arcane, so obscure, that it alienated most voters. I remember canvassing in Patrician Villas off the Stillorgan Dual Carriageway and this man said, 'Look, love, I just don't understand it. I'm not going to vote', and I remember walking away thinking, 'This is wrong, this is wrong; this is not how democracy is meant to be. This is not how amendments are meant to be put into the Constitution.' And I blame my own side as much as I blame the other side because we never punched it through. I don't think either side did—we became involved in the minutiae. I think the politicians did that on purpose frankly. To put a dampener on the building passion of the debate.

This was a view White shared:

I think that's right and I think you can see that from looking at how the campaign went. It was very odd that politicians took a very, very minor role on both sides in the course of that. There was the huge importance of people like John O'Reilly [leading behind-the-scenes strategist of the pro-amendment campaign] and the emergence of people like William Binchy, because it was probably the first time in Ireland where lobby groups actually ran the whole thing on both sides. That's very interesting about it. I think it's the first real occasion when you've got a big political context without politicians—the leading lights on both sides were unknown people. They were political nonentities on both sides. This is a change, and is something you see happening far more often after 1983. But of course it suited politicians in 1983 to play no part—even Haughey who, of course, was leader of the opposition then, when the thing was going through, said very, very little. He considered saying nothing, as some writers have suggested; he considered making no broadcast but changed his mind at the end and said he would.

According to Hourihane, the X case forced those who had been silent to deal with the fall-out from the original referendum:

This is when everything tragically came home to roost because the hypothesis which both sides had dreaded actually took human form, and one of the things I want to emphasise is, for example, the arrogance of the medical profession. What happens if an underage girl is raped and they say, 'Don't you worry—we'll take care of that', and suddenly somebody went through the letter of the law—in fact, the guards—and then it was a nightmare come true ... It was always argued that it was bad law, that was the argument, and it was a pyrrhic victory for the other side; it was a mess, it left a legal mess. Also, on a cultural level, what the '83 amendment had done was it had dragged it into the public domain in a way that it had never been before. So, for example, pro-life people went round to schools and children were coming home from primary schools saying to their parents, 'What's an abortion, Mammy?' That would never have happened beforehand. So it became much more of a battleground and a publicly discussed subject. No one foresaw that.

White added:

And I think what was attempted in fact was to abstract the issue at the time in 1983. It was a classic attempt to abstract it from the reality of people's lives. The anti-amendment campaign were saying to people, 'Look, let's not have a referendum' and one has seen the counter point of view come up more recently also, that what's wrong with a referendum? Fianna Fáil and Bertie Ahern said that in 2002 as well.

Hourihane continued: 'I think personally, if there hadn't been the amendment in 1983, it would have been in 1984. That's what I think because I don't think those people were letting go and I don't think anybody knew enough—the politicians didn't know enough to stop them—to say, "Forget it; we're not doing it."'

White responded, 'You're probably right, when one looks at '83 and '84. It does seem to me that '83, for me anyway, looking back, constitutes or represents a high point for that particular viewpoint and they've never got back up onto that high step again.'

Both had plenty of ideas as to the legacy of the referendum, and what might have happened if it had not taken place. Hourihane remembered:

> People like Michael Cleary and so on. Cleary was bringing disabled people into studios and saying, everyone's a disgrace. Then the disabled people against the amendment came and they brought people in. There were very strong personalities. Mary McAleese was one of the people who emerged from this. I do think that if there hadn't been this amendment, I think that perhaps secularisation would have moved in a different way, instead of ricocheting from scandal to scandal. I think the process would have been different. Alex is right when he says the powers are at the peak of their confidence at this time—we were all John Charles McQuaid's children; the priests couldn't believe the campaign—they were astonished; and I think a lot of the liberal people within Catholicism knew this was a disaster for them—a disaster. I think things like, for example, there would have been perhaps more secularisation moving in different areas—perhaps the church's grip on medicine and obstetrics would have been loosened in a more gentle way, and perhaps we wouldn't have cases now that are happening in church-run hospitals which are an alliance between the church and things like the medical hierarchy. That was demolished—partly demolished subsequently by litigation, but it's still not a pretty sight.

Did the fact that the 1983 referendum occurred make it easier to legislate for the decriminalisation of homosexuality and the introduction of divorce?

According to White,

John Kelly, the late Fine Gael TD and former Attorney General, said something very interesting in the Dáil in 1983—it was prior to the referendum vote being taken and I think he himself actually said that he was going to vote for it, as I recall. But he made a very interesting speech, and a very thoughtful speech in the Dáil and he said something along the lines of, the promoters of this proposal may have unwittingly created 'a large secular platform in Ireland from which, in the future, we could expect there to be repeated attacks'—that was a phrase he used, and that they would launch these attacks in the future and that they would, in fact, come back and change it; that they would be emboldened. They all know who they are now—they were a group that had been constituted almost by the fact of the 1983 amendment. So, I sometimes think, when you look back over the peaks and troughs in human affairs or politics, sometimes one's inclined to think that maybe it needed those sort of events and I'm not saying it was a good thing that it happened—I personally believe that it was a very bad thing. When you look back, you think maybe that's what was needed in order to give strength to others.

Hourihane regarded the referendum as having done significant damage to politics, owing to the absence of leadership, and mentioned that the figure cited in 2001 for women giving Irish addresses when undergoing abortions in Britain was double that of 1983:

To me, one of the biggest results of the amendment was that parliamentary politics lost its thrust. Ever since, social change has come from outside the Dáil, and the politicians have been running after the public. I think that's one of the big changes. The Dáil never got to grips with this—it disgraced itself. The momentum moved outside the Dáil to the courts, the tribunals, whatever. But, of course, the one set of people it didn't make any difference to were the women who were going to England for abortions. And all those figures were always underestimated. So it made no difference. No one gave a curse about them, and the politicians still don't.

Chapter 3

What if there had been no *Magill* magazine?

One of the most dynamic, original and controversial figures of modern Irish journalism, Limerick-born Vincent Browne came to national prominence in the late 1970s, charting new ground in investigative journalism with *Magill*, a monthly current affairs magazine he established with Noel Pearson and Mary Holland. The first edition appeared in October 1977, and included contributions from Holland, Conor Cruise O'Brien, Ulick O'Connor, Paul Foot and Bruce Arnold, and an advertisement informed readers that the best way to have a wonderful time was to drink Harp and lime.

Once it was firmly established, the magazine sold well, though as Browne recalled, 'The first few years were traumatic commercially . . . and survived through the generosity of Edward Pinelas and Gordon Colleary and the careful and dedicated management of Cecily O'Toole.'[1] It was challenging, provocative, angry and frequently revealing, shedding light on many of the dark corners of Irish society. Its success was never guaranteed, and the editorial process was rarely uncomplicated, but it did manage to provide an outlet for many talented young journalists, including the two guests on this programme, John Waters and Fintan O'Toole, who both edited *Magill* after Browne left the magazine to edit the *Sunday Tribune*. O'Toole was in the editor's chair from April 1985 to December 1986, and Waters from January to October 1988.

Browne may no longer have been editing, but he still retained ownership, usually got his way, and frequently chided his successors by denouncing their efforts. 'IT'S SHITE!' seemed to be his most common complaint.[2] In a sense, this programme was a very public form of therapy for both Waters and O'Toole.

The climate of Ireland in the late 1970s and early 1980s was also conducive to good coverage of politics and the economy, given the number of general elections, the despair about the nation's finances, and the fact that many felt it was time to begin to analyse critically what had gone wrong, and, indeed, to hold people to account for what had gone wrong. Reading *Magill* was certainly a good way of learning about politics and power in Ireland: the processes and the abuse. The other advantage of such a magazine was that it facilitated the writing of much longer articles than was feasible in newspapers.

Browne wanted to go beyond the deferential approach to politicians that he found evident in Ireland. At the opening of this show, an archival clip was played of an unusually serene Browne talking about the role of the political journalist, in which he claimed:

> My experience is politicians will only tell you bits and pieces of gossip; that a great deal of it is unreliable and is trivial in any event. What is much more important is to compare what politicians do with what they said they'd do. That is what the primary function of political journalism is supposed to be about, and also to sharpen up issues in a much more clear-cut way than is done. I actually think this issue of constraints and access is greatly exaggerated journalistically. Journalists excuse a lot of deference and timidity in their journalism by reference to that.

Browne's successors rarely lasted long in the job; indeed, it seemed it was necessary for them to leave after relatively short periods in order to preserve their sanity, a reflection of the fact that Browne, though he could be hugely generous, funny and compassionate, was notoriously difficult to work with and satisfy, and seemed to have an exceptional capacity for aggravation—destructive and charismatic in equal measure. It has also been suggested that these magazines have a limited shelf-life. Brian Trench, who edited the magazine briefly in the late 1980s, remarked around the time of its first closure in 1991 that, 'Publications such as *Magill* may have a "natural" life cycle and that the magazine might have reached the end of that cycle.'[3]

Browne relaunched *Magill* in September 1997, and it was a commercial success, with monthly sales of over 40,000, but he sold it to Mike Hogan in November 1998. In October 2004, he launched a new weekly current affairs magazine, *Village*. It struggled to make an impact, and six months after it was launched, Browne wrote: 'A survey we did a few months ago showed only 10 per cent of the adult population were even aware of *Village*. That's how it was when *Magill* was first launched in October 1977. I had forgotten. It is claimed now there are fewer stories around than there were 25, 30 years ago, less room for a current affairs magazine. That certainly is untrue. There are now more instances of corporate criminality than there were then, more evidence of Garda misconduct, continued chicanery over party political financing, the Tribunals have given us vivid insights into the scale of political corruption and there is no reason to believe it has gone away.'[4]

John Waters grew up in Roscommon in the 1960s, before moving to Dublin, and I wondered why, in the first instance, he had wanted to write for *Magill*:

Well, *Magill* was the cutting edge of journalism. To be editor of *Magill*, I always thought, was the best job in journalism at the time. Vincent was such an extraordinary crusader, at a time when politics was fluid and changing, in the late 1970s and early 1980s—Charlie Haughey's arrival to power, a series of elections—politics was just in your face in a way then that it isn't now. You were breathing it in every day and watching Vincent making his crusading appearances on the *Late Late Show*, and the style of journalism in *Magill* was so different to what was in the newspapers, which was like it was written by clerical officers rather than journalists. There was real writing in the magazine and it was much more narrative and fluid and relaxed and a subjective view of Ireland; so to be part of that— it excited me—that it was bridging that factoid world of the newspapers and the fictional world of the novel and it really appealed to me. I don't know if Vincent would have agreed with that analysis of *Magill*, but certainly that was the way it appealed to me.

What was the attraction for O'Toole? Was it the anger that Browne was articulating; his capacity for telling many politicians that they were useless gobshites? Did that appeal to him and would the challenge to the establishment have been delayed if there had been no such magazine?

It was enormously important in the context of what was still a very hierarchical, authoritarian society where, really, the boundaries of public discussion of public issues were still actually very, very narrow. There was still an assumption that people in power deserved to be deferred to. It wasn't simply broken by what the magazine was doing; obviously there was a whole set of changes around what TV was doing ... people like Brian Farrell were starting to ask questions on television in a different kind of style. There were all sorts of changes around, say, how someone like Gay Byrne might leap on someone on the *Late Late Show*. But it hadn't really transferred itself into print—you had a change in broadcast ideas which, oddly, had remained pretty much outside of the print arena which was still the arena in which people got most of their basic information. So what Vincent did simply was to define media, particularly print media, as having an automatically antagonistic relationship with whoever was in power. The famous cover of the magazine that I remember was after one of the elections in the early 1980s—an issue that came out with the headline: 'How much longer must we stand this awful government?'—that was the attitude Vincent brought.

This, it seems, was a recurrent theme; another one of Vincent's favourite phrases was along the lines of, 'There is no doubt that this is the worst government we have ever had; the question is, would the alternative be even worse?' But was this a good thing or a bad thing for Irish journalism? Was this ingrained hostility more destructive than constructive?

According to O'Toole, 'There was that sense of attitude which, in the long term, has its limitations and its dangers, but I think in that time and in that place it was an extremely necessary one.

Simply to invigorate the idea of the public realm as one in which people had to earn their spurs; that you could no longer assume that because you had authority by virtue of your office you were therefore entitled to be treated as somebody very precious.'

Was Browne targeting the recruitment of journalists with a mindset similar to his own or was he going to allow them to inaugurate their own style? In assessing this, Waters drew attention to some of the paradoxes associated with Browne and *Magill*:

Well, it was strange, because Vincent always had a particular model of journalism which he repeats to this day which doesn't really bear out what he actually did as editor. He talked about the importance of facts of information; disparaged the notion of writing and opinion, and yet if you look at *Magill*, it was very much to do with opinion—in a broad sense and in a very narrow sense, in terms of the writing and also the style of the writing which was very, very high quality, including Vincent's own incidentally, and Vincent's opinions were uppermost in the whole thing, so there was this almost confusion. *Magill* started around the same time as *In Dublin*, and Fintan began with *In Dublin*, and I started with *Hot Press. Hot Press* was a slightly different stream because it didn't come to politics until some time later, but certainly *Magill* drew on the Dave McKenna thing (he was editor of *In Dublin*) and he created this new style where you brought in the importance of subjectivity in writing . . . of having a view of society, an attitude towards society. I won't say Vincent poached that style, but it was convenient for him that it happened at the same time, and he drew on a new generation—people a few years younger than him who had a particular attitude towards society, which was the first generation for a long time which actually stayed here and wanted to claim ownership of society and wanted somewhere to express those views about it. There was a synchronicity between that and Browne's agenda and these two things existed somewhat uncomfortably together for as long as it lasted.

O'Toole had a similar assessment, but what was interesting about this discussion was the different nuances and the importance of individual journalists in changing the way people thought about things. In this regard, if Gene Kerrigan had not been involved, it would have been a weaker magazine:

That's absolutely right; I think it was an uncomfortable relationship. I think that's the key thing and that's why people like John and me didn't actually last that long! Vincent knew what was going on in the sense that there was an opportunity to write about things in a more complex way about our society. I think because he was of an earlier generation in journalistic terms, he was closer to the idea of journalism as a first draft of history than maybe John or I who were maybe more influenced by American new journalism— the idea of subjectivity; the idea that how you write it was as important as what you said—and there was always a certain kind of tension around that, but if you look back now, the single most direct achievement of the magazine in those years was nothing to do with Browne; it was to do with him in that he gave a platform for it, but it was the writing of Gene Kerrigan, and the work that he was doing on the criminal justice system actually had an enormous influence and led to a real shift in public perception. What was critical in these stories was that Kerrigan was writing at an incredibly high level of craft, in terms of the actual literary quality of what he was doing, in the way he told stories. There was a famous story he did on Karl Crawley who was a particular criminal who had been through the system in all sorts of ways . . . and the way it was written: if it was a short story you would have put it in the great short stories of twentieth-century Ireland; but it was true— everything in it was true, it was consistent with the facts; it was actually honed in that sort of way, yet it was written with an extraordinary literary style and actually if you were to look back and ask what did *Magill* change so directly, it changed the fact that, within a couple of years of those pieces, Dublin juries in particular looked at Garda evidence in criminal cases in a different way; you actually started getting cases where juries rejected Garda evidence, where judges reject Garda evidence, and it seems to me that was directly to do with the way Gene was writing.

Browne obviously had his own particular interests, if not obsessions, as editor; Charles Haughey was clearly one of them. But there were also other themes frequently analysed: the state of psychiatric hospitals, the rise of the Christian Right. Did it change when the young Colm Tóibín took over in 1983 at the age of 27? Did the magazine evolve in any significant way? Waters remembered:

I was once talking to Vincent about this and he had the view that there was a difference between his editorship of *Magill* and subsequent editorships . . . he freely admitted that the magazine became more consistent after he'd stopped being editor but that it didn't have the spectaculars that he used to commit (the atrocities, I suppose you might call them!) Now, I think there's a truth in that but it's not as true as he might suggest. When you go back over *Magill*'s history and the mythology of investigative journalism, how much of *Magill* was actually about investigative journalism in the sense of pure factoid, getting information? Not that much! We used to have this joke—there was the Arms Trial, there was a long piece about the Workers Party . . . and after that you were into the other reasons why people bought *Magill*—as Fintan said, I think Gene was the secret weapon of *Magill* for many years—Gene would somehow get hold of a book of evidence and turn it into a novel. It was the kind of stuff you would set aside an evening to read, like reading a book, and I think that was part of the appeal; and the other writers followed that—Nell McCafferty, June Levine, etc, but it was really about writing about Irish society in a new way, rather than simply finding out new things about it.

The youth of the editors was also notable in the aftermath of Browne. Was this a help or a hindrance? If they had come to it when more mature, would it have made for a better magazine? O'Toole remembered:

I was pretty young and pretty stupid! I wouldn't have done it otherwise—I think that probably goes for everybody else who subsequently edited the magazine, but Colm's editorship—those two years produced the best sequence of magazines in any genre in the history of Irish publishing, I think. If you look back on them, they were superb—brilliantly written and very diverse in terms of the kind of subjects they were trying to deal with—and I think it came from the fact that Colm's view of Irish society was a much broader one than Browne's. Browne had magnificent obsessions with the details of political power and the way it worked, but every journalist who ever went in to work there was always given a list of articles to write and it was the same list of articles and issues— Charlie Haughey's finances topped it—and they were all stories which never got done because they were undoable at the time, and

Vincent's great anger was about the stories that couldn't be done, whereas I think Colm Tóibín and I said, 'We can't do those things. We don't have the resources, or the legal situation is such that you can't do them, so let's try and concentrate on trying to have a broader perspective on what Irish society is like.' I certainly wasn't as good at it as Colm had been and I think there was a certain kind of shift in that the energy around investigative journalism had become very different (and difficult). I actually did manage to get one junior minister sacked—Eddie Collins, junior minister for Industry and Commerce—directly as a result of a piece I wrote in the magazine, and yet what happened was that when it was raised in the Dáil (which at the time was a sensational story), the Ceann Comhairle ruled it completely out of order and there was no public discussion of it whatsoever and there was that sense of what's the point in trying to do these stories because they simply have no purchase on the way Irish society talks about politics.

Garret FitzGerald recalled this resignation in his memoirs, and one can understand the frustration that must have been caused to people like O'Toole; FitzGerald's account, in a sense, proves O'Toole's point. He claims that Collins 'through inadvertence and clearly without any improper intent' had attended some board meetings of a family company which he had resigned from on appointment to his ministerial position. He was present at such a meeting when an application for assistance from a state financial institution was discussed. FitzGerald claimed he had to sack Collins so that 'no suspicion of impropriety be allowed to exist . . . and for my own part it was perhaps the most painful personal decision I had to take as Taoiseach, and one that has left me most unhappy ever since.'[5]

Waters shared the view that 'the stuff that Colm Tóibín did went deeper, went down into the cultural issues and the more psychological issues in a way, and there was almost a satirical level at the top where you could see the tension erupting between Browne's model and Tóibín's, and I used to find it very funny, because Vincent had this obsession—you couldn't say "I" in an article; you weren't allowed to be subjective; he wasn't interested in your opinions and Tóibín used to satirise this by writing a diary piece and saying "this reporter did this" and "this reporter did that" and it was almost like taking the mickey out of Vincent's model of journalism in a certain sense, and yet there was this sense that we were all informed by Vincent's crusading zeal and the enthusiasm. One of the great things about Vincent as an editor was that he was hugely enthused about his own ambition to find things out, and you would be standing in a bar and he'd be jumping up and down with glee at the damage he was going to cause!'

But what was it like to be at the coalface? At editorial meetings? This was perhaps where the most difficult aspects of Browne's character came to the fore. The real 'what if' here was what if Browne, when he ceased being editor, had left the rest of them to get on with it? There was no chance of that, however. The editorial meetings, according to O'Toole, were 'hellish. He's a very ambivalent figure; he's the only person I've ever met for whom the term "larger than life" actually applies, in that he has outsized ego, outsized generosity, outsized openness, outsized ability to bring people in, to let people do things, but also this kind of outsized mania at certain times in terms of the actual running of a project that in a way was doomed once he left it, in one fundamental sense, in that he didn't leave it enough; if he had simply gone, or sold the magazine at that stage, or if it had been possible to come up with some other way of structuring it so that somebody like Colm Tóibín could have continued to edit it without being completely pestered by the person for whom it was his own personal baby; he wouldn't mind the baby, he wouldn't feed it and yet he wouldn't let anyone else feed it or bring it up either, so he was like an absent father who would turn up every so often and say, "How dare you raise that child as a Protestant", and have these really strong views, but it was completely unstructured and with no actual relationship to the function of bringing out a very good monthly magazine with a staff of two or three people.'

According to Waters, this was an almost impossible situation:

I used to resign once a month at least, and at the end of that kind of row, a discussion would ensue and I'd say, 'Vincent, it's your magazine. Why don't you edit it?—I'll work for you, but this can't go on; we can't both be editors of *Magill*', and he wouldn't let go of it because he had that vision for what it was, and in a way that's what killed it in the end because it couldn't grow with the society . . . in certain senses, if it had stayed with Vincent's vision, it would have continued to be successful because he has moved with the society in his own way, but he was not directly involved all the time, but constantly making these kind of dawn raids on the magazine . . . I remember he'd be passing, on the way to Galligan's restaurant, and you'd be looking out the window and he would look up at you and make these typewriting gestures at you as if you were shirking your work. It was humorous—he's an extraordinarily funny man and this is the great thing—the character of Vincent was extraordinary. There was this sort of amnesia that used to set in with you regarding Vincent—after a while you'd have an experience and think, 'It's not that bad', and then you'd go back and it would be, 'Oh my God, it's worse', and it was. . . .

But, perhaps more important than that, did working with Browne make them better journalists? And was it the case that if there had been no *Magill*, many young journalists would not have had the space or time to practise their craft? Was there an attractive alternative journalistic life outside *Magill*?

'There were other places,' noted O'Toole,

But there weren't other places that actually paid you anything much and at least Vincent kind of paid something, so yes, it did make it possible for a whole generation of journalists to actually become professional journalists which they would have found very difficult otherwise. It also hardened some people an awful lot—in some ways, having to deal with all this means that if you survived, you probably were better. It made me a better journalist in one real sense, in that I remember being at one of those general election press conferences when Haughey was in power and was going for re-election, and the entire press corps was there and Vincent was there at the back and he just kept saying, 'What is the source of your money?' and 'How did you get to be rich, to afford that house?' which was the big neon light of Irish politics. I mean, it was bloody obvious there was something really, really, wrong. Not only would nobody else ask it, but eventually, after two or three times, the rest of the press corps turned around and told Vincent to shut up—that they had work to do and this work did not include asking Haughey how he got his money, and the only person who actually stood up and said, 'Excuse me, Mr Haughey, your job here is to answer questions' was John Bowman—only he and Browne felt that the job of the journalist was to ask the question the politician didn't want to answer, and the more he didn't want to answer it, the more critical that the question kept being asked . . . but the rest of the press corps were absolutely determined that this wouldn't happen and Browne was absolutely right about that—he was trying to reveal the truth about something that, when it was revealed, everybody said, 'Ah sure, we always knew that, it was obvious'—it wasn't obvious, in that the press refused to make it obvious, and whatever Browne's foibles and faults and mis-demeanours, there's an incredible importance in the kind of madness it takes to stand up in a room like that to keep asking that question and demand that it be answered.

Waters also identified significance in the fact that:

There was a certain importance about its coverage of Northern Ireland, because it had a certain nationalist/republican slant, rightly or wrongly. It was quite sympathetic and open to the nationalist side of the North and it kept that valve open at a time when it was closed elsewhere because of section 31, which didn't just close down broadcast media; it also infected print media, and the argument can be made that by keeping that valve open, it allowed the possibility for armed republicanism to be talked down from the ledge subsequently, resulting in the Peace Process and so on. Now, that's a big argument, perhaps, but I think the important thing is Vincent's vision—he was right almost all the time; his instincts were so good; he would write long, long, lists of stories that could be done which were absolutely fascinating in themselves —that any one person could have so many angles on Irish society and they'd all be really good ideas and he'd have a particular idea as to how each story could be done and, by and large, he would be right . . . I remember writing a column for him in the *Sunday Tribune* and it took five weeks to get it published because he kept throwing it back at me and saying, 'That's not what I want. I don't want your opinions. I don't care what you think.' So he had a very rigorous view of journalism. I think the problem was that there wasn't enough time—he hadn't enough hours in the day to do everything he wanted to do and he could never get people who were precisely of the same mind as himself and, if he had, they wouldn't have been any good because they'd just be doing what he said, so that was the problem fundamentally. But at the same time I don't believe I personally would have come to what I am as a journalist if Vincent hadn't existed. I mean, *Hot Press*, yeah, but there was a certain limit to that; it was only when Browne brought me over the line and started kicking the head off me that I started to really think about how to do things and where to go with it. So I think he's a hugely important figure and the magazine was hugely important. Ireland might have developed something similar anyway, but it would have taken longer and I don't think it necessarily would have been as good.

Was it also the case that it would have taken women longer to establish themselves in Irish journalism, had it not been for Browne—was he responsible for the liberation of women in that regard? I asked O'Toole the question, slightly tongue-in-cheek.

'It was odd,' he suggested,

> . . . and Browne had some very ambivalent positions around some of those issues, but one of his great values was a genuine commitment to the idea that journalists should not necessarily be people from middle-class backgrounds who go to university and then go on to do postgraduate courses. One of the ironies of Irish journalism is that its social base narrowed hugely in the last few years, and, from a very early stage, he did have that notion that women could be journalists and was very committed to that; now, it's a pity that Mary Holland was pushed aside as well, so there's all sorts of ironies around this, but someone like Pat Brennan, who was very important in the first five years, had a very important impact. The great sort of heroic, mad gesture of setting up a women's version of the magazine, which was actually a very good magazine, even if it lasted only three or four months; the very fact that it existed did open up a very different agenda and allowed it to be stated that this was an acceptable thing to do. So, very often, Vincent's contrariness was much more important than his moments of being lucidly organised; that he was actually much better in a way for being the kind of maddening character that he was—he was so contrary and self-contradictory that he actually achieved a certain kind of freedom which was that he didn't

actually owe anything to anybody. Ideologically, he was all over the place—he was the person who put right-wing economics on the agenda in the mid-1980s, at the same time as demanding more money be spent on social welfare and highlighting poverty and mental hospitals.

Browne's new project—the weekly current affairs magazine, *Village*—had just been launched a fortnight before this programme. Many people believed it was a suicidal venture, not just because of the pressures of doing it weekly, but also because of the climate of Irish journalism, and, perhaps, a certain fatigue with regard to revelations and tribunals. Waters did not think the climate was suitable for the success of the new venture:

> The climate is different. You don't have such clear-cut issues any more in terms of the church, and the nature of politics—they're more diffuse, and to have a single view of them now which would equate to a journalistic agenda is not as simple as it used to be, so I'd be less optimistic about a publication like that being successful now.

For O'Toole:

> The depressing thing is that one of the things that animated us all who were around *Magill* in those years was the belief that if you could tell the truth, it would make a vast difference—that Irish society would actually be fundamentally changed—and the really depressing aspect of the last ten years is that we're all know-alls; we know *ad nauseum* the details of the financial transactions, and in some ways it's made absolutely no difference, and in some ways it's made it worse because you don't have that sense in journalism that it is worthwhile trying to open up these dark secrets and put them out there. The power of the secret, in a sense, has been disarmed and diffused by the Tribunal culture.

Chapter 4

What if John Charles McQuaid had not been appointed Archbishop of Dublin in 1940?

Few would doubt that John Charles McQuaid, appointed Archbishop of Dublin in 1940, was *the* towering figure of twentieth-century Irish Catholicism. From his appointment, until his retirement in 1972, there were virtually no areas of Irish Catholic life that he did not influence, or at least attempt to influence. Clergy and politicians alike could ill-afford to ignore his views or defy his commands, as he kept abreast of developments in the spiritual and secular spheres.

His interests, some would say obsessions, were meticulously recorded in his voluminous personal archive, held in the Dublin Diocesan Archives. A keen educationalist, he vastly expanded the size of his Dublin diocese and was active in promoting Catholic social welfare services amongst other things. McQuaid was very much an enforcer of what today is often depicted as a suffocating, repressive and authoritarian church. By the end of the 1960s, the climate of international Catholicism was at odds with his pre-Vatican II outlook, and he looked askance at growing ecumenical trends, and criticism of his style of leadership became more vocal.

Perhaps this was one of the difficulties in finding an objective assessment of him—the perception of him, and perhaps de Valera, as having outstayed their welcome has led to hostile assessments in recent years, and their place in history has been

castigated by those who in the 1960s began to experience intellectual disenchantment with 'traditional' Ireland. Novelist John
Banville summed up this attitude well when he wrote in 1995 that
this was an Ireland that was 'a demilitarised totalitarian state in
which the lives of its citizens were to be controlled, not by a
system of coercive force and secret policing, but by a kind of
applied spiritual paralysis maintained by an unofficial federation
between the Catholic clergy, the judiciary, the civil service and
politicians'.[1] In contrast, Deirdre McMahon, in a perceptive
overview of McQuaid's time as archbishop, has warned against
the 'crude caricatures of hidebound Catholic reaction with which
McQuaid has become identified since his death in 1973'.[2]

Born in Cootehill, Co. Cavan, in 1895, McQuaid was educated
at St Patrick's College in Cavan and later Blackrock College and
Clongowes Wood, before he entered the Holy Ghost novitiate at
Kimmage Manor in 1913. He went on to study at UCD and completed a doctorate in Rome. Ordained in 1924, he was appointed
Dean of Studies at Blackrock College in 1925, and served as a
young president of the college from 1931 to 1939, before being
appointed a relatively young member of the hierarchy in 1940. It
was an appointment that caused shock, as it was the first time a
priest from outside the ranks of the regular clergy had been
appointed Archbishop of Dublin since John Thomas Troy in 1786.[3]

Clearly, the work of de Valera and the words of the Irish
minister at the Vatican had had their effect; the latter had written
of his hope that 'the need for a person of no ordinary attainments
and character is realised as they realise the defects of the last
incumbent owing to ill health'—a reference to Edward J. Byrne.[4]

A phenomenally hard worker, McQuaid hand-wrote thousands
of letters each year, and presided over a diocese that expanded
during his archbishopric from 81 to 115 parishes, as well as co-
ordinating the welfare activities in the diocese when it came to
clothing, fuel and housing. He forged close links with the English
hierarchy through the establishment of an emigrant welfare
bureau and also devoted much time to the physically and
mentally handicapped and the building of hospitals, alcoholism,
and his vigilance committee which sought to monitor the

activities of those on the left. As McMahon points out, many benefited from his public and private charity, and she argues that his life and career 'cannot be understood without encompassing this context of change in the life of his church and his country'[5]

The two guests on this programme had a particular interest in McQuaid for different reasons. John Cooney, a veteran journalist, who before the programme freely admitted that he was somewhat 'obsessed' with McQuaid, had published his book, *John Charles McQuaid, Ruler of Catholic Ireland*, in 1999, having spent the previous few years researching in the Archbishop's archives in Drumcondra (Dublin Diocesan Archives). Margaret MacCurtain, often affectionately known as Sister Ben (from Sister Margaret Benvenuta OP), historian, feminist and frequent critic of the institutional church, spent thirty years teaching history at UCD, a college where McQuaid wielded considerable power. While both of the guests shared certain assessments of McQuaid, they had different perspectives on what motivated him and how historians will remember him.

As an introduction to this programme, a rare archival clip of McQuaid's voice was played; he was extremely media-shy, and, to my knowledge, was never a guest on a radio or television programme. This clip recorded him speaking after returning from a pilgrimage to Lourdes in 1949:

> ... our first diocesan pilgrimage from Dublin has been so successful. I have not seen such recollection and piety amongst any group of pilgrims. I have not heard a murmur of complaint since we left Dublin.

It was perhaps appropriate that the clip chosen, though relatively innocuous, contained references to piety and the absence of dissent —precisely, it seemed, what McQuaid is now remembered for.

I reminded John Cooney of a reference McQuaid had once made to history, to the effect that he dismissed it as nothing but 'the sad recording of the decline in man's natural inclination to worship the Supreme Being'. Cooney seemed to think that this was ironic, if not downright disingenuous on McQuaid's part:

> You mentioned McQuaid didn't like history or the verdict of history. I think that's the wrong reading of McQuaid by some

historians. While he believed ultimately that he was accountable to God and not journalists or educationalists, nevertheless, he wrote to one journalist, Louis MacRedmond, who wanted an interview, and said that, 'Unless you had access to my personal archive, you could not describe my episcopate. They will remain closed for a long time after my death and they will contain many surprises for those who have already attempted to assess my years as archbishop of Dublin.' So McQuaid was very conscious of his place in history. The very fact that he kept 700 boxes of detailed documentation is proof of that. He is a historian's dream because he has nice crisp assessments. His whole system was based on an espionage system, so he thinks like J. Edgar Hoover on whom he very much modelled. So in the whole of his archives you get the anatomy of the whole of Irish society, not just the church.

But was it also the case that he should never have inhabited the archbishop's house in Drumcondra; that he was not seen as a front-runner, and his appointment was unexpected and certainly not inevitable? Why was it such a surprise to the clergy? Just who were they expecting to be the next archbishop?

According to Cooney:

His appointment was a real shock to the clergy. He had been very active in church–state affairs, in education, in Catholic social action and Catholic affairs generally through his friendship with Eamon de Valera, through the Catholic Headmasters' Association, through also making himself available. On the way up he was almost the man who would do the job on any particular thing; he was a bit of a back-scratcher, in a way, almost sycophantic—to be of service.

So was there a degree of political intrigue in his appointment?

Well, he has positioned himself centrally with Dev in the drafting of the 1937 Constitution, but what McQuaid was not really seen as was as a candidate by the clergy, because of the Emergency, because of the long illness of Archbishop Byrne, and I think the diocese of Dublin had been run down, had been let go a bit and it was open to factionalism. There was a group called the Billiards Room Cabinet which was effectively the secretaries of Archbishop Byrne who were running the diocese, so that when the list of the three candidates which goes from the diocese to Rome for submission was sent, it was assumed one of *them* would be appointed. But right from the minute Byrne has died, de Valera, along with Paschal Robinson, the Papal Nuncio in Dublin—they have virtually decided that McQuaid is the man that they need, and who'll be in line with government policy. Remember, Fianna Fáil have been in power for eight years—they've got over the period of anti-clericalism. De Valera's determined to be the Catholic statesman. McQuaid has been critical privately with Dev of the inaction of the hierarchy, of the lack of direction of the clergy and the laity, so they see him as the man.

And what of the diocese he inherited? Obviously it was a much smaller entity than the city and its extended suburbs we are familiar with today. MacCurtain gave a sense of Dublin in 1940:

> He had the privilege of being headmaster as well as president of Blackrock College, but once you stepped outside the precincts of those beautiful parklands, Blackrock was a poor village in the 1930s and 1940s. It was one of the villages that ringed round the small capital city of Dublin, similar to one of the Eastern European capitals at the present time, in that it was poor; the slums were cheek by jowl with O'Connell Street and St Stephen's Green. There were lay groups like the Legion of Mary, which was still in its pristine vigour, and the Society of Saint Vincent de Paul—all of them carried with them notes of the dire, stark poverty and the homelessness of this small capital.

It was undoubtedly a concern with such poverty that gave rise to a premium being placed on welfare, and McQuaid's establishment of the Catholic Social Services Conference. This is perhaps a side of McQuaid that we do not hear enough about. MacCurtain elaborated on this:

> One of his first tasks was to outline a programme of Catholic social welfare, but we must remember, too, he was an extremely interesting educationalist. He came a decade after the promulgation of 'Catholic Education' by, I think, Pope Pius XI. So, education was a strong factor in his suit. In his concept of education, there was

character building, there was moral values, and there was, extraordinary for its time, this sense of social justice. For that reason he did listen to people like Frank Duff and León Ó Broin [Secretary of the Department of Posts and Telegraphs, historian, scholar and ecumenist]. He listened to various conduits of what it was that made the city of Dublin so complex an entity, and he had to move in quickly to set up an agenda of Catholic social welfare.

Of course this could not be done in isolation, and required the co-operation of many different groups. McQuaid seems to have had a need to control the lay movements who were instrumental in welfare and charity work. MacCurtain acknowledged that: 'Yes, I think it's true that his sense of controlling every organisation was uppermost; he was authoritarian, but it was more than that; in some ways, he never dropped the role of headmaster: he had to be in charge.'

An archival clip was then played of one of the individuals who had dealings with McQuaid—Vincent Grogan, who at one stage was the Supreme Knight of the Knights of Columbanus. Was McQuaid different in private? Was he easy to get on with?

> In private, I have to say that my own relationship with him was never easy and indeed never happy. I did find in private he was very much inclined to be—is overbearing too hard a word? But certainly to be intractable and certainly not malleable in his point of view. I think he did feel that those, who perhaps like myself in a modest way, that those who were in a position to influence public opinion should do so in entire obedience and in deference to a very literal point of view that he took about Catholic doctrine, for example.

Cooney was particularly eager to expand on this; indeed, it seemed to him that this was ultimately what McQuaid was about. Is it fair to say that he expected that same obedience from politicians as well?

> Oh, absolutely. While he was willing to embark on social pro-grammes with government, he saw himself basically as the senior partner, and the role of the state was primarily to provide the finance while he got on with the infrastructure; in effect, he was

building a Catholic state within a Catholic state and he expected
the politicians to get on with the supply of money, leaving him in
charge with the religious orders, particularly in education and
the hospitals. His central inspiration, I think, was *Quad Anno*
[*Quadragesimo Anno*], the encyclical by Pope Pius XI, which wasn't
just about social action, but that you should incarnate in the world
Christ the King, the Kingdom of God, which meant in McQuaid's
eyes that the temporal powers should be effectively subordinate to
the spiritual power.

Cooney was quick to turn to what he regarded as the most
interesting and, indeed, unattractive of McQuaid's traits:

Where things go off the rails a bit, I think, is that he's not just
prepared to deal with the social issues, to make Ireland a better
society. His weakness is that he's totally obsessed with sex, and it's the
imposition of a very severe code of sexual conduct, the opposition to
'filthy' books and the opposition to the great writers, the snooping on
people about their sexual mores, the obsession with purity, segre-
gation of boys and girls, that girls have to be primarily trained in
domestic education, to be housewives and so forth, the very fact that
he's against mixed sports. His whole attitude to Irish society becomes
therefore about him being 'the spy in the cab': he's almost like
Ceaușescu [former Romanian dictator] or any of these Eastern
European leaders—he's bringing Ireland more and more under a
kind of spiritual terrorism that is austere, that is backward looking
and which is also pretty strict theologically. By the late 1950s, he's
pretty well taken on everyone in the state. He's against the
Protestants or giving them a real role or say in the Commission on
Unemployment [of which he was appointed Chairman in June
1943]; he's opposed to Noël Browne and the Mother and Child
Scheme. He's opposed to the playing of soccer by the Irish team
against Yugoslavia—the list is endless. When you look at his
archive, you can see he's got priests and laity; even people like
Frank Duff of the Legion of Mary are effectively his spies.

Is this not an overly simplistic, almost cartoon reading of the man
and his influence; is there not a danger here of reading history
backwards, of judging the man according to the standards of the
twenty-first century? MacCurtain responded by saying,

Listening to John, the sense that I pick up is that John is painting the image of McQuaid that we knew in the 1960s when the '60s was freewheeling. But McQuaid as he came into his full strength in the 1940s, and particularly in that first hearing of his voice in Lourdes in 1949, was very much the Victorian teacher, the headmaster who loved Victorian novels—Dickens much more than Thackeray. Also, he had a dark view of life. His MA in UCD in Classics—he was a good Latin scholar—was on Seneca [first-century Roman philosopher, statesman and pre-Christian moralist] and Seneca is one of the dark Latin writers. The obsession with sex that went on? I don't see it primarily as being the major preoccupation of McQuaid. I think the history of the repression of sex in Ireland in the 1940s and 1950s has yet to be written about.

Cooney was in no mood to compromise on his view of the Archbishop and his obsessions, and strongly disagreed:

> . . . because when you look at the McQuaid papers from the 1940s and 1950s, right from the instant he's in power, that obsession is there. If you take his first pastoral—it's based on the idea that the primary duty of parents is to instil discipline in the children from day one.

But wasn't it also the case that there were those who were capable of standing up to McQuaid, or resisting him and what they perceived as his bullying? MacCurtain had direct experience of this. She relayed the story of when 'he disapproved of my stance':

> It was a small essay I wrote in the old *Hibernia* on the place of theology in the universities, about 1963, when the beginnings of the Vatican Council began to permeate back and there was great excitement about theology in these decades. I suggested that because of the nature of the charters of the universities, the only place you could have a faculty of theology was in Trinity, and this offended him deeply, so much so that he wrote to my Mother General (even the very term is militaristic!)—my superior at that time—to say that he wanted to see all my notes for university lectures as well as anything I would write for the papers . . . I was very annoyed and so was she. I reminded her that we were a papal order under the jurisdiction of the Vatican and that the bishop in

this case could only act in an advisory capacity to her. She had forgotten that. She was a fearless woman, Jordan Cleary, and she phoned him—she did not write and you won't find this in the archives—and said this was her business and she was not going to demand lecture notes from me or anything that I would write in the future. So, it was a tremendous vindication, but I did feel in UCD that from then on, I somehow fell under the gaze of Monsignor Horgan [Dean of the Faculty of Philosophy at UCD], that he was aware of this and that I was suspect from then on, so that later on when we had the student revolution in 1969/70, I'm quite sure that Monsignor Horgan went back and said, 'That troublesome nun is at it again!'

There is a tendency, I suggested to Cooney, to forget that there were other bishops in Ireland during the era of McQuaid. What if someone like Cornelius Lucey, Bishop of Cork, or Michael Browne, Bishop of Galway, had been in his position? Cooney seemed to think that were others even more implacable than McQuaid:

I think if Michael Browne had been Archbishop of Dublin, it would have been even worse! 'Cross Michael' he was known as; likewise, Connie Lucey was very strong, but he was very much a Cork man. I think the trend was towards Catholic ascendancy inevitably. If there had been a more moderately minded bishop, we might not have had the sort of thing that went on behind the scenes with McQuaid. He had a famous phrase (and I'm sure he meant it in terms of his relationship with Margaret too!) when he said he liked 'taking people quietly'; this was his code for putting the knife in the back of certain people, so he was a sinister figure, he had his hit men doing it. Now, would another archbishop have had that? I doubt it; perhaps we would have had more balance. If you look at the 1940s and 1950s, at two of the great experiments taking place in Dublin: one was spiritual and social—the Legion of Mary and Frank Duff, and McQuaid was giving Duff, by and large, a hard time; and when it comes to the Second Vatican Council, it's left to Cardinal Suenens of Brussels to suggest to Pope Paul VI that Frank Duff is such a world figure that he should be part of the observers—it's not a suggestion from McQuaid. Secondly, if you look at the ecumenical debates which took place in Dublin in the 1940s with the Mercier Society—mainly civil servants, politicians,

Church of Ireland members and Roman Catholics who met regularly to debate theology—that was too extreme for him, as was debate with the Jewish faith and dialogue with writers.

On the subject of the Vatican Council, a recording from the archives was played in which an upbeat McQuaid talks about differences of opinion, and the 'airing of opposite points of view. Such an airing is what we're here for. The whole point of any debate is that it should reveal all that has to be said on any side of the question.'

Was it fair to say that McQuaid was not able (never mind willing) to grasp the changes heralded by Vatican II, despite his seeming welcome of debate? According to MacCurtain:

> No, I don't think he really did understand them, because McQuaid's Catholicism was based on the total obedience and loyalty which permeated Catholicism in the twentieth century and particularly during the pontificate of Pius XII. And also, his idea of loyalty was militaristic; he was, I think, a military man; he would have made a wonderful commander-in-chief had he not been archbishop. But leaving that aside, he was interested in developments in the media and communications. Joe Dunn was appointed a director of the new *Radharc* ['Vision'—the religious broadcasting unit] team during that last decade of his episcopate and there are letters in Joe Dunn's book, *No Tigers in Africa*, which exhibit the playfulness between Dunn and his archbishop. Nonetheless, I don't think McQuaid really took on board what was happening in terms of the dismantling of the old church.

Cooney added:

> He loves gadgetry, and television attracts him in one way, but he can't control it and this is the big difference between the 1940s and 1950s when he's been in controlling situations, because it is a deferential society and the media were very deferential, so he got away with it. Once we get into the 1960s, there's the feminist movement, there's the Beatles, the development of television, and there's a more abrasive press coming through. At the same time, he's been hit in Rome by two major developments that really spin him out of control—one is that his belief that Protestants have always been sects, not members of the church of Christ, is absolutely

obliterated when ecumenism is accepted, and secondly, he has grown up in the old French tradition that 'error has no rights', that the very fact that the declaration of liberty comes through—he sees this as an absolute betrayal because he has believed for decades that the most iniquitous thing since Luther's so-called Reformation, was the Declaration of the Rights of Man during the French Revolution. So his whole world explodes, and at the same time everyone around him is becoming excited about these ideas, wanting to implement them, yet he can't adapt.

By the end of the 1960s, McQuaid was being subjected to more criticism, not least by Fr Malachy Martin in his book, *The Pilgrim*, written under a pseudonym, which effectively accused him of an innate hatred of Protestants. In this sense, was he simply a prisoner of his own upbringing and theological training and dogma?

MacCurtain, slightly roguishly, offered the following:

> Well, you see, he was a Cavan man and you have to understand that the Cavan men of that generation were great haters, in the context of sectarianism (and I hope I don't offend Cavan listeners!) He had that deep, deep suspicion of the Protestant as 'the other'—a thing that came from his upbringing in Cavan—and he could not comprehend a church that was now welcoming Protestants as brothers.

Cooney elaborated:

> His whole philosophy before and after the Vatican Council is that Catholicism is the One True Church—he sees Pope Paul VI as diluting the faith, but he's in a minority. He's panicking that he can't control it so he's getting more and more argumentative and he's getting caught out more and more. Although he's disdainful in public—saying that he's not worried about it, that he's going to go on and preach as he always has—deep down, it's eating away at him and becomes a real source of anguish for him, and you have to have some sympathy for him, because in Rome's eyes he's become so notorious as the bishop who is not implementing the Council changes. So the Vatican decides to give support to the proposal to seek an alternative once he becomes 75, and has to give his resignation, and the worst moment of his life is when he hears that the successor is to be Dermot Ryan who has been the arch rival, the young Turk who has challenged him.

In 1971, McQuaid's final pastoral as Archbishop of Dublin was on the issue of contraception, entitled *Contraception and Conscience*. Was this apt given that so many women were now defying church teaching in the aftermath of the issuing of the encyclical, *Humane Vitae*, which reiterated the Catholic Church's opposition to contraception, and that feminism was one of the movements with which he would have been uncomfortable? In reaction to this, very different perspectives emerged from the two guests.

MacCurtain offered the following:

> I think he was too old at that stage even to grasp the significance of what he was issuing—that the subject of contraception had become so uncontainable that this final pastoral is almost lip-service.

Cooney strongly disagreed with this, and surmised that if there had been no *Humane Vitae*, he would have slipped from view at an earlier stage:

> I just don't agree with that. I think the whole passage of *Humane Vitae* in 1968 gives him a new lease of life. He thinks that Pope Paul VI is beginning to see sense again and that the Council's aberrations are now a thing of the past and that we can go back to the real uniformity. He's becoming a hard-hitter again—he stops any attempts by Mary Robinson, John Horgan and Trevor West in the Senate from mobilising Jack Lynch to bring in a full contraception bill, and he's also motivated by the fact that his mother had died just a few days after his own birth, so he's absolutely obsessively against contraception.

MacCurtain, however, seemed to believe that the game was up at that stage; that a momentum had developed which he was not in a position to resist:

> But he's overtaken by history. In a sense, we're on the verge of European union and it's the women's vote that is crucial in that referendum, and the whole tenure of the Commission on the Status of Women, parts one and two, had the effect of bringing Catholic and Protestant women together in a united stand. He was up against too much.

Chapter 5

What if Ben Dunne had not gone on a golfing trip to Florida in 1992?

The decade of the 1990s was one of revelations; so much so, that, in a memorable phrase, journalist Fintan O'Toole suggested, 'the gap between current affairs and history had narrowed almost to nothing.'[1] It was often by accident rather than design that the truth (or partial truth) emerged. Nowhere was this more apparent than in the exposure of Ben Dunne's misdemeanours (snorting cocaine and cavorting with a call girl) while on a golfing holiday in Florida in February 1992. In the aftermath of the exposure of his activities and arrest, Dunne was contrite and honest, and there was some sympathy for him, given his personal difficulties and his kidnap ordeal at the hands of the IRA in the previous decade.

However, business is business, and, within a year, the Dunnes Stores empire, which included a family trust valued at £600 million, was at war, and Ben had been removed as chairman of the company. Subsequent litigation over the family trust led to an examination of his business and economic affairs, which revealed that payments had been made to Michael Lowry, a Fine Gael minister, and former Taoiseach Charles Haughey. Investigations and tribunals were to follow. Subsequently, the McCracken Tribunal was to find that Ben Dunne had made five payments to Haughey: £182,630 in December 1987, £471,000 in July 1988, £150,000 in June 1989, £200,000 in February 1990, and £210,000 in November 1991 (all those amounts were sterling).

At the end of 1987, when Haughey's moneyman, Des Traynor, had been looking for a consortium to get Haughey out of financial trouble, Dunne, it seemed, had offered to meet the full requirements, and was reputed to have said, 'I think Haughey is making a huge mistake in trying to get six or seven people together. Christ picked 12 apostles and one of them crucified him.' As Vincent Browne noted wryly, writing in the re-launched *Magill* magazine in September 1997, 'Ben Dunne would be the apostle to crucify Charlie Haughey.'[2]

It was perhaps apt that Browne came to write in detail about all this, given that he had harangued Haughey on various occasions during his years in politics about the origins of his seemingly massive wealth. Haughey certainly would have had little trouble spending the money; according to the report of the McCracken Tribunal, his outgoings were nearly £5,500 per week from August 1988 to January 1991 (and this expenditure did not include mortgage payments)—a total of £708,850. Justice McCracken wrote in his report, 'If politicians are to give an effective service to all their constituents or to all the citizens of the State, they must not be under financial obligation to some constituents or some citizens only.'[3]

The emergence of the details of payments did not surprise many of those who had closely observed Haughey and Irish politics in the 1980s, and the reaction of Haughey's sternest critics was predictably trenchant. Dick Walsh observed: 'Haughey was not, as many of his admirers thought (and think), some latter-day Robin Hood. He may have been out to rob the rich—AIB and the people from whom his agents begged or borrowed money. The funds didn't go to the poor; he served himself . . . we have had at the head of affairs in this state one of the most devious, ruthless and selfish politicians we've known. In politics and business, he kept (and was kept by) a circle of friends who knew that once they played the game, everything was up for grabs.'[4]

In twentieth-century Ireland, tribunals were rarely resorted to, so when they began to probe the murky underworld of the relationship between businessmen and politicians, there was particular interest in what they would be able to prove and what the consequences would be. As Eunan O'Halpin pointed out, until

1991, when the Hamilton Tribunal into the Beef Industry was established, 'judicial inquiries had for two generations been employed solely for inquiries into disasters such as the Whiddy Island explosion of 1978 and the Stardust Fire of 1981 which were without significant political or administrative subtexts'.[5]

There were two precedents for their use in a more political context: in 1947, one was established to examine charges of tax irregularities made against Con Ward, the parliamentary secretary to the Minister for Health. He was found to have committed no serious wrongdoing, but it did end his ministerial career. The following year, Oliver J. Flanagan suffered no such consequences; he had made allegations that Fianna Fáil was involved in influencing the affairs of Locke's Distillery. The tribunal not only found no substance to these allegations but also suggested that Flanagan had deliberately lied. Flanagan did not give a damn, and had no need to; he garnered over 14,000 first-preference votes in the general election of that year, double that of the next highest candidate, and sent a triumphant telegram to de Valera: 'Laois/ Offaly's answer to Locke Tribunal leaves no doubt as to belief in existence of corruption.'[6]

O'Halpin suggests that, after this, Seán Lemass apparently vowed never again to agree to such inquiries based on party political allegations.

The Beef Tribunal report had also disappointed many; it had uncovered massive tax fraud and other reckless practices and decisions made by businessmen and governments, but it was also widely regarded as an 'unwieldy and opaque document', exhaustive in detail and devoid of clear conclusions. In contrast, the 1996 Tribunal of Inquiry (Dunnes Payments), otherwise known as the McCracken Tribunal, and established to deal with allegations about the financial links between Dunnes and Charles Haughey and Michael Lowry, was regarded as a success, because its business was done quickly, clearly and effectively.

It also revealed that there was much more to be discovered and probed, leading to further inquiries, which prompted the President of Ireland, Mary McAleese, to comment in 2000: 'The sordid side of the country's secret life is now under the spotlight and we are deeply challenged by the evidence of so many different forms of evidence.' But the tribunals also had their critics—former Fianna Fáil Senator Des Hanafin suggested in the same year that the fact of protracted tribunal hearings 'demoralises, shakes confidence in politics and even destabilises the state. All politicians and public servants are smeared and held up to public odium'.[7]

But what if Dunne had not travelled to Florida in 1992? Would we still be in the dark? And Would Haughey have stayed out of the headlines and enjoyed a peaceful retirement?

These intriguing questions were addressed to two journalists, Sam Smyth and Pat Leahy. Smyth, a journalist with the *Irish Independent* and presenter of Today FM's *Sunday Supplement* show, wrote a book based on the fallout from the affair—*Thanks a Million Big Fella*. It was also Smyth who revealed in the *Irish Independent* in November 1996 that Dunnes Stores had paid for a large extension to Michael Lowry's house in Tipperary. Lowry was subsequently forced to resign his ministerial position. Leahy, as a young political reporter with the *Sunday Business Post*, had written extensively on the main characters being investigated by the tribunals and the political implications of their findings. He was subsequently appointed political correspondent of the newspaper.

This programme opened with a clip of Ben Dunne speaking in 1992, offering his apologies and explanations; he had been advised, it seemed, to come clean and be contrite, which worked very well for him, despite the fact that the story appeared on the front page of the *Sunday Tribune*, while Vincent Browne was still editor—an unusual front-page splash for that paper. In the archival clip, Dunne was succinct about why he had taken cocaine: 'I dabbled because I was weak.' He elaborated on the unenviable position he had found himself in:

> There was a situation that had arisen where I had taken some cocaine during the few hours before which made me panic and to leave my room and to look for security. When security arrived, I wasn't at all happy that these were regular security men. I was on the balcony of a seventeenth-floor hotel room. I was fighting in my mind for my survival and that's why I was staying in public

view . . . I can blame no one but myself. No, I'm not a cocaine user, in a weak moment I took the goddam stuff and in no way am I looking for pity . . . It was hard to be arrested as a dealer, but it is something I will overcome. I was weak, and that is why I took it.

I asked Sam Smyth to revisit the scene of that infamous night, given that he had made a trip to Florida to research his book. He was particularly interested in what might have happened had Ben Dunne decided to jump:

Well, the day or the very early morning when this became public . . . I was there myself in the hotel and I spoke to a lot of the guests including the members of U2 who were in the foyer of the hotel on the morning—this all happened at around 5 a.m. It's the most expensive hotel in an area where there is no shortage of very expensive hotels . . . It has a central atrium which goes right the way up the building, and below this there's a white grand piano there, and Ben Dunne was directly above this grand piano when he was threatening to jump, which meant that, had he jumped, he would have hit bottom C, I suppose, on that! These security people were genuinely afraid he was going to jump; he did appear afraid, he was paranoid, and there was a young woman by his side . . . she could not understand what was going on. It was a very dramatic time. The entire place ground to a standstill; the police were trying to talk Ben Dunne down, and eventually, when they overpowered him, there was a very memorable description where he was hogtied; he was being carried out on a stick by those policemen, as someone said at the time, like a pig going to a barbeque. It was quite an extraordinary scene.

Smyth elaborated on his follow-up investigations:

Afterwards, I spoke to the District Attorney for the area, a very amiable man who just couldn't believe that this was the equivalent of, say, Donald Trump—how he could possibly get involved in such a thing—as the police remarked at the time, he was caught with a huge amount of cocaine, which was of such a quality that it wouldn't have been got at a street corner or something that was got casually; it had to have been arranged by someone who had an inside knowledge of the drugs trade. It obviously totally changed

his life, but you know, like the butterfly flapping its wings in China
. . . it caused a hurricane in Dublin.

That hurricane, of course, proved ultimately to be a political one—
was there any indication in his life to date that Ben Dunne had any
interest in politics, given that he was associated in the public mind
with the carrying on of the supermarket empire started by his late
father?

> There was no suggestion that he had any particular interest in
> politics—he was known as a big gruff fella, I suppose 'ignorant' in
> the original sense of the word—not to know—he was rude, crude,
> quite generous to those around him, but he had no political
> aspirations, but perhaps a curiosity about politics . . . but, obvi-
> ously, he also knew the value of something you're going to buy, and
> he clearly went out and bought politicians, though it has to be said
> that whether or not he bought Haughey, there's no proof . . . he
> gave this money to Haughey because Haughey was a hero to many
> men like Ben Dunne—he was laconic, he didn't say much, there
> was always a whiff of danger about him.

Did Smyth believe that if Dunne's fall from grace had not occurred,
Haughey would have enjoyed a much more peaceful retirement?
Would the rumours and questions have been kept at bay as Haughey
had managed to keep them for so long during his political career?
After all, unlike some other politicians, when Haughey went, he
went and stayed quiet; there were no controversial interjections or
any suggestions that he wanted a role in public life after retirement, bar perhaps starting the annual regatta in Dingle, Co. Kerry,
where many revered him. On this question, the two contributors
had divergent views. According to Smyth,

> It's very possible he would have been undisturbed, or if Ben Dunne
> had died, because if he had jumped, it would be my view now that
> probably it would have been a personal tragedy; presumably there
> would have been an investigation by the auditors of the company.
> Whether or not it would have been pointed out to his sisters that
> he had paid these sums, it's hard to know; my own view is, I doubt
> it very much, and, knowing the ethos of Dunnes Stores, I don't
> think it was the way they did their business ever to do anything

public. I think they would have been very angry at Ben Dunne for giving the money to Charles Haughey but I don't think they would have caused any trouble and, despite what many people speculated on at the time, it's my view that the Dunnes had nothing to do with the leak that led to the culture of business changing in Ireland.

Were Irish journalists gleeful as well as enthralled with the news coming out in the aftermath of the Dunne drama?
According to Leahy,

Without wishing to sound overly callous about those we write about on a weekly basis, of course we were. I suppose the remarkable thing about Ben Dunne's adventure is all the consequences that stemmed from such a peculiar event so far away ... the Buchanan, McCracken and ultimately Moriarty Tribunals ... But I'm not sure I agree with Sam when he says Haughey could have remained aloof in the absence of Ben's adventures, because aside from that line of revelations, there's also the parallel line—the Flood and Mahon Tribunals which stemmed from Michael Smith and Colm Mac Eochaidh's anonymous ad looking for information on planning corruption ... that of course led to James Gogarty's revelations about Ray Burke, Tom Gilmartin's accusations against Pádraig Flynn, and ultimately to Frank Dunlop.

But Smyth maintained that Haughey would not have been caught:

... except for the smaller fish which was Michael Lowry ... It was on the day that Lowry resigned that when the microphones were switched off, Michael Lowry said to the two reporters there, as people often do when they're caught, 'Well, if you think I'm bad, there's another fella got a million.' This ricocheted around; I remember one of the sobriquets was 'Mr you know who'.

A sarcastic Leahy interjected:

Sam's being characteristically modest, of course, in omitting to mention that it was he who broke the story. I think it's difficult to imagine a landscape where, given all the attention focused on all these more minor figures—some major, such as Burke and Flynn, but all these councillors—that Haughey's finances would not have been subjected to the most extreme scrutiny by journalists and tribunals. While it may be the case that we would not know he received one million from Ben Dunne, I don't think he would have remained untarnished.

This also raised the issue of the difficulty journalists were having in getting to the bottom of the rumours that had been around Haughey since the 1960s, and, more generally, about 'funny business in planning', and the threat of libel that went with attempting to expose what was going on. As Smyth put it, for many years,

> ... nobody could ever nail it. It was dogs in the street stuff; everybody seemed to know about it, but nobody seemed to know how to nail Haughey ... he had been retired for four years before all this came out; he was throwing tea parties and growing chrysanthemums at his home in Kinsealy ... while there was always question marks about him, I think people were quite prepared at that time to let him go with the 'I have done the state some service' ... but the mood had changed, particularly after Michael Lowry was caught in flagrante delicto—these things become a frenzy. They go looking for others ... and then a mood was created which allowed the planning stuff to be probed ... before, people were very frustrated; the journalists who were involved could not get this dealt with ... but the mood had changed and people were much more prepared to believe that yes, there was widespread corruption.

Is a more important 'what if' the one regarding the actions of Michael Smith, a former chairman of An Taisce, and Colm Mac Eochaidh, a barrister specialising in environmental and planning law, who had placed the advertisement concerning planning corruption? What if they had not, on 3 July 1995, placed their ad on the back page of the *Irish Times* ('sandwiched between a death notice and an advertisement for a suit sale'[8])? The ad offered a £10,000 reward fund for information leading to conviction or indictment 'of a person or persons for offences relating to land rezoning in the Republic of Ireland'. Journalists had to contact their solicitors, Donnelly, Neary and Donnelly, in Newry, after the ad had been placed 'on behalf of two anonymous clients'. They had not wanted to do it in the jurisdiction of the Republic. Did they know exactly what they were looking for? Smyth, who met them in Buswells Hotel in Dublin after he had contacted their solicitor, suggested:

> They weren't even sure themselves; it was a fishing expedition . . . and the one thing that has never been said is that they offered a £10,000 reward and I'm not sure if that has ever been paid.

It was also the case, of course, that politicians, particularly those who could not keep their mouths shut, or resist blowing their own trumpets, could also add new twists to the tale, even if they did so advertently. If Pádraig Flynn had stayed away from the *Late Late Show*, would Tom Gilmartin have stayed away from the tribunal? In his usual manner of the lord regaling the peasants with tales of his greatness, Flynn was responding to Gay Byrne who had asked in a casual way about the £50,000 Gilmartin claimed he had given to Flynn. The clip from this show was then played: Flynn dug the hole, and then kept on digging (and digging). If only Dermot Morgan had been around to satirise this memorable exchange:

> 'Well, I wanna tell you about that. I've said my piece about that. In fact, I've said too much, because you can get yourself into the High Court for undermining the tribunal, so I'm not saying anything more. Except to say just one thing. I never asked for money from anyone to do anyone favours in my life.'
>
> *Gay Byrne*: 'But you know Gilmartin?'
>
> 'Oh yeah. Haven't seen him now for some years. He's a Sligo man; went to England; made a lot of money; came back and wanted to do a lot of business . . . didn't work out for him. He's not well; his wife is not well; and he's out of sorts.'

Flynn then reiterated his earlier contention, but amended it, very pointedly:

> 'I never took money from anyone to do a political favour in so far as planning is concerned.'

Gilmartin was enraged on hearing this and made it clear that he was by no means 'out of sorts' and would be telling the Tribunal what he knew. But just who was he and why was he now at the centre of all this? Pat Leahy elaborated:

> Tom Gilmartin was a property developer based in Luton and he came over in 1989 and he wanted to get involved in two major developments—one on Bachelor's Walk and one out where the Liffey Valley Centre is now, and he met several people—and much of this is still to be fleshed out at the tribunal. He met most of the senior members of Fianna Fáil and he gave Pádraig Flynn £50,000. Flynn was Minister for the Environment at the time and treasurer of Fianna Fáil. Gilmartin claimed, coming out of a meeting with Fianna Fáil, 'You guys make the Mafia look like monks.' It seems Liam Lawlor was one of the individuals who Gilmartin claimed he got money from. Lawlor wanted to be made a director of the company and put on a monthly retainer . . . in the heel of the hunt, things didn't work out for Gilmartin because other developers came in and the bank foreclosed on him.

What was Sam Smyth's take on Gilmartin?

> My recollections of hearing the evidence at the time suggested to me that here was an Irishman who had gone to England, made enormous sums of money, came home and along the way somebody said to him, 'The way to get things done in Ireland is to give money to politicians.' He came into town with his plans and word got around that there was this gobshite [Leahy interjected: 'an ATM cash machine!'] handing out money and everybody took his money, which suggests to me something else: Is it as corrupt to take someone's money and *not* do something for it, as it is to take money and *do* do something for it? This is one of those conundrums that comes up from time to time, but it seems that every time Gilmartin turned up, someone took his money. What there's no evidence of is anybody doing anything for it.

Pat Leahy suggested:

> If there is a single thread running through all of this, it's the perception among some of the business classes that large areas of public

policy, and particularly at local level with regard to the planning process, were for sale, and the brokers in that sale were the politicians, and if the 1990s was the decade of revelations, it was revelations to that effect.

One curious thing is that, despite the allegations being flung about senior politicians taking large sums of money from business people, it seemed to do little damage to them or their parties when it came to elections. Why were the opposition parties not able to make more headway, with Fianna Fáil continually in the news for all the wrong reasons?

Pat Leahy acknowledged:

It didn't appear that the opposition could make capital out of it . . . we mentioned Colm Mac Eochaidh—he stood for Fine Gael in the general election in Dublin South East in 2002 and got whacked, and Fine Gael actually lost his seat. Poll after poll shows that people don't really seem to care about sleaze.

In Smyth's view, it was not about individual politicians being punished, but rather:

'A plague on all your houses' is the message coming through on successive opinion polls . . . Fianna Fáil actually went up two and the opposition dropped a point each, so it seems to be that people grew disillusioned with the political process more so than with any particular party. Yet, paradoxically, they seem to like their local TD.

This was a difficult time for Fine Gael, which was beset by question marks over the future of John Bruton. Was Michael Lowry seen at any stage as the heir apparent within that party?

According to Leahy,

I think that's the most fascinating 'what if', because I think that definitely Michael Lowry could quite easily, if he hadn't been taken down, have become leader of Fine Gael. John Bruton was always from 1992 teetering on the edge as leader of Fine Gael. Had he gone, Michael Lowry, who was Fine Gael's most successful fundraiser ever, by a mile, could have been unstoppable within the party. Now, had Michael Lowry become leader of Fine Gael, he could easily have been Taoiseach or Tánaiste in a Fianna Fáil/Fine Gael coalition, because Fianna Fáil always regarded him more as one of theirs than a righteous Blueshirt!

Sam Smyth wasn't quite as enthusiastic about this theory:

> Oh, I don't know. I think he almost certainly would have been leader, or if not leader, the principal power broker within Fine Gael because he gave money to the potential leaders following Bruton— he gave money to Michael Noonan and Ivan Yates; it was always cash, and any time Fine Gael needed money, he was there. Bruton, coming from a wealthy background, always had a certain disdain for the grubbier end of politics, when you had to ask people for money, and Lowry was one of those people who had no difficulty in knowing the way business is done. I don't know if anything specific was ever done for it, but I have absolutely no doubt that there is an understanding that if I give this money, I get preference for it—that's the way it was done, and Lowry was popular within the party. Before he was taken down, he was John Bruton's favourite; he was the one that the rest of the party were bouncing ideas off . . . I remember before the story that brought him down, there was a profile in the *Irish Times* suggesting he was the brightest of them all; he was young; he had everything going for him.

One individual who had not been mentioned in the discussion was Bertie Ahern. Had there been a feeling in journalistic circles that the revelations about Haughey might result in a punch for Ahern that would knock him out, given that he was seen as Haughey's protégé? According to Leahy,

> There was a sort of belief from the Haughey revelations on, that Ahern could at any minute be taken out by a train coming down the tracks of the tribunal, so to speak. Ahern is a guy who has had to put up with that sort of expectation but nothing has ever landed on him and I think that expectation that there is a train running down the tracks towards Ahern is somewhat dissipated as time passes . . . the tribunals if anything have got further away from his government, his cabinet . . . I don't think there is that expectation any more.

Smyth's reflections on this painted an interesting picture of a thoroughly ordinary Taoiseach with little interest in money:

> If there had been something there, I suspect it would have been found out a long time ago . . . Bertie Ahern is the sort of guy that could run on €25 a day—three pints of Bass, a takeaway pizza and a video—and that is the image he has. He actually works very hard; he's quite monastic in many ways—he just works very hard all the time. I think if there's an accusation that can be levelled against him, it's that he was there and saw others doing bad things and turned his head away, averted his eyes—that's the main criticism of him.

And what of the tribunals themselves—do they work? Have they been worthwhile?

Both seemed to agree. In Smyth's view, 'Yes, they do exactly what they say on the tin; they take forever and they will tell you things: what they don't do is what some of the politicians wanted them to do, and that is to punish Fianna Fáil.' According to Leahy:

> Yes they work, but I think that the current expectation that the Mahon tribunal is going to go on for another 10 or 15 years will see a desire for a move towards a less formal, less quasi-judicial form of investigation that would be able to conduct their inquiries without the necessity for formal legal representation on each side, without the necessity of years and years of tedious inquiries . . . the lawyers love them which is generally a sign that they're not good for the rest of us.

Chapter 6

What if Bishop Eamon Casey's secret had not been discovered?

This show opened with an archival clip of Bishop Eamon Casey inviting the guests on an RTÉ television show to join him in a sing-a-long, as he began to belt out, with great gusto, 'If you're Irish, come into the parlour', and then moved on, scarcely pausing for a breath, to a fine rendition of 'The Foggy Dew'. One of the guests in the studio audience during that performance was Fr Michael Cleary. Both men were well known, as a result of their energetic personalities and high media profiles, particularly around the time of Pope John Paul II's visit to Ireland in September 1979, when Casey had presided at the mass in Galway at which Irish young people were finally told publicly that they were loved.

Both men, as we now know, had been carrying deep secrets—both were fathers. But there, perhaps, the similarities ended. Eamon Casey's private life became full public knowledge in May 1992, dramatically announced on RTÉ's *Morning Ireland* programme, and broken in the print media by Conor O'Clery, then US correspondent of the *Irish Times*. Michael Cleary's secret did not emerge into public glare until after his death in 1995.

Casey is a fascinating subject for a number of reasons. Throughout his extraordinary career, he wore many hats. Not just a singer, he was also a political and social activist, often a champion of the dispossessed, but also a man who lived life to the full, ate and drank well and drove fast cars, and all of this while being one of Ireland's favourite bishops, first of Kerry, where he was appointed in 1969, and later of Galway and Kilmacduagh. The secret that emerged in 1992 was that he was father of Peter Murphy and lover of Annie Murphy. More recently, when this programme was broadcast (October 2004), he was in the news again as a result of his decision not to return to Galway to commemorate the twenty-fifth anniversary of the Pope's visit there in 1979. Casey, it seemed, was determined to stick to his isolated penance abroad, first in South America, and, after 1998, in England.

He had managed to stay out of the limelight after his dramatic resignation in 1992. For some, this was a case of the Bishop of Galway fleeing and leaving his fellow bishops to 'pick up the pieces';[1] for others, it was the only possible course of action open to him, given the disgrace and humiliation he had brought on himself, particularly when it emerged that he had dipped into diocesan funds in order to finance his son's education (the funds were subsequently repaid).

Born in Kerry in 1927, Casey was educated in Limerick and Maynooth before being ordained in 1951. He first served as a curate in Limerick, and in 1960 joined the emigrant apostolate in Britain, where he became director of the Catholic Housing Aid Society and set up 65 branches throughout Britain. He was a founder trustee of Shelter National Campaign for the Homeless and became chairman of Shelter in 1968. As Bishop of Kerry, he was active in introducing social services, and sponsored the 'full life for youth' initiative, aimed at nurturing the talent of the youth in his diocese. He remained active in emigrant welfare; in 1971, he masterminded a national collection in support of Irish welfare centres in Britain, raising an extraordinary £280,000 in a single day.[2] Nor was he shy in excoriating governments about their failings in this regard; after all, from the late 1950s onwards, the government, in refusing to fund emigrant welfare, had made it clear that the church was on its own in this regard.[3]

Casey's other interests were reflected in the various commissions of the bishops' conferences that he served on, including mass media, social welfare and the Third World, and he was critical too of the government in relation to its paltry response to Third World development and, indeed, American foreign policy. He was also prominent in the right-to-life debate in 1983, rejecting the assertion that the referendum on abortion was sectarian, arguing that the right to life was 'antecedent to all churches. It is there before there was ever a church'.[4]

Perhaps his approach to agitation and community development can be best summed up by his contention (and this he tried to deliver on), that 'one powerful single voice is more important and more effective than a number of voices, each of which is in competition with the other, for both the public purse and public attention'.[5]

But what sort of man was he, and what difference would it have made to him personally and to the institutional church if Annie Murphy had never arrived in Kerry, or if the secret affair and child had remained under wraps? The two guests on this programme, historian and Dominican sister Margaret MacCurtain, and archivist and critic Catriona Crowe, fleshed out answers to some of these questions. I started by asking Margaret to share her memories of him in the 1960s and the 1970s; to give some sense of the kind of man he was and how he saw his place in the Irish Catholic Church:

Well, when the Papal Nuncio told him he was appointed Bishop of Kerry in the summer of 1969, I remember his reaction—he said he was dismayed! He was the youngest bishop; he was unconventional; he had a wonderful track record in London because he had started the whole housing situation, not just for the homeless Irish but also for the British . . . he really was a free spirit and he knew he was coming into one of the most traditional dioceses in Ireland. He was a very bright man, but he had not been plucked out of academia, and he was dismayed. He knew his weaknesses and he knew his strengths, but, in fairness to him, when he went in, he was like a breath of fresh air, because one of the first things he did was to raise the profile of Saturday-night dancing and céilís, which is very important in Kerry . . . and then the serious side of him came in 1973 when he supported Trócaire and became its chairman, so it looked as if he was set to become the moving spirit in the Irish hierarchy, and my sense of him was influenced by hearing, I suppose, about the nights in Glenbay—I never attended them, but people would love him dropping in, in his fast car, driving at 95 miles per hour . . . it was said that once he drove from Killarney to Tralee and didn't even notice that the gears had gone on his car—he travelled so fast! He was very much the trendy 1970s but with a deep, deep seriousness about social action.

This concern was obviously something that had evolved from his work as an emigrant chaplain, the position he had been appointed to in 1957. It was from this position that he launched what became, in effect, a framework for a housing movement. According to MacCurtain, 'He was appointed to a kind of "safe seat", if you like, as chaplain to emigrants in Britain, and he could have gone to the middle classes, but instead he went to Slough; he saw what was happening and established Shelter, and from that he went into the whole issue of the homeless in Britain; it was prophetic when you think of the numbers that came in the 1980s—that he set the trend for a policy that became a government policy.'

What if Casey had chosen a political life instead of taking the religious route—would he have been an effective politician? MacCurtain believed that he would have made 'an excellent politician'. I asked Crowe if those who identified with left-wing politics or worked as community activists saw him as a distinctly 'left-wing bishop'?

Very much so, and for those of us who were battling with the institutional Catholic Church, particularly around its misogyny and restrictions against women in the 1980s, even though Casey seemed to share some of those ideas, he was a huge breath of fresh air in terms of his espousal of social justice, not just in Ireland but in the Third World as well. Remember, he was at Archbishop Romero's funeral in San Salvador—another bishop who was committed to social justice in a very dangerous country. Casey supported Third World issues, through Trócaire in some cases, but also off his own bat, right throughout his career. In a way, he was very, very different from what had preceded him. In Ireland, we were used to the very dour, strict authoritarian bishops like John Charles McQuaid in Dublin or Cornelius Lucey in Cork. Now, I know that's a very black and white picture, but that's the kind of image one had. Casey combined the qualities of a prince of the church with the broth of a boy. He liked the authority that he held and he thought it was very important, but he also liked to enjoy himself.

An archival clip was played in which Casey talked about his own vocation, and the fact that he did not feel there was any particular time at which he received his calling. He suggested that the sort of family he came from had a lot of bearing on it, in terms of how he saw the role of the priest, as that of 'go-between between man and God'. It was all very humble sounding, but if his personal life had not ended the way it did, would Casey have gone further in his church career? Was he cardinal material?

According to MacCurtain,

It's interesting that Bishop Duffy was very gracious when Casey resigned and said he had great gifts of leadership; now whether these gifts would have brought him to the central authority of being a cardinal, I'm not sure, because he was impulsive, he was a driven man and he was not a listener—also, I don't know if he would have understood, politically, if he would have been able to mesh in in the Northern troubles in the very subtle way that Cardinal Daly was able to do. I think Cardinal Daly has been greatly under-estimated in his dealings with both unionists and nationalists during his time as cardinal, whereas Casey was an instinctive kind of man who went on his instincts more than his intellect.

Was this a view shared by Crowe?

Well, apparently he used to wear red socks quite a lot which may have been an indication that he aspired to be a cardinal! But I think, realistically, even though he was one of the warmer-uppers at the Pope's visit to Ireland in 1979, I don't think the present pope [then John Paul II] would have chimed with him on some of the social justice issues. There might have been difficulties there and I think Margaret's analysis of the personality stuff is possibly right as well, but I think perhaps he might have gone further in the Irish church. He was building quite a serious power base—he had a huge amount of support from young people, for example, and the person who reminds me most of him now, in every respect, except I suppose 'the scandalous one', in inverted commas, is Willie Walsh, who is someone that is hugely admired by young people, which is something that the church needs now so badly, especially with the recent scandals. But I think the impulsive side of him could have made problems for him in terms of advancement within the church.

What about that public perception of Casey as a man very much in touch with youth? When looking back on 1979 and the Pope's visit, and his articulation of love for young people, is there a danger of sentimentalising it? Was it really important that young people were being told the Catholic Church loved them?

Mac Curtain suggested, 'It was in one way, but there's another way of looking at that. I wasn't in Galway, I watched it on television—with hindsight, maybe this is too dramatic, but I thought he was a troubled man, even at that stage.' This reminded me of an interview which he had done with Ivor Kenny in 1986, in which he referred to being 'a battered instrument'—was this the accumulation of pressure and guilt as a result of the great secret?

> Yes, by 1979 it must have been a tremendous effort, more for him than for Michael Cleary, to keep up that kind of façade of jollity and bonhomie, and loving affectionate nature, which I think was basically what he was, but behind it was this tremendous secret that he carried.

That secret, when it emerged, also brought Annie Murphy into the homes of Irish people via numerous interviews and soul-baring media sessions in which she detailed how she first met him in April 1973. An interview from the archives was played in which she remembered, 'It really was kind of love at first sight; I just felt this tremendous feeling. I don't know what it was but I had never felt that in my life.' Her son, Peter, also emerged into the limelight and recalled how, 'I was kind of shocked when she told me at the age of 9. Even at the age of 9, I knew what a bishop was, what he did and what he can and can't do and I was what he cannot do . . . it would be nice if he could just have acknowledged me.'

A contemporary vox pop with members of his diocese, recorded in May 1992 by an RTÉ reporter, also revealed the large degree of sympathy that existed for Casey. Is it fair to say that there was more sympathy than anger and disgust?

According to Crowe, 'There was a great deal of sympathy, and, of course, anybody human has sympathy for someone in a position of disgrace. But it's a very complex situation, all of this. I spent yesterday on a plane, reading Annie Murphy's book, which I have to say is a really terrible book. It's a mixture of coyness and far too much information about things we don't need to know.'

Undoubtedly the book, *Forbidden Fruit*, co-written with Peter de Rosa, contains passages of excruciating drivel, such as the following:

> There stood the Bishop, my love, without clerical collar or crucifix or ring, without covering of any kind. The great showman had unwrapped himself. Christmas of all Christmases. This was for me more of a wonder than all the mountains, lark song and heather-scents of Ireland. He stood before me, his only uniform the common flesh of humanity . . . he looked forlorn, almost like a child lost in a dark wood . . . I witnessed a great hunger. This was an Irish famine of the flesh.[6]

'We don't need to know any of that Annie' was Crowe's stern response. 'She shouldn't have written the book and she herself felt afterwards that she had been manipulated by her publishers. I'm not sure if that's true or not. She's disingenuous in it; there are awful accounts of her collaborating with her son, Peter, to video him in New York, which isn't either appropriate or right.'

Crowe then went on to give a very perceptive analysis of the significance of the revelations and what occurred afterwards:

> But at the heart of the story, what we have is a really harrowing account of a woman having a baby and being pressurised by her lover and many other people to give the child up for adoption, which raises huge issues about Irish society at that time. We also have the first and only account of what it was like to be in St Patrick's Home on the Navan Road, and it is incredibly moving and very, very anger-making to read what happened her. We can't judge people, and one wouldn't want to, but I think some important issues came out of this very old-fashioned scandal, as it turned out to be . . . Peter Murphy was not the first child of someone sworn to celibacy, but it raised issues, for example, about

absentee fathers in situations where women are raising children on their own—what that does to the child; what it does to the mother. In terms of the church itself, it raised the issue of the loss of good authority; Eamon Casey would have been seen as someone who wielded good authority within an institution that needed to change, and then, of course, the huge identity issue which became in the 1990s one of the main issues in Ireland, crystallising around subjects like the foreign adoption issue that uncovered itself, and institutional care—children, now adults, searching for information about their identity and looking to repair broken and fragmented relationships. Now, Peter Murphy is different in the sense that he knew who his father was, but he wasn't recognised by him until very late in the day, so a lot of issues come up from this that I think are still obsessing us in Irish society.

MacCurtain also believed that the Casey affair had shed light on an issue that had been relevant for a very long time:

What I am concerned about is that we probably have forgotten that in the time of Pope Paul VI, a lot of priests got dispensations personally from that pope, and the big issue for discussion, even for the synod of bishops in 1971, was a married clergy. It was this big topic for discussion among bishops all over the world, particularly the African bishops and the South American bishops; and the second thing I think we have to face is that already, post-Vatican II, the Catholic Church was in crisis . . . by the 1990s, the Catholic Church was visibly in crisis, and what was so pleasant listening to the vox pop was the compassion of ordinary people for what was a complex tragedy, involving two people and a child . . . It's true that we are aware in Ireland that the names 'Mac an tSagairt' and 'Mac an Easpaigh' existed in the Celtic church where celibacy was not an issue, but also there is the fact that in these times, the whole issue of clerical celibacy has been magnified by the present pope, I think to a kind of apex of church authority . . . in my opinion, in relation to Bishop Casey, it's a very tantalising question—was he right or was he wrong to remain a member of the Irish hierarchy?

Casey, at a later stage, referred to the fact that he had received 1,500 letters, and they were all supportive, bar two. Given the level of public support and sympathy that seemed to exist, could he not have stayed in Ireland, and if he had stayed, would it not have been better for the Catholic Church? Crowe's belief was that it 'would have been unbearable for him to stay. There's a clean economy about his fleeing the way he did. It was very hard on Annie Murphy and his son, but, on the other hand, they knew what to expect. There was a huge media storm about it. There was compassion from ordinary people for Casey, which I think is admirable, but the other side of the coin is that Annie Murphy received boatloads of hate mail, which isn't fair.'

Was the treatment of her by Gay Byrne when he interviewed her on the *Late Late Show*—during which he seemed to question her fitness as a mother—a further injustice?[7] Crowe was adamant that:

> If there was ever a little moment where the underlying misogyny of Irish society was revealed, it was in that moment—one doesn't have to believe she was right to go public or right to seek money in the way she did, but to treat her the way Gay Byrne treated her was surprising and shocking.

Given the flood of revelations about the dark underbelly of the church in the 1990s, isn't there always the danger that the name Casey will be used in the same paragraph as the names of people who brought shame on themselves and the church because of child abuse? And isn't that particularly unfair, given how active Casey was in Limerick as a curate in tackling the issue of child abuse? Isn't it the case that, nonetheless, he will be on that history page?

'Unfortunately, it is the case because it all coalesced in the 1990s,' according to MacCurtain.

> In a way, by remaining Eamon Casey the Bishop, he acts really as the weakest link, and he acts as a kind of a shield for the hierarchy in the 1990s because they have become embroiled in stalling strategic strategies around the issue of child abuse. Were Bishop Casey in a sense more respected, more vibrant, he could have acted as a kind of mediator between the issue of married clergy in the church—which is a very important issue for the future.

Crowe saw the Casey affair 'as a much more old-fashioned scandal. I suppose the next one of this sort that came up was Fr Michael Cleary in 1995, but that was different too because Phyllis Hamilton was 17 years old when she came to him and very vulnerable. Annie Murphy, to give her credit, does not claim to be a victim, except with regard to her son not being recognised, but she was an adult when she engaged in the affair, and she acknowledges that she wasn't victimised in that sense.'

There were many other events that occurred in the early 1990s, including the X case controversy, and the whole question of the rights of women with regard to pregnancy, and, indeed, the extent to which the church respected them. Could Casey, if Annie Murphy had not come to Ireland, have been someone to take a constructive role in terms of the relationship between women and the church?

'Frankly, I doubt it', responded MacCurtain.

> For the reason that what's really happening to the Irish church, and it's going to be slow, is that a new model of church is slowly emerging and it's going to be a model of church where the laity have far more of a role in terms of leadership positions than could have been possible or imagined in the 1980s or even the 1990s. Women are going to be more vocal but they are also, theologically and professionally, going to be more articulate around issues and may well leave bishops of the calibre of Eamon Casey speechless in the way that they can argue a position.

But if history remembers Casey for something other than the Annie Murphy saga, surely it will be with regard to his political activism and as a trenchant critic of American foreign policy in the Third World? An archival clip was played of Casey being interviewed about the visit of Ronald Reagan to Ireland in 1984, in which he criticised what he saw as the lies that Reagan was pedalling about El Salvador, particularly when Reagan had referred to its 'duly elected government'. Casey pointed out that there had not been an elected government in that country since 1944. In relation to Reagan's weasel words, Casey criticised 'the total absence of any concern for human rights. We see the endemic oppression and poverty there as an affront to human dignity.' This seemed to be topical also in terms of the church's role in politics, in speaking out about human rights abuses—the Iraq war was a case in point. What about the noble tradition of the Irish church speaking out on these issues, particularly in the context of the missionary work of Irish priests and nuns—could the Irish church still have a strong role to play in all of that?

Mac Curtain replied:

> I have been at Merriman summer schools where Bishop Willie Walsh has been fearless in the way he has spoken out about issues of church and state. He probably hasn't got the media attention Casey did. I think that was Casey's finest moment actually, when he revealed his opposition to the Reagan visit. I'm not sure bishops should be silent; it is a wintry period in the church in general, with an ageing pope who himself was very fearless vis-à-vis communism when he took on the freedom of Poland in the 1970s before he was elected pope . . . so in terms of the model of a bishop speaking out, I hope it will never disappear from the Irish church.

Crowe suggested that there were reasons to be hopeful of a change in direction:

> One has hopes for Dr Diarmuid Martin. I think that the way that he has begun to respond to the institutional scandal issue bodes well. It really needs to be taken in hand. Now that he has got his head, I really think we are going to see more of a commitment to social justice from our Archbishop of Dublin and I sincerely hope so because it is very, very badly needed.

In the midst of all this, is it time for Bishop Eamon Casey to return to Ireland?

'Absolutely' was the unanimous response.

Chapter 7
What if there had been no 1916 Rising?

This programme was broadcast on the eighty-ninth anniversary of the 1916 Easter Rising. The same week, a new book, *Witnesses: Inside the Easter Rising*, by Annie Ryan, was published, an indication that new perspectives on the Rising were still emerging. This book was based on the files of the Bureau of Military History (BMH), consisting of statements taken in the 1940s and 1950s from people involved in the events of the period 1913–21. Under the auspices of the Department of Defence, the work of the Bureau was wound up at the end of 1957, and, in March 1959, 83 steel boxes were locked into the strong room of government buildings, containing the 1,770 statements, as well as collections of contemporary documents, press cuttings and photographs.

What had not been resolved was when the boxes could be opened; there is no record of a formal government decision as to when the files would be released—an issue which led to frustration on the part of historians. In 1967, historian F. X. Martin bemoaned the 'official iron curtain . . . cutting off the findings of the Bureau from all outsiders . . . The papers of the Bureau have now become a miser's hoard'.[1] Despite his fulminations, and the revisiting of the issue on many occasions, the bureau's files were not released until March 2003.

Unsurprisingly, there is a huge variety of statements—some short, some long, and some containing implausibly detailed recollections, but most of them are measured, sober and, perhaps most importantly, are from the rank and file members of the many groups involved in the Rising. As Margaret MacCurtain points out, the statements give support to the contention that 'Easter Week 1916 does not belong to any one group exclusively—the Irish Volunteers, the IRB, Cumann na mBan, Sinn Féin, the RIC or British public opinion—but defies co-option'.[2]

The statements give a strong sense of what motivated participants, what they did (and did not do), the extent to which they believed that they were part of a national revolution, and the degree to which they triumphed and suffered. Never before has such a range of first-hand experiences of the Rising been collated and analysed. Ryan succeeded in illuminating the sheer diversity of human experiences in 1916, and in particular highlighted the role of women in the Rising, and provided more insight into the re-organisation of the Irish Republican Brotherhood prior to the Rising. Later in 2005, Charles Townshend published a more comprehensive overview of the Rising, *Easter 1916: The Irish Rebellion*, and it, too, sought to incorporate the BMH files into a fresh narrative of the events of Easter week.

Most of the witnesses were very young at the time of the Rising, and their statements give a strong sense of the social and political exclusion felt by a determined minority during the First World War. Of course, thousands had enrolled in the British army, and it would be a gross exaggeration to suggest that the majority of Irish people felt remotely revolutionary in 1916, but there did exist an expanding group of young and politicised dissidents. Trade unionist and member of the Irish Citizen Army, Helena Molony, was one of them, and she recalled resentment towards Arthur Griffith's Sinn Féin movement, with its emphasis on passive resistance, and the sort of home-rule Ireland envisaged by its members:

> The social ideas of Sinn Féin did not appeal to us. They wished to see in Irish society (as their official organ once expressed it) 'a progressive and enlightened aristocracy, a prosperous middle class, and a happy and contented working class'. It all sounded dull, and a little bit vulgar to us.[3]

The sense of confusion and bewilderment created by Eoin MacNeill's decision to countermand the order given to the Volunteers to assemble on Easter Sunday, after the organisers of the Rising had deceived him, is recalled by many. Some felt in the loop, others outside; Paddy Browne, a member of the staff at Maynooth College, recalled that, 'I had not the slightest notion that anything was going to happen, I did not know anything about dispatches going around the country', whereas Min Ryan remembered 'a sort of seething undercurrent' of anticipation.[4]

Not for the first or last time, however, British government ineptitude ensured that the mood of the Irish public was transformed. The decision to execute the rebel leaders and arrest 3,400 suspected sympathisers in May 1916 ensured that the Rising was the prologue to a much more prolonged and effective Irish War of Independence.

The events of 1916 thus raise intriguing 'what ifs'—not just because the Rising could quite likely have not gone ahead, but also the question of whether or not it could have occurred at a different time, and if so, how different would the impact have been? Historians have in fact been raising counterfactual questions about the Rising for many years. In 1973, Joe Lee pointed out that the decision of Patrick Pearse to accept an unconditional surrender was of the utmost significance, because if such a surrender had not occurred, 'there would hardly have been executions, as the Volunteers would probably have died in action.'[5] Twenty-two years later, in the book mentioned above, Charles Townshend suggested, 'The argument that the decisive national mobilisation would have happened in 1918 with or without the 1916 rebellion remains a powerful one. Opposition to conscription was the key motive for the expansion of both Sinn Féin and Volunteer membership during the war. At the individual level, it may be asked whether without conscription Michael Collins (to take one notable example) would have returned to Ireland from London at that point. At the institutional level, no other cause could have brought the Catholic Church so firmly into the Sinn Féin-led national front. And on the face of things, at least, it could be argued that the 1916 rebellion made the imposition of conscription—and hence the dramatic upsurge of national unity in 1918—less rather than more likely'.[6]

In 1991, at the time of the seventy-fifth anniversary of the Rising, there was controversy about the low-key approach of the state to its commemoration—clearly, it had gone out of fashion, but undoubtedly there will be those determined to ensure that the centenary in 2016 is a much more grandiose affair.

The two historians who contributed to this programme represented the research of two different generations into the Rising. Michael Laffan, Head of the School of History at UCD, has made significant contributions to the debate about revisionism in Irish history and is author of the definitive history of Sinn Féin during this period, *The Resurrection of Ireland*. Marnie Hay had just completed a doctorate on Bulmer Hobson, an IRB activist and strategist, and a contemporary critic of the Rising, and has read many of the Bureau of Military History statements. As Towsnhend has pointed out, Hobson was effectively 'written out of the nationalist story' because of the stance he took in 1916.[7]

Laffan began researching this period at a time when historians like F. X. Martin were insisting that the Rising was neither necessary nor inevitable, and that it was disingenuous to suggest otherwise. Is this a view that still has wide currency?

> I think almost all people nowadays would agree with that; almost all historians would agree it wasn't inevitable, it wasn't something inexorable; it was partly the result of chance; the rebels were extra-ordinarily lucky. True, MacNeill countermanded the manoeuvres which were to form the pretext, the background and the occasion for the Rising, but leaving that aside, otherwise they were very lucky—the British could have stopped it. British naval intelligence knew what was going to happen but couldn't release the information to the cabinet or Dublin Castle, so they were very lucky it went ahead. You might say, to be blunt and brutal, they were lucky that the British responded as they did; if the British hadn't responded in a normal way—and the executions were perfectly normal, after a Rising when rebels parade their alliance with your enemy (the reference to 'gallant allies in Europe'), the attempt to smuggle German arms—all that was designed to provoke as well as to help the Rising succeed and it did provoke the British into a response.

The response was very modest executions by the standards of most rebellions, but enough to change public opinion. It needn't have happened; the Rising needn't have happened or the British could have responded differently, so the old idea; the pre-1966 idea that the Rising was something natural or predestined has been exploded a long time ago.

Was it the case that, when you consider the level of militancy in Ireland—the marching with arms and the drilling, both north and south—the British government had, in fact, shown a great deal of tolerance in the lead up to Easter 1916? Laffan was adamant that:

> Never had Ireland been more benignly and moderately ruled than in early 1916 and the classic example is this—discrimination by the British government in favour of the Irish against the English, the Scots and the Welsh—they were all conscripted from January 1916 onwards. The Irish were let off because Redmond and Dillon and the Irish Parliamentary Party leaders asked that the Irish should not be sent off to be killed in France, so not only in comparison with the Irish past or other countries in Europe, but even within the UK, the Irish were privileged; Ireland was doing very well out of the war. There wasn't any pre-revolutionary situation in Ireland at all.

Was there a perception that Eoin MacNeill was an out-of-touch academic with his head in the books and someone who did not really have an insight into the mentality of the IRB, or is that depiction of him unfair?

> He was suspicious and, of course, he was quite right; he had every reason to be suspicious—not suspicious enough from his point of view. He wrote the famous memorandum that F. X. Martin published in 1961, showing an insight into the mentality of the rebels, almost forecasting what they would do—that they would fail militarily but succeed posthumously and change public opinion after their deaths—and he ruled that out as something that was unacceptable to him at least, so he had an idea of what they were planning. Maybe he imagined that he could outmanoeuvre them; if so, he was totally wrong and they—people like Seán MacDermott and Tom Clarke—were much tougher, more ruthless, and they

Gay Byrne on the set of *The Late Late Show* in September 1985. Was he still the 'Great Liberator' or had the power moved to the radio show? (*Derek Speirs*)

Some of the foot soldiers of the Irish cultural wars of the 1980s, campaigning in favour of the proposed pro-life amendment to the constitution, 1983. 'It was like living in Franco's Spain' (Ann Marie Hourihane). (*Derek Speirs*)

Garret and Charlie square up. The cover of *Magill* magazine, 7 June 1981. 'There is no doubt that this is the worst government in the history of the state. The question is: would the alternative be even worse still?' (Vincent Browne, editor). (*Derek Speirs*)

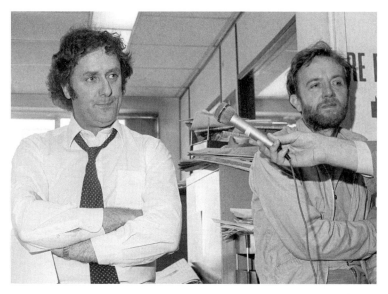

Vincent Browne looking sceptical as usual. 'The only person I've ever met for whom the term "larger than life" actually applies' (Fintan O'Toole). Journalist Paddy Prenderville looks on. (*Photocall Ireland*)

Dr John Charles McQuaid, Archbishop of Dublin, 1940–72, holding his hat, but not the Cardinal's hat. 'Bringing Ireland more and more under a kind of spiritual terrorism' (John Cooney). (*Courtesy of the National Library of Ireland*)

Ben Dunne walks the tribunal plank, April 1997. His solicitor, Noel Smyth, looks on.
(*Derek Speirs*)

Annie Murphy, one time lover of Bishop Eamon Casey. She helped to end 'an Irish famine of the flesh'. April 1993. (*Derek Speirs*)

'Wear a condom just in Casey' (and never overlook a marketing opportunity). O'Connell Bridge, Dublin, June 1992. (*Photocall Ireland*)

Dublin in ruins, April 1916, after the Easter Rising. 'The rebels were extraordinarily lucky' (Michael Laffan). (*Camera Press Ireland*)

Eamon de Valera in Cobh for the return of the Treaty Ports, July 1938. 'They were trophies brought home triumphantly from London, and he got 77 seats, one for every man executed during the Civil War!' (Tom Garvin) (*Irish Examiner*)

outmanoeuvred him. So, yes, he was a bit unworldly, but he doubtless felt he could use them, just as they felt they could use him. In the end, both sides were disappointed, but Clarke, MacDermott and the rebels got the better of him ultimately.

Despite a lack of concrete evidence, historians have been quite emphatic about the contemporary reaction to the Rising in Dublin, which, it seems, does not do justice to the variety of opinion that existed—was there a uniform view about the Rising? According to Hay,

> No, not at all, even before the Rising happened, even when you are looking at the Irish Volunteers when they were started in November 1913, there was talk from then that they might be used for rebellion and there was a lot of dissent about when a rebellion would be right. For some people, it was felt that, if it was defensive—if the British tried to bring in conscription—that would be a reason, that would be a justification for a Rising, or if the British tried to disarm them, or if they got enough help from the Germans. So, there were reasons put forward, but what you have is a division within the Volunteers—the people who were willing to rise in those circumstances—and Bulmer Hobson and Eoin MacNeill would have been among those. And then you have the others who just feel, we need to have a Rising—no circumstances, no justification, we just need this.

So how did the putative rebels deal with the thorns in their side, such as Hobson?

> Well, they kidnapped him on Good Friday, because they felt he had the ability, especially as he was Quarter Master General of the Irish Volunteers, to scupper the whole thing, and I think they recognised that he was going to be more difficult to manipulate than MacNeill, and you find all these quotes in the Bureau of Military History to the effect that they saw Hobson as this kind of evil genius and that he was this great influence on MacNeill and that's why they had to get him out of the way. They took him to a house in Cabra Park, which belonged to a man called Martin Conlon who was a member of the IRB, and they held him hostage in the front room.

A clip from the archives was played of Bulmer Hobson, reflecting on his experiences and explaining his attitude and position, and the sort of conflict he felt was feasible in the circumstances of 1916. His feeling was that 'if there was going to be a fight and we realised all along that there was going to be a fight at some stage, that a guerrilla fight gave us the opportunity of never coming to a decisive engagement, of keeping the thing going if necessary for years; whereas, you threw all into the one throw in going into an insurrection and, after all, seizing the public buildings in Dublin, you could do nothing but sit there until you were shot out of them and that actual process took only a few days—they were anxious for a demonstration in blood; they were anxious to sort of strike a blow and to me that was just a gamble; it might turn out well; as it turned out it turned out that the effects were pretty good, but if the English had not executed them it would have been a complete fiasco.'

Hobson, in this clip, seemed measured and philosophical about the issue—was this just because of the passage of time?

According to Hay,

> I think he is. He's had enough time at that point to have his viewpoint about it, but one of the things that struck me when I was looking at his reaction to the Rising over the course from 1916 onwards up to the 1960s—it was almost as if he had his pat answer, and it doesn't change much; his feeling all along was that it was the guerrilla warfare that was going to work and, it seems, well before 1916, as early as 1909, he is putting forward that view. But I think inside, he was very angry; I think he felt that his own thunder and what he thought should happen was stolen from him, but I think he did try to be fair, to be balanced about it, and I think a lot of his ideas that he brought forward in the 1960s have been the viewpoint around 1916 that historians would accept today, but it took 50 years for his ideas to be accepted.

Given that Laffan would have commenced research into this period in the 1960s, he had an opportunity to interview many of those who were involved. What was his impression of them?

> Yes, way back when I was a research student myself, I did interview some of the survivors and they were proud, in some cases slightly

bemused, inclined to forget of course—some of them would ask me to remind them what they had done and what they had said! There was a feeling that it worked. It might not have worked, and in retrospect the sequence was right—the gesture doomed to failure and then the Bulmer Hobson-style guerrilla warfare that polarised public opinion yet further and ultimately wore down the British will to hang on to southern Ireland.

Do historians see the arrests as having more significance than the executions and just how many people were involved? Surely this is the most important 'what if'?

Well, yes, there were about three and a half thousand arrests or more, because ever since the Liberals had taken over in 1906, they had wound down the secret service in Dublin; they had regarded it as superfluous. The IRB were regarded as just a shower of drunks reminiscing about the past and dreaming about the future—the result was that all their information was out of date and the people they rounded up after Easter week or even during Easter week were people who ten years earlier had been full of republican enthusiasm and excitement, but now had become, in many cases, solid, respectable people, and when their neighbours and their families saw these harmless people being rounded up, they were outraged and indignant and they felt there was no justice, that there was yet another monstrous miscarriage of British injustice on a par with the executions, but in many cases it was simply because the files were out of date.

The executions ensured, of course, that more people than ever before were aware of the names of the leaders, particularly Patrick Pearse, which is precisely what he had hoped would happen. But is it now the case that more credence is being given to the claims contesting his leadership role and the idea that he, above all others, should be associated in the public mind with the Rising? Hay thought:

Absolutely. I think there's the popular view of him as this saint, but I think he was accepted as the front man; that was his role and he liked that role in terms of his public-speaking ability and things like that, but in terms of any real leadership, underneath it all you have the IRB—Clarke, MacDermott and Plunkett and Connolly, who was the only one who had any real military experience—but I think in the popular imagination, 1916 is so tied up with Pearse, and to a lesser extent Connolly, which obscures what was really going on in terms of the leadership.

And what of the lesser-known characters who got involved, even though they were outside the IRB conspirators' circle? Unlike Bulmer Hobson, Michael Joseph Rahilly (known as The O'Rahilly), the man who convened the meeting that led to the formation of the Irish Volunteers in 1913, did take part in the Rising, died in action and ensured that he would be remembered as a nationalist martyr. One archival clip played was of his son, Aodogán, talking about The O'Rahilly:

> I don't know to this day whether my father was in favour of MacNeill and the countermanding order, or against it, but he would have argued that in an organisation, you must have the discipline—if the Commander-in-Chief issues an order, then you obey it. Once the Rising was started by an organisation that he [The O'Rahilly] was largely responsible for creating, he couldn't just sit there and watch them fighting. Obviously, other people like Bulmer Hobson could, but my father felt he had to go out and take his part. At the very end, when my aunt went into Liberty Hall, she went up to Pearse and gave him a good pinch in the arm and said to him, 'This is all your fault!' Now, clearly she was expressing her brother's views—so he obviously resented that Pearse had taken on himself the leadership and the control.

Wasn't this just a further example of the sheer confusion that existed prior to and during the Rising? According to Laffan,

> There was an enormous amount of confusion. The basic plan for the Rising was a sensible one: manoeuvres as a cover for that contradiction in terms, that oxymoron—a secret mass uprising! All the Volunteers would be out, not knowing what they were going to be doing, then they would be told, 'Lads, there's a Rising on; go, seize that building; shoot those soldiers.' Some would go home, others would join in and you'd get far more people involved in the Rising than could have taken place in any other way. It didn't work,

but it was a clever plan. When it fell to pieces, there was utter dismay. Tom Clarke, for example, determined that they would go ahead on Easter Sunday and not wait another day; the others more sensibly said, 'Look, we need time to readjust our plans', but in the case of The O'Rahilly, he carried MacNeill's countermanding order to Volunteer units in different parts of the country, then came back and, in spite of his efforts, the Rising was going ahead, and famously said, 'Since I've helped to wind the clock, I'll be there to see it strike' and drove his car into O'Connell Street, dumped it as part of the barricades opposite the GPO and went in to fight [he was subsequently killed in Moore Street]. So there was a great deal of confusion, and that's another way in which I think the rebels were incredibly lucky, in that they overcame the confusion. They had to make their gesture—they knew by Easter Monday there was no chance of success. They went ahead making the gesture, and, as things turned out, that was enough—to have fought for six days, to have put up a good fight, to have been seen rightly as having been brave; to have avoided disgrace of a sort that many observers thought was their natural predestined fate—all that was enough, provided that things after their death would follow a favourable course, as they did. There, of course, they were gambling, but the gamble paid off.

It is also the case that this gamble did enormous damage to the Irish Parliamentary Party. Indeed, people like Bulmer Hobson suggested that if the Rising had not happened in 1916, the conscription crisis in 1918 might have been a more favourable time for it to happen, in that the IPP could have reasserted itself in a leadership role around that controversy. Hay responded to this suggestion:

> I think that's absolutely true. The IPP sort of lost their impetus over the course of the war because home rule had been put into cold storage for the duration of the war and, I think, for the IPP, they needed something new to provide leadership, to get people back on board and I think that would have done it for them.

One of the more recent developments regarding the historiography of this period has been the attempt to place the Rising in a European context—to acknowledge the huge number of Irish people serving in the British army, but also the extent to which the rhetoric and actions of the Rising reflected a European glorification of bloodshed. Just how important was this?

Laffan noted:

> There's a book that was published about 20 years ago, called *The Generation of 1914*, which looked at a number of intellectuals in various European countries—Rupert Brooke in England and various others on the continent—all glorifying war, all bored by the peace and prosperity—philistinism as they saw it—of the pre-First World War age, of the Edwardian age in this part of the world. They wanted excitement, drama, and they had an old-fashioned image of conflict—cavalry charges like Waterloo, not the horror of trench war as people had learnt to recognise it and appreciate it for what it was by 1916, so there was that mentality, and Pearse was just an Irish representative of that general European mood. So old ideas of seeing us in Ireland and Irish republicanism as a unique phenomenon have been modified and toned down now as we look at other countries, at the excitement that war did provide. There's a famous photograph of a large crowd welcoming war in Munich, and recognisable, ecstatic with joy, is the young Adolf Hitler. Here was what he was waiting for; here was the excitement, and he loved the war. He was devastated, heartbroken when it ended; he loved the conflict and the camaraderie of the trenches. People who didn't share many of his views still were excited by war and conflict, though in many cases it had worn off by Easter week, 1916.

Hay further developed this theme:

> Building on that, I think it's correct about Ireland being part of a wider European phenomenon and I'm thinking particularly of Na Fianna Éireann, which was the nationalist and youth organisation —mostly boys, but a few girls as well—which was involved in the Rising and later on, and it was frankly imitating the British boy scout movement, but instead of promoting imperialism, they were promoting Irish nationalism and it was part of that focus on manliness and discipline—this feeling that somehow people, especially youth, had become very decadent. So I think we often forget that Ireland is part of a wider trend in the late nineteenth and early twentieth century.

There was another dimension that Laffan wanted to stress, to the effect that:

> In the context of 1916 and the war, we should remember that not only were Irishmen not conscripted, but emigration was banned, so there were large numbers of women and men in Ireland without any jobs—people who would, in other circumstances, have emigrated, and I think one thing historians don't ask often enough, or hardly ever, is what would have happened if conscription had been imposed in Ireland as well as Britain in January 1916? Would a lot of those unemployed young men have been taken off to the army without protest? When the British tried, in the spring of 1918, it was far too late; in the spring of 1916, it probably wouldn't have been too late, and some of the people who fought in Easter week against the British might by then have been fighting for the British in France.

Hay added, 'The only thing there coming out of that, and I think it's a very good point, is that by 1916, within the Irish Volunteers, one of the things that there was agreement on was that if the British tried to impose conscription, they would fight back, so you would have had some who would have gone along, but we could have had an earlier Rising perhaps.'

Laffan accepted that that was a possibility:

> And that of course was the official policy of MacNeill and he wasn't a pacifist—you couldn't be a chief-of-staff of an army if you were a pacifist. What he said was, we would rise if we were attacked and an attack can take each of two forms—whether suppression of the Volunteers or conscription—and that would be a sign for action, but whether they would have been ready in 1916, who knows?

The last issue addressed in this programme was that of the legacy of the Rising: the extent to which it was used, perhaps abused. There was certainly a tendency in the context of violence in Northern Ireland in the 1970s and 1980s to give credence to a school of interpretation suggesting that Irish independence could have been achieved earlier and without bloodshed had there been no 1916 Rising. Addressing this, Laffan noted:

Well, yes, historians always ask themselves what might have happened. We don't dwell too much on counterfactual history; there's enough to keep us busy in what actually did happen! But it puts things into perspective by showing alternatives, by stressing that what happened didn't need to happen; it could have turned out differently. Of course, people saw parallels in the 1970s and 1980s with the 1910s—they saw a moderate political movement under threat; they saw new ideas emerging as a result of violence; they saw repetitions. There was very often a feeling of *déjà vu*— we've been here before; internment in 1971, for example. There was a natural, almost inevitable tendency on the part of republicans in the late 1960s, 1970s and 1980s to look back and try and appropriate the past, or suitable useful aspects of the past and, of course, there was a corresponding determination on the part of others— democratic politicians, elected governments—to say, we too represent a republican tradition; it's not as if Sinn Féin and the IRA are the only heirs to Easter Week—they would be among the very many heirs, but we, the democratically elected governments of the Republic, we too represent that tradition.

As mentioned, there was some disquiet about the muteness associated with the seventy-fifth anniversary—was this in a sense a backlash against what was (often erroneously) perceived to be the triumphalism of the fiftieth anniversary commemorations/celebrations in 1966?

'Definitely', according to Hay.

I think because since 1966 there's been so much, in terms of historians' research, documentaries reconsidering 1916 and looking at it from different points of view, that simply wasn't done before 1966 and because of what happened in the North, there's almost a sense of unease about it that certainly wasn't there in 1966 and I think things may swing away from that; so often commemorations say more about the time that they are occurring than the time they're supposed to be commemorating.

Would Laffan expect there to be a more robust commemoration in 2016 or will the relative silence in 1991 be evident again?

I don't think so. It's a long way off yet, but I think there will be more serious, more sustained commemorations than in 1991 for the seventy-fifth anniversary, particularly if Northern Ireland doesn't resort to widespread violence of the sort that was in 1991. So, yes, I think we can expect a lot of commemoration, examination and discussion and, above all, putting 1916 and the First World War and the interaction of violence and political activity into context.

And what about the definitive history of the 1916 Rising?
    According to Hay, 'That's yet to come.'

Chapter 8

What if the Treaty ports had not been returned in 1938?

The rise of Fianna Fáil after 1926 represented a stunning political comeback by the defeated republicans of the Civil War, and their victory in the general election of 1932 created fear amongst their opponents at home and abroad. De Valera, it quickly became clear, was intent on rewriting, if not tearing up, the Anglo-Irish Treaty. The ultimate aim, it seemed, was to ensure that the Irish Free State could exercise an independent foreign policy, a goal that had an added urgency as international conflict seemed more likely by the end of the 1930s.

Securing the return of the Treaty ports to Ireland was a central part of de Valera's quest for increased Irish independence and made it easier for him to declare Irish neutrality at the beginning of the Second World War. This programme posed the questions: what if these ports had not been returned, and, indeed, what if Ireland had been invaded during the war?

The programme opened with an archival clip of de Valera informing radio listeners of the progress of his diplomatic efforts with the British government regarding the issues of partition, the return of the Treaty ports and the ending of the Economic War with Britain, which began after the Irish government withheld the payment of land annuities owed to Britain, who responded by penalising Irish exports into Britain. Similar penalties were then imposed on British produce coming into the Irish market.[1]

The London agreements of April 1938 had principally concerned three issues: the transfer back to the Irish government of
harbour defences (Lough Swilly, Bearehaven and Cobh) retained
by the British government under the Anglo-Irish Treaty of
December 1921; the settlement of the Economic War (Britain
preferred to call it a 'financial dispute'); and future trade arrangements between the two countries. De Valera's strongest words,
however, were reserved for the issue of partition, which he referred
to as an 'open wound'. His negotiations at that stage were not
going to resolve this particular issue; of much more importance
was the issue of Ireland's defence, given the impending conflicts
in Europe.

As far back as 1935, de Valera had said publicly that 'the Irish
people did not want to be dragged into any European or other
war, but the Irish people would be prepared to strain themselves
to the utmost to defend their own territory and to see that no
nation suffered because of their freedom'. In the Dáil in June 1936
he also stated, 'we want to be neutral',[2] though of course, as he
acknowledged, the problem of the occupation of the Treaty ports
would have to be addressed for that to be possible.

How Irish foreign policy was framed and executed in the 1930s
is the subject of a book published by the Royal Irish Academy in
2004 which brings together over 400 documents that go to the
heart of de Valera's quest to establish an independent role for
Ireland in international affairs during a tumultuous decade. What
is striking is the sheer clarity of thinking that existed within
government and the civil service about this matter, and the
growing realisation within the British government that it would
have to deal with a de Valera who was there to stay, having won
two general elections in quick succession to establish Fianna Fáil's
grip on power.

Ronan Fanning suggested recently that those preoccupied with
economic and social history have been intuitively hostile to de
Valera, but that his extraordinary achievements in Anglo-Irish
relations should not be overlooked, as without them, 'we might
never have achieved independence and we certainly would not
have achieved it before the Second World War'.[3]

De Valera addressed the League Assembly of the League of Nations in Geneva in 1932 when the Irish Free State held the presidency of the League Council, and highlighted his disquiet about the larger powers dominating international organisations:

> Let us be frank with ourselves. There is on all sides complaint, criticism and suspicion. People are complaining that the League is devoting its activity to matters of secondary or very minor importance, while the vital international problems of the day, problems which touch the very existence of our peoples, are being shelved or postponed. People are saying the equality of the states does not apply in the things that matter, that the smaller states whilst being given a voice have little real influence ...

But de Valera and Joseph Walshe, secretary of the Department of External Affairs, were mostly concerned with wresting control of foreign policy from the British government. Walshe, obviously completely devoted to de Valera, gave him crucial strategic advice regarding how to deal with Britain and urged him to take complete control. In June 1933, he wrote:

> In the trying years before us especially the same mind must directly control what are, really, only two facets—the external and the internal—of the same group of activities of our State life.

All negotiations were heading towards one thing—for Walshe, as he put it in March 1932, that '"Ireland" will be our name, and our international position will let the world and the people at home know that we are independent.'[4]

The two guests on this programme were Eunan O'Halpin, Professor of Contemporary History at Trinity College Dublin, and Ireland's leading historian of defence and security policy, and Tom Garvin, Professor of Politics at UCD, who has written prolifically on Irish nationalism and society in the twentieth century. O'Halpin had recently published a book on MI5 and Ireland during the war which revealed that Irish neutrality in many ways suited Britain, allowing the British to keep a close eye on their German counterparts and to thwart German espionage against Britain through neutral Ireland. The book made it clear that the relationship between Irish and British intelligence agencies was a lot warmer than that between the two governments.

Cambridge historian Christopher Andrew noted in his fore-word to the book:

> MI5's main anxiety in collaborating with the Irish was that they might discover British wartime intelligence operations on Irish soil. Irish military intelligence however, was aware of them (though it did not tell the British) and proved remarkably tolerant of their continuance. As with some other apparent contradictions in British–Irish intelligence collaboration, this was by no means a unique occurrence.[5]

But before any of this occurred, the British had to get to grips with the fact that, in 1932, de Valera was in power. I asked O'Halpin how the British government reacted:

> When Fianna Fáil came to power, there was huge unease. Britain had no diplomatic representation in Dublin other than a trade representative. They didn't really know how to read Irish politics. They saw de Valera, potentially, at best, as a kind of Irish Kerensky [Russian revolutionary and army commander in 1917], with the Bolsheviks behind him and the IRA pushing Ireland over the edge. They fairly quickly, within a year, came to realise that Dev might be in some ways disagreeable and antagonistic towards Britain, but he was above all a politician with whom it might be possible to do business. It's clear as you work through documents from 1932—from late 1932 on—that the British government, although on their side they're managed by a very incompetent minister, Jimmy Thomas, the former railway man, that they're coming to see more and more that Dev has to be negotiated with; he can't be patronised, he can't be bullied, and they can't appeal to his better sentiments as a member of the British Empire, and they actually have to do some business. And so, even as the Economic War breaks out and intensifies, in the background there are negotiations going on to the point where by 1935/36 most of the key departments within Whitehall, in Britain that is, particularly the Treasury, are very keen on an all-round Anglo-Irish settlement that will undo the economic damage which both sides are feeling as a result of the conflict.

Just how important was the economic issue?

I'm not sure to what extent Dev was pushed by economic factors, but I think the British were more conscious of the economic damage being done all round than Dev was. I think Dev felt it was a price worth paying, and in some ways the argument about the cost of the Economic War is still ongoing. Most countries got highly protectionist anyway but we were talking about it within a protectionist framework—to what extent Britain and Ireland could work out a sort of mini free-trade area in certain commodities. Wales, for example, was very hard hit by the Economic War because of coal, so it wasn't just Irish beef exporters who were suffering the damage. And in Whitehall at the time, the head of the civil service and head of the Treasury, Warren Fisher, was passionately 'pro' in understanding with the Irish and was very indiscreet in his approaches, particularly to the Irish High Commissioner in London, a former colleague of his, about these things, and it was clear that the British were very keen. Neville Chamberlain as Chancellor of the Exchequer, and then later, from 1937, as Prime Minister, thought that a pretty definitive deal could be done with Ireland, not only in economic matters and financial matters but also on the big question of British security which underlay the ports issue.

That eventual deal was immensely satisfying from an Irish point of view. Garvin saw this settlement as:

Vital. The final result of negotiations was very favourable to Ireland and it also of course included the return of the Treaty ports. De Valera ran to the country almost immediately afterwards—two months after the agreement was signed—and he gained, I think, 16 seats. They were trophies—absolutely—brought home triumphantly from London, and he got 77 seats, one for every man killed during the Civil War! There was a degree of bombastic triumphalism on the part of ministers like Seán T. O'Kelly, and, to quite an extent, Ireland did actually have the British over a barrel for a very simple reason—there was going to be a very large war in Europe and it was also evident from First World War experience that there was a huge danger of Britain and Ireland being cut off from food supplies overseas, which of course were vital for British sustenance during any sustained conflict, and also Ireland was to be turned back into the British Isles larder again as it had been during the

First World War. If there was any hitch in Irish trade with Britain because of political differences of one kind or another, they would have to be ironed out, and by 1938 the British understood that perfectly. De Valera was very clever—he played a blinder; he played a very hard line and he got the ports back; he got them back for free, so to speak; and he got a very favourable trade agreement with Britain in 1938. He was a very clever politician, could be very pragmatic and very stubborn, and stubborn in times when he knew he could get his way. He had a reputation for an almost implacable stubbornness about certain things, a kind of quasi-principledness and that reputation in itself weakened his opponents against him because when they got some kind of a concession from him—an unexpected concession—they were so surprised that they tended to give him more than perhaps they had intended originally to give, and he was an extremely good negotiator.

To what extent did it impact on British politics—was it for some an irritating sideshow? O'Halpin responded:

I don't think it was that irritating or that much of a sideshow for the ministers who really pushed it, particularly in 1938. Chamberlain as Prime Minister saw this as important; he didn't see it as a minor issue. He saw it as one brick in the wall that he was attempting to build in terms of British security. We talk about the ports all the time, but effectively what you are talking about is naval facility; you're talking about aviation facility in association with those naval facilities. You're talking airfields; you're talking all sorts of what would have been radar later on, and signals, equipment and these things. So getting British military presence out of Ireland wasn't simply a matter of taking over a couple of decrepit old gun emplacements up in Donegal or down in Cork—it was the ancillary facilities which, in practice, in the battle of the Atlantic would have been far more important, particularly airfields. The trade-off was—and de Valera had said this in some sense since 1920—that Ireland would make sure that she wasn't a threat to British security, which meant in turn that you had to prevent third parties using Ireland as a means to attack Britain, and that became an issue in terms of security, in terms of intelligence, but it also became a military security issue, because Ireland, as we know, didn't have the wherewithal to defend more than a couple of hundred yards in modern military terms of the island, or even of the 26 counties. It's that side—the lack of preparation on the defence side—that's the striking weakness on the Irish side of the argument—that if you give us back these facilities, we'll make sure Ireland is basically impregnable to any attack from an enemy of yours.

By June 1940, the situation in Europe had altered dramatically, once Hitler had decided to go on the rampage and Churchill had become British prime minister. Clearly, despite the declaration of neutrality, it would be decisions taken outside Ireland that would determine its fate. Joe Lee suggested that in some ways a British invasion was more likely than a German invasion, if one is to believe Churchill's boast of the restraint they showed, and his references even before he became prime minister to the 'so-called neutrality of so-called Eire'. Lee suggested, 'that raises one of the most intriguing what might have beens of Irish history, and by no means an unhistorical one, in that it was deemed a live possibility at the time.'[6]

A clip from the archive was played, with de Valera speaking about a possible invasion:

Today we are a people united as perhaps never before in our history. Unless we are attacked, any change from neutrality would destroy this unity. It is our duty to Ireland to try to keep out of this war, and with God's help we hope to succeed. If it should be however, that we are attacked, our people and our friends every-where in the world will already have known of our determination to resist, and that to the utmost of our power. To such a situation we shall endeavour to bring the same spirit which has made our history a story of one of the most devoted struggles for liberty in the history of mankind.

But whether it was a German or British invasion, what would have been the likely course of events? Garvin observed:

Well, after the fall of France, the two southern ports were wide open to German attack, particularly German aerial attack, and I suspect that Cobh and Bearehaven would have suffered the same fate as Portsmouth, or Southampton, with long-range German bombers coming in and just plastering Cobh and Bearehaven and pushing Ireland perhaps into the allied side in the Second World War. It's unimaginable what would have happened—I cannot see how the Germans would have held their hand once they had France; they had not just Britain, they had Ireland in their sights as well and I think the situation is now almost unimaginable because history turned out a very different way, but I do not know how de Valera could have got out of that one.

O'Halpin elaborated:

Well, Ireland wasn't really in a position to defend her shores against any serious conventional attack either from Britain or from Germany. At the outbreak of war we had a very small army— professional army—under 7,000 soldiers, many of them not very well trained, almost no heavy equipment, almost no anti-aircraft weapons. We'd no modern defensive aircraft. We had no naval service at all in 1939—there simply wasn't the basis there for any organised successful defence, even with the expansion of the defence forces in 1939, and particularly in 1940, and the huge popular enthusiasm that that reflected. By 1942, the Chief of Staff reported that the army was, in his view, in a sense now militarily ready for an invasion, but it still didn't have any armoured vehicle worth the name, still didn't have any anti-aircraft artillery, still didn't have a long shopping list of elements that any modern defence force would have needed.

Historians, of course, have the advantage of hindsight and access to documentation. O'Halpin remarked:

Another point, though, which I don't think many would have been aware of, was how close Britain and Ireland became in military terms from June 1940, where you've elaborate arrangements being put in place, belatedly—far too late—but belatedly put there, so that if there was a serious German raid, there would be the agreed Anglo-Irish response, and obviously, on the security and intelligence side, co-operation became very deep very quickly. You could really describe that as a secret alliance between Britain and Ireland that was concluded at that time. The British army in Northern Ireland were issued with tri-colour armlets, you know, in case if the

Germans came in, they would come in through Wexford and Waterford and try to go up the east coast. The Irish Army was supposed to hold them off for two days or so and the British were supposed to back them up after day two or something like that.

And what other information is now available to historians? O'Halpin elaborated:

On the details of military co-operation, a lot of that material is now coming out into the public domain. In all these negotiations, the Irish difficulty in talking to the British was what can the Irish realistically do? What can they realistically contribute? Because the problem would be that if the British thought the Irish couldn't do Job A, then the British would do it, whether the Irish liked it or not, and if you were facing a serious German attack—say of 5,000/ 10,000 paratroopers or something—the Irish simply wouldn't have had, because they didn't have anti-aircraft weapons, they didn't have any armour worth the name . . . simply couldn't have done it on their own, so the British would have been in and the question is would the British wait till the Irish said, 'Please, sir, will you come and join us?' Or would they have intervened first and thereby arguably have been the first invader and therefore the object of an Irish attack.

Given that Britain did not believe Ireland could do a reasonable job in defending itself, were the British strongly tempted to invade the country? O'Halpin surmised:

I don't think so, because obviously one of the points about the whole defence issue is, in 1940, Britain, as we know, made an offer. Churchill made an offer to de Valera of Irish unity in return for the ports going back under British control, and associated facilities. And that offer was clearly very serious; it was done very quickly— it was done without consulting Northern Ireland in any great depth, because obviously they would be appalled—but it was a serious offer; it wasn't a sort of an effort to trade. It was famously reiterated again in 1940. When the United States came into the war, Churchill sends de Valera the famous telegram: 'A Nation Once Again, Now is the Hour' and so on. So, in some ways, with Ireland having the ports, the British thought they could bargain Irish unity in return for Irish participation in the war, and because of domestic problems, but also I think because Churchill saw that de Valera saw neutrality in a sense as an absolute for a small state. Dev in the last analysis said no, and I don't think that was simply because he thought the North wouldn't play, and that the British wouldn't deliver, but he saw neutrality as the proof that this indeed was a sovereign state.

What was Garvin's view of the significance of this offer?

I suspect that de Valera in the back of his mind wasn't sure who was going to win, Hitler or Churchill, and he might have suspected that by Christmas he would be negotiating with Hitler rather than with Churchill because several people whom I have come across writing in 1940, powerful people in this country, said they expected to see Hitler in London by Christmas. So there was a lot of defeatism as far as Britain's fate is concerned, in Ireland at that time. You must remember that de Valera probably thought that Churchill couldn't deliver and mightn't even be there to deliver in a few months' time, so why negotiate with somebody who's politically bankrupt? He was miscalculating then if what I suspect is true. I think partition was always the thing that de Valera could do nothing about and also it was an area of Ireland about which he was profoundly ambivalent, because in some ways in the back of his mind, I think, he didn't really think of the unionists as Irish. He actually talked several times about transfers of population, transferring—believe it or not—the population of Liverpool for the unionist population of Northern Ireland. So deep down, I think, he really regarded unionists as foreigners, and I'm not sure he really relished the idea of having a million outsiders, or enemies—political enemies—inside a 32-county nation state. He also believed he wasn't going to get it anyway and basically de Valera had no idea what to do about Northern Ireland.

Just how representative was James Dillon in opposing Irish neutrality? He was the only TD to oppose the policy and was censored and (temporarily) thrown out of the Fine Gael party for his efforts. Was he seen as just a maverick; had there been more like him, would the policy of neutrality have been more roundly criticised?

'He was regarded as a representative of a very small minority view,' according to Garvin:

> Perhaps 10 per cent or 15 per cent of the population who were actively pro-allies—make it 20 per cent—I'm guessing. But I think most people were in favour of neutrality and the republicans were violently in favour of neutrality, if you like, many of them pro-German, and the rest of the population were just non-militarised—they just wanted nothing; they didn't want to hear about the war; the war was something that was going on over there, something very horrible. 'They've all gone mad out there'—said one Fianna Fáil senator in 1939 during the debate on neutrality. They've all gone mad 'THERE' and we are 'IN HERE'—Irish isolationism was a very powerful cultural sentiment at that time, for one reason or the other.

How did the IRA view government policy, and when had de Valera's attitude to the republicans shifted? Garvin suggested,

> I don't think his political outlook changed in 1938/39. I think it had changed in the early 1930s. He realised that the IRA were impossible, that they were pre-political people, that they were incompetent and that they were a liability. On the other hand, he himself had his party built out of the old IRA, and many of the people in his party and his active supporters thought like the IRA, and there would have been a significant minority among the voters, and a significant minority among his own people were actively pro-German, not necessarily because they were Nazis, but because your enemy's enemy is your friend basically, and also traditional sentiment in favour of Germany because of the First World War and the declaration of 1916—'our gallant allies in Europe', and all that sort of thing. In other words, de Valera had to keep them on side. I'm almost certain that that is also the reason why he signed the book of condolences or whatever it was at the German Legation in 1945. He was trying to keep his 10 per cent IRA sweet because he had three by-elections coming up and he was challenged by Seán MacBride's new republicans and that is something that doesn't seem to be noticed by the historians. He was actually fighting elections the whole time and he fought them very brilliantly. It was one of the reasons he stayed in power so long. He was able to use crises—home or international—in a way that appeared irresponsible but which got him electoral votes each time.

For O'Halpin, this interpretation of the message of condolence on the death of Hitler was too generous:

Saving Tom's presence, I think it was an appalling gaffe. I think it was unnecessary—the head of the Department of External Affairs, who advised him not to do it, had been earlier in the war unctuously sort of deferential to Germany and Germany's interests. I think, though, with regard to the issue of German connection and German activities in Ireland linked to the IRA or not, we have to realise—and I've been going through a lot of material in Britain recently—how very important and how significant this was for the British for their security interests, not only in 1939, but particularly in 1940 when they saw it as the preamble to a possible German attack, but also in 1943/44, especially when Churchill has steam coming out of his ears about Ireland, not any more because of the issue of the ports and Britain's survival, but because he's worried about security, because security was the overall thing. It's not a minor issue, it's not a footnote, it's not dealt at the middle level; these people—the British intelligence agencies, the British security agencies, the Deputy Prime Minister, Sir Clement Attlee, for whom we have a lot to thank in terms of keeping the lid on Churchill a bit, and Churchill himself—came back again and again and again to this issue of people in Ireland helping the Nazis, of German activity in Ireland and the like. So it wasn't simply an early-war thing that had to do with the ports; for Churchill it was a huge issue, certainly until the end of 1944, which is one of the reasons why in 1945 he has a good old swipe at Ireland in his VE Day speech. We should also note though that Winston Churchill was incapable of uttering a dull phrase—he was a drama queen—any minutes he writes, any comment he makes on a file is written in a highly stylised way, and so anything Churchill says you have to discount hugely, because there was nothing on which he would not make a magisterial pronouncement.

De Valera's reply to Churchill's contention that Britain had shown 'restraint and poise' in not invading an Ireland that had 'frolicked' with the Japanese allowed him to undo some of the damage that had been done as a result of the visit to the German ambassador; the fact that his reply was relatively understated was also effective—or the idea that, in his own words, it was delivered in a much 'quieter atmosphere'. He robustly defended the Irish pursuit of freedom and the determination to keep that freedom. The reply included the following words, broadcast on 16 May 1945, in which de Valera indulged in his own counterfactual questions:

> I would like to put a hypothetical question—it is a question I have put to many Englishmen since the last war. Suppose Germany had won the war, had invaded and occupied England, and that after a long lapse of time and many bitter struggles, she was finally brought to acquiesce in admitting England's right to freedom, and let England go, but not the whole of England—all but, let us say, the six southern counties.
>
> These six southern counties—those, let us suppose, commanding the entrance to the narrow seas—Germany had singled out and insisted on holding herself with a view to weakening England as a whole and maintaining the security of her own communications through the Straits of Dover.
>
> Let us suppose, further, that after all this had happened, Germany was engaged in a great war in which she could show she was on the side of the freedom of a number of small nations. Would Mr Churchill as an Englishman who believed that his own nation had as good a right to freedom as any other—not freedom for part merely, but freedom for the whole—would he, whilst Germany still maintained the partition of his country and occupied six counties of it, would he lead this partitioned England to join with Germany in a crusade? I do not think Mr Churchill would.
>
> Would he think the people of partitioned England an object of shame if they stood neutral in such circumstances? I do not think Mr Churchill would.

What was the response of the Irish people?
'They loved him,' said Garvin.

There is surviving newsreel footage of middle-class gents standing in bars and around fireplaces puffing their pipes and nodding to each other satisfiedly, 'quite right—Dev stood up to him!' That's why they loved him. Even people who didn't support him admired him for that kind of behaviour.

What was the response of the US government to the stance taken by Ireland during the war? O'Halpin observed:

> In terms of the ports, for example, the American administration was much less understanding of Irish political problems and just didn't see why, from 1940, Ireland didn't row in with Britain, why they didn't grant naval and air facilities and so on. Once America entered the war, then it became almost a personal thing because, as far as Roosevelt could see, here was this ridiculous small country entirely dependent for defence on Britain and yet refusing to contribute to the defence of the British Isles, and, worse still, endangering the lives of American servicemen. The Americans had come to Derry in July 1941 and the Americans put much more pressure in some ways, much more publicly, on Ireland than Britain did in the course of the war, on issues to do with the ports and also with security co-operation; and their representative in Dublin, David Gray, became very critical of de Valera. Generally, the administration in Washington just thought this was ridiculous —why weren't the Irish in? And 'If you're not with us you're against us.' And I think in the immediate post-war years, it certainly didn't help Ireland—the memory of the State Department in particular of what they saw as a kind of posturing. 'You shelter under the British defence umbrella, but you refuse to contribute to Anglo-American security.'

Garvin concluded:

> You must remember the American context here—the Irish and the German ethnic groups in the United States were, of course, anti-British and pro-German right up to the coming of the Japanese to Pearl Harbor, when suddenly they all changed sides, and you could see this in the Irish/American, German/American newspapers of that period, that they're sort of balancing between Britain and Germany up to Pearl Harbor, and then suddenly they're pro-American back to the 'dough-boys' and all the rest of it, and I suspect that, in ways, American neutralism was being counter-balanced by the behaviour of the American administration in Washington, because they had been doing exactly the same thing that de Valera was doing up until Pearl Harbor when they got a kick in the behind from the Japanese.

Chapter 9

What if the Blueshirts had attempted a coup in 1933?

This programme was broadcast on the seventieth anniversary of Eoin O'Duffy's departure from the centre stage of Irish politics, when he abruptly resigned after a year as leader of the new Fine Gael party that had been launched in September 1933. O'Duffy had been a prominent IRA leader during the War of Independence and subsequently became chief-of-staff of the Free State Army during the Civil War, before becoming Commissioner of the Garda Síochána. He is best remembered as leader of the Blueshirts, a group that had its origins in the Army Comrades Association, formed in 1932, which evolved into the National Guard in the summer of 1933.

O'Duffy became leader of this group in July 1933; its members were identifiable by the wearing of a blue shirt, and by the raised arm salute. A proposed mass march in Dublin in August 1933 was banned by the government, and the National Guard was outlawed later that month, with de Valera invoking the Offences Against the State Act and military tribunals set to administer justice. According to historian Dermot Keogh, 'It is not possible to know what O'Duffy would have done if he had found himself at the head of a large crowd in the grounds of Leinster House, but the likelihood is that he would have tried to seize power.'[1]

Fine Gael was created out of an amalgamation of the National Guard, the Cumann na nGaedheal party and the Centre Party, dedicated to the interests of farmers. For some, the Blueshirts represented the most effective opposition to Fianna Fáil and were defenders of free speech; for others, they were unbridled fascists who were stopped in their tracks when a government clampdown ensured that democracy was safeguarded.

Referred to in contemporary news reports as 'De Valera's dynamic opponent', O'Duffy has thus divided historians in much the same way that he divided his contemporaries in the 1930s. Having been dismissed as Garda Commissioner in February 1933 (republicans had long campaigned for his dismissal), he became one of the most polarising figures of a polarising decade, accentuated by de Valera's electoral triumphs, the release of republican prisoners, the Economic War with Britain over the withholding of land annuities and, of course, the legacy of the Civil War, exacerbated by violence, intimidation and threats to freedom of speech and expression.

The Blueshirts were often confused as a result of the gulf between the overtly political ambitions of their leadership and the more mundane if immediate concerns of their grassroots membership. Mike Cronin, the most recent historian of the Blueshirts, noted that 'the gap between the populist rhetoric of Fianna Fáil and the reality of the experience of the Blueshirt members who suffered at the hands of Fianna Fáil is very real, and did most to motivate those wearing the shirt'.[2] At leadership level, the Blueshirts were not monolithic, with the bombastic O'Duffy following a different agenda from the likes of Richard Mulcahy and Ernest Blythe, who had been prominent members of the Cumann na nGaedheal governments in the 1920s and whose primary allegiance was to party politics.

At an academic level, Michael Tierney, Professor of Greek at UCD and a former Cumann na nGaedheal TD, James Hogan, Professor of History at UCC, and Alfred O'Rahilly, another Cork academic and prominent Catholic social theorist, did much to justify the movement by linking it to developments on the continent and the teachings of papal encyclicals. However, marrying the various layers, particularly given O'Duffy's refusal to accept the wisdom or advice of his political peers, was to prove futile.

Were they really fascists or 'potential para-fascists' as Cronin characterised them (and what does that mean)? And if the march on Dublin had gone ahead in 1933, could there have been the possibility of an attempted coup?

Undoubtedly, the issue of free speech and the hardships that stemmed from the Economic War foisted on the farming community resulted in much violence and mobilisation; at one of the earlier meetings in Limerick, there were an estimated 14,000 Blueshirts present. Following the withholding of land annuities by the government, the British government introduced the Special Duties Act, in July 1932, which placed a 20 per cent duty on all trade in live animals and dairy products, and the value of Irish exports dropped by £18 million, with an estimated 20,000 jobs lost. The Irish government retaliated with the Emergency Duties Bill, which penalised British exports into Ireland of coal and steel. Cronin also records that, as a result of the campaign to prevent the government's collection of annuities, there were 197 violent attacks in Cork between July 1934 and January 1935.[3]

There was also a strong sporting and recreational side to the movement; indeed, successfully managing the 1932 Irish Olympic team is perhaps one of the few things O'Duffy can be credited with during his turbulent career. As a recent biography by Fearghal McGarry makes clear, there was a huge element of fantasy and contradiction to O'Duffy's career—a moralist, or 'preacher of national virility' as McGarry put it, he was also a closet homosexual; he was an advocate of teetotalism but also an alcoholic. There were many factors that drove him towards extremism, including the cultural environment in which he grew up, Catholicism and anti-communism, and his ideas on sport and masculinity. The man who led the IRA, the Garda Síochána, the Blueshirt movement, the Fine Gael party (even though he believed that political parties had outlived their usefulness) and an Irish Brigade to fight under General Franco in the Spanish Civil War, eventually collapsed under the weight of his own contradictions, and died in wartime Dublin, a broken man.[4]

There was a healthy tension between the ideas of the two guests on this programme in terms of how they viewed Ireland in the

1930s and what potential they believed existed for O'Duffy to damage Irish democracy and politics. Brian Hanley, author of *The IRA, 1926–36*, was certainly aware of how O'Duffy was viewed by his republican opponents and had the fresh perspective of a younger scholar. Maurice Manning's book on the Blueshirts was first published in 1971 and he had perhaps a less severe interpretation of the movement and what it stood for.

What exactly drew Manning towards a study of the movement at that stage, when he was a research student in the late 1960s— was it a subject around which a certain taboo still existed?

Well, there was very little investigation into that period of history at that time and I was probably one of the first generation coming out of the post, post civil-war time, and I think there was a sense of the whole period being frozen—people didn't want to talk about it; it was too recent and too raw, and so for younger generations of historians and political scientists like Tom Garvin and myself who were starting our careers, they were obvious subjects to start looking at. Now, it was a difficult one to do because there were no state papers, no archives. So a great deal of work had to be done by interviewing people on both sides, which was great fun. People weren't used to being surveyed and interviewed in those days, but they were very willing to talk, and so in the process I met virtually all of the major characters on both sides during that period.

Manning was impressed by what he regarded as:

A sturdy generation on both sides, and, to put it into a context, there was a certain similarity with Northern Ireland at the present time, based on total distrust of the democratic integrity of both sides, and it was much the same talking to these veterans of the 1920s and 1930s. If you were Fianna Fáil, you believed that the Cosgrave party, having lost two elections, was going to get power back by any means; if you were a Cosgrave supporter, you believed you were a person who had established the state, upheld democratic institutions and now Dev was going to unleash the IRA on you and was going to win power that way. They were both wrong, but that's what they both believed and it's this distrust which is at the root of everything else in the 1930s.

This was a reminder of how charged the decade was, given everything that was going on, but was it an adequate analysis to boil it down to a battle between fascists and democrats or was it based on more mundane concerns?

> I think Fascism was very much a side issue. If you were a Cumann na nGaedheal supporter living down the country, and if you were a farmer in particular, what you saw was first of all the government letting loose the IRA as they saw it—the IRA very definitely breaking up meetings and intimidating their opponents. The slogan 'No Free Speech for Traitors' was the mantra at the time, so you felt for your life. If you happened to be a farmer, on top of that situation, because of the Economic War, was the possibility that you faced economic ruin; you couldn't sell your cattle . . . you went from fair to fair and brought your cattle back. I think it was Oliver Flanagan in a colourful phrase, many years later, who talked about 'the ghosts of the slaughtered cattle marching down Merrion Street to haunt the government'—there was that sense that everything was from where the person subjectively stands and that was how people saw the events of the time.

But can the Blueshirt era be characterised as a time of petty, localised skirmishes, or even faction fights underpinned by local feuds that in reality had little if anything to do with theories of government? Hanley acknowledged that:

> Certainly there was a very definite local element, and in many ways the legacy of the Civil War obviously overshadowed the conflicts of the Blueshirt era, but I do think that the international context is very important. There's no doubt as far as I'm concerned that a strong section of the pro-Treaty elite had by the 1930s decided that the party system had failed because it had returned a government they didn't like—a Fianna Fáil government—and that therefore the various forms of government, a fascist form of government, held an attraction. People look back and wonder, 'Did that mean a Hitler form of government'? In Ireland of the 1930s, it didn't necessarily mean that; people like Michael Tierney, James Hogan and Ernest Blythe were interested in the various forms of the corporate state abroad, particularly in Italy, and did see that some of those ideas were applicable to Ireland; you also had, tied in with

that, an intense sense of betrayal and resentment among the pro-Treaty elite that they had been rewarded for, as they saw it, saving Ireland from anarchy in 1922 by being voted out of government in 1932, and right through the conflicts of that era, you find amongst the supporters of the Blueshirts, particularly among the strong farmers, an intense sense of class resentment . . . that Fianna Fáil are rewarding classes of people they think shouldn't be rewarded—that is, landless labourers, small farmers, urban labourers, who seem to be benefiting and were benefiting from Fianna Fáil in government. The strong farmers who dominated the backbone of the Blueshirt movement in many parts of Ireland simply regarded these people as people who shouldn't benefit from government, so all of these things come into it. But I do think the idea of fascism is important to the leadership, certainly O'Duffy himself, and also to the intellectuals, who, for a brief period of time, held sway over the leadership of the Blueshirt movement.

One of the archival clips used during this programme was of a prominent Blueshirt veteran, John L. O'Sullivan. He insisted that the reason he and others joined was that their meetings were being broken up, because anybody speaking on behalf of Cumann na nGaedheal could not be guaranteed free speech; that essentially, it was an organisation that would give protection to speakers. Manning suggested it was this theme above all others that was:

universal, and it's borne out by the fact that meetings were being broken up—it's not an accident that the only meetings being broken up were Cumann na nGaedheal meetings or Centre Party meetings—no Fianna Fáil or IRA meetings were being broken up, so people were not going to break up their own meetings; certainly it was believed; it was their experience, and it was the fact. So it was a big unifying theme in all of the Blueshirts I spoke to and it was the main complaint made by the leaders of the party at that time and it included somebody like Frank McDermott, the farmer who had come into Irish politics as leader of the Centre Party. He was going to be above all Civil War politics—he was a superior sort of person—but he very quickly said, 'Look, our meetings too are being broken up' so it was a fact.

What does this suggest about republicans during this period, and the arguments of people like IRA chief-of-staff Moss Twomey? Was their sole mission to break up the meetings of others? What did Hanley detect as being the priorities of the IRA in this regard?

> Well, the argument is quite complex, because the Republicans could have said that, up until 1932—and the ACA predated the victory of 1932—that people like Eoin O'Duffy had already secretly pressed in late 1931 for a military coup if the election results did not go as desired, so his commitment to free speech and democracy is open to question, and he also pressed for greater powers for the gardaí to effectively ban opposition parties during that period, so certainly there's a great sense of fear during that period among many pro-Treaty supporters. The reality is that street violence becomes very intense during 1932, but it becomes even more intense during 1933. But I don't think you can get away from the fact that some of this is driven by unrealistic fears but also about the pro-Treaty side's own rhetoric about having saved Ireland from Bolshevism and anarchy. People like T. F. O'Higgins argue that Fianna Fáil was the vanguard of communist policy in Ireland; Dev was seen as the Irish Kerensky [Alexander Kerensky, Russian socialist revolutionary and army commander whose troops were defeated by the Bolsheviks in 1917]; once Fianna Fáil are in power, they'll fall very easily, and that the very obvious sense of fear amongst the rank-and-file supporters of Cumann na nGaedheal intensifies this fear that they were going to be purged. And, in general, Fianna Fáil didn't purge its enemies once it came to power. Within the IRA, the reaction is very mixed; generally, the organisation's leadership tried to prevent its members being involved in street fighting because they saw their task in terms of building themselves up as an army and waiting for the next round of conflict with Britain. Many of their supporters spontaneously took part in riots and violence at meetings and this, in fact, is one of the issues that began to fragment the IRA itself during 1932, but there isn't any evidence to support the idea that the IRA deliberately set out to destroy free speech for its opponents during 1932; they actually wanted to see what Fianna Fáil were going to do first.

Manning believed much of this assessment to be 'fair':

I think it's the rhetoric of both sides and the total lack of belief in the democratic integrity each has for the other, but Dev just almost had to watch on and first of all let the Blueshirts make fools of themselves . . . there wasn't ever going to be a coup, but the very fact that Dev put it up to O'Duffy to call off the march and the fact that O'Duffy did, did huge damage to the credibility to the Blueshirts at a very early stage and Dev played it very well—he was quite happy to play the Blueshirts off against the IRA and vice versa; the military tribunal he brought in to use against the Blueshirts, he was very happy to use in a much more draconian way against the IRA afterwards, so he did play both sides against each other.

But if the planned march had gone ahead, would it have led to violence; the opening up of the prospect of bloodshed and worse? This is where both speakers found themselves at odds. According to Manning:

There might well have been violence, but when you try and put the thing together as to what might actually have happened—what would they have done if they had seized an empty Leinster House on a Sunday afternoon? There were no plans for a coup d'état and the reality was that, had O'Duffy tried to seize power, it would have failed within days, because most of his own party, Fine Gael, were constitutionalists, before and after—they would have disowned him, as they did within a year. The army was not going to go along with someone in whose judgement they had little respect. In relation to the gardaí, he had talked about the possibility of a takeover; I've heard it described as 'drunken dry run' because I think it was late at night up in the Phoenix Park in the Garda depot, but he got no support there at all and the civil service was totally loyal to whatever government was in, so it wasn't even a starter.

An interesting archival clip was played featuring a discussion on the proposed march; it comprised an interview in which John L. O'Sullivan, mentioned earlier, and Peadar O'Donnell, then active in the IRA, reminisced and presented it all as a harmless bit of fun. O'Sullivan insisted that the Blueshirts had no plans to wreck the state; that the march should not have been banned; that there was no question of the army defying the government of the day and that 'there were no arms going to Dublin with the band of people who were travelling to Dublin (though there might have been a good hardy stick)'. More surprising was to hear Peadar O'Donnell insist that there were no arms in Dublin to resist them, that as a member of the IRA army council, he had thought, 'it was ridiculous that it should have been banned because it was really a very harmless display'.

Had the two gone soft in their old age, becoming misty eyed, and downplaying the real fears that existed? Hanley scoffed at the skewed memory on both sides, particularly because:

At the time, Peadar O'Donnell was arguing in *An Phoblacht* that the march should be smashed off the streets. I don't think the IRA would have made an armed attack on the march. I think it's very revealing when John O'Sullivan says they knew marching to Dublin wasn't going to be great, because the Blueshirts were very weak in Dublin and in urban areas generally, and they would have met both spontaneous opposition and also opposition from Republicans. So I think there would have been violence at the march, but even if there had been violence, the march can still be a success if it goes ahead. I disagree with Maurice on this one. If the march had gone ahead, there wouldn't have been a military coup, but there would have been a propaganda coup for O'Duffy; it would have strengthened O'Duffy's leadership. O'Duffy had been described by Batt O'Connor, who claimed Michael Collins had said to him that O'Duffy was 'the coming man', the man who would lead the pro-Treatyites if anything happened to Collins, and there were people in the army, and ex-soldiers particularly, whose impression of O'Duffy would have been greatly strengthened by a successful march in Dublin. The intellectuals who were flirting with European fascism—his credibility would have been enhanced with them had he led a successful march, and even the constitutionalists within what became Fine Gael, people like Cosgrave, would possibly have given him a little more leeway had he led a successful march and successfully defied Dev, and I think had that march gone ahead, it would have enhanced the Blueshirt movement.

Manning was not remotely convinced of the veracity of this counterfactual analysis:

But the march was no more than that—it was a march, a demon-stration, a parade, that was all. I don't think in itself that it would have shown that the movement was strong or not strong. I don't agree that it would have had the same knock-on effect, and in enhancing O'Duffy. There's a curious thing about O'Duffy, which is that by the end of his tenure with the gardaí, under the Cosgrave government, there were serious question marks over his judgement and a belief that he was losing the run of himself, getting too big for his boots and so on, and there were plans to have him moved to a different job. There was talk of him becoming a Free State Commissioner somewhere or other, but there was unease about him. Nonetheless, by the time he was sacked by Dev, and I think rightly sacked by Dev because he had to have a police chief in whom he had complete trust, he offered him a job at the same salary, as Director of Mining for the Free State, which wouldn't have been all that onerous! I would be very critical of the Cumann na nGaedheal people who came to O'Duffy at that stage.

Was it simply the case that they were using O'Duffy to further their own ends?

I think so. I wouldn't quite call them the elite, but people like Tierney and James Hogan and Blythe were looking at other models —they were the Moore McDowells of the time, giving a right-wing analysis of what was going wrong in Irish society; they said, 'Right, we have our independence with the Treaty, we have a class-ridden society, we are deeply divided, we're not growing economically. Is there something wrong?' And they began to look at other models. Now, they dismissed Hitler out of hand—'That's closer to Fianna Fáil,' is what they said at the time! They looked a bit at Mussolini, but basically it was at *Quad Anno* [*Quadragesimo Anno*], the papal encyclical of the Corporate State and there were some—Tierney, Hogan (though he was a bit idiosyncratic) and certainly Ernest Blythe—who would have liked that sort of model for Ireland but it never cut any ice.

Hanley, too, was interested in not just the class element, but also the international question and the fact that, in many ways, O'Duffy was a mass of contradictions:

There is no direct comparison, but if you looked at Hitler in 1932 in Germany, large sections of the German elite would have regarded him as an Austrian upstart, a mass of contradictions, as well. O'Duffy had been a very successful IRA commander; he had credibility with the IRA and with Northern nationalists because he was one of the few pro-Treatyites who had argued very strongly and in a very sectarian fashion on their behalf. He had credibility as commissioner of the gardaí—initially; he was seen as having done a very good job. So, in many ways, he was a good strong leader for this movement and, again, I think the context of the time is very important—you have both intense bitterness in many ways against a large section of the Irish people, and questions are being asked: 'Who are these people to vote us out of power?' 'Who are these people to allow de Valera in?' And there's this whole range of xenophobia that cuts through Blueshirt propaganda at the time: 'How can Dev govern Ireland—he's not even an Irishman; he's a half-breed,' as O'Duffy says. You have this issue of class on the part of some members of the pro-Treaty elite—Paddy Hogan [former Cumann na nGaedheal Minister for Agriculture] before the 1932 election said, 'People are afraid of de Valera and his followers but, actually, I don't think I'd be that afraid because they're incapable of governing—you have to have breeding to govern!' So there is that sense of 'who controls the country now?' In that context, post Civil War, and internationally, you can't get away from Mussolini and Hitler—when people saw a uniformed march on the streets, that is what they thought, and some Blueshirts thought that as well. Maybe many of the ordinary members didn't think about it very deeply, but people like James Hogan who said at the time, 'I'm greatly in favour of the Fascist state', did think that this was the way forward in Ireland.

Manning acknowledged that:

There was a much bigger class element in the whole thing than I think was realised at the time. Brian is absolutely right when he says that many of the people in the Cosgrave party underestimated de Valera. There's a famous phrase of Michael Tierney's, I think, when he said, 'People say give Dev enough rope and he'll hang himself,' and Tierney says, 'We gave him enough rope and he hanged the rest of us!' Fianna Fáil was an extraordinary political machine in 1932 in its organisation, in the intensity of its feeling and in the loyalty to Dev, and in its determination, and I think that the Cumann na nGaedheal people underestimated them. But there's another factor which I think is important and it's a phrase that wasn't used at the time, but I think it's 'burnout'. These people had been ten very difficult years in power; they had achieved enormous things; many of them had been involved from 1916 on and, by that time, they were burnt out and many of them wanted to remake their lives in various ways. They weren't very well off either—there were no parliamentary pensions then—and I found in talking to a lot of them, obviously they were recollecting, but that was a factor, and it is mentioned in the Dáil debates at the time—even Seán MacEntee [Fianna Fáil minister] pointed out in the late 1930s that conditions in this regard were bad.

Many in the Fine Gael party, of course, wanted to forget about the Blueshirt era as quickly as possible. The historian Mike Cronin likened their relationship with Blueshirts to that of a bridal party cringing at the antics of a drunken uncle in the corner. But that is only part of the story. For some of those who were involved, right up to the 1980s, they refused to see the Blueshirts as anything other than defenders of freedom and democracy. An archival clip was played containing the booming, unmistakable voice of James Dillon, one of the great orators of twentieth-century Ireland, who led Fine Gael from 1959 to 1965, and who, in 1983, informed a Fine Gael audience, to rapturous applause:

> I want to recall with pride that we fought a desperate battle for the preservation of free speech in this country, and let it never be forgotten that we could not have won that battle but for the Blueshirts who helped us to win it. And as they fought, they were fighting not for party but for democracy, and democracy won. No thanks to those who were opposed to it!

Manning, who has written a biography of Dillon, noted that what was significant about him was that 'he hated the Sinn Féin tradition. His story is significant because he came into politics to get away from the Civil War, to remain above it all, and within a year, he realised there was no half-way house—you were either for

Dev or against Dev and Irish politics was black and white in the 1930s, and there wasn't any room for common ground.'

In looking at the early days of the Fine Gael party, was it not just as well that they jettisoned O'Duffy at an early juncture, given that he could have been a serious electoral liability?

Mischievously, Manning commented, 'Well, even when you listen to the archival clips, you don't get the sense of a charismatic leader, and I once got into terrible trouble by saying it's very hard to be a charismatic leader and have a strong Monaghan accent!'

Hanley, however, was determined that this episode would not be remembered fondly or that the programme would end on a light note:

> Retrospectively, that might seem to be the case, but it wasn't in 1933 and if you look at why Fine Gael lost out, it wasn't just due to O'Duffy's erratic personality; it's the forces that made that personality so important, which was the often spontaneous opposition to the Blueshirt movement. Remember again that when you have clashes locally, you have small farmers and labourers fighting people who employ them or want to employ them, and this element of class conflict. Many farmers remember with horror and real bitterness this period because of the hardship it caused them and the fact that cattle were taken from them and they couldn't sell them and beef was given out free in the cities to urban labourers who'd never eaten beef before. What party did that benefit? Fianna Fáil, of course, and politically, Fianna Fáil won this battle and also won the battles against republicans. But I think retrospectively, to see the Blueshirts as simply a combination of tragedy and farce doesn't do justice to the forces that were at work at the time and the very real conflicts it represented within Irish society.

Chapter 10

What if de Valera had stood down as leader of Fianna Fáil in 1948 instead of 1959?

T his programme opened with an archival clip of an impassioned Eamon de Valera speaking at the Council of Europe in 1950:

> We have heard here recently suggested that the best way of beating communism is not necessarily by force—that there is something else also which is required; that we have got to show the people who are going to resist communism that there is a way of life which is worth defending. We believe that that is true and we want to be, in Ireland, to be in a position in which we will feel that we are defending *all* the things that are worth defending; that we are defending the liberties of our people, and as long as the powerful nation which is near us by force divides that ancient nation and subjects a large proportion of the people that are cut off to a foreign rule against their will, then as long as that exists, so long will Irishmen feel that if there is liberty to be defended, it has first to be defended on Irish shores.

Following defeat in the 1948 general election, de Valera made many such anti-partition speeches abroad, having spent the previous 16 years attempting to maximise the political independence of the Irish Free State, following the creation of Fianna Fáil in 1926 and the party's victory in the general election of 1932. He was one of the most influential and polarising figures in the history of modern Ireland. There were many things that were distinctive about his career, not least his political longevity. Although Fianna Fáil lost the 1948 election, de Valera, then aged 66, had no appetite for retirement. He continued to lead Fianna Fáil until 1959, serving a further two terms as Taoiseach in the 1950s, before Seán Lemass eventually replaced him.

The critical assessment is that he stayed too long and stalled the modernisation of Ireland because of allegiance to out-of-date political and economic philosophies. But if he had stepped down in 1948, would it have made any difference to Fianna Fáil, to the country and to the perception of the significance of his legacy?

The question of the perception of de Valera also raises the issue of how he was regarded by different generations. In his memoir, *Pictures in my Head*, the actor Gabriel Byrne describes how, as a young boy, he saw de Valera in very old age being transported around like some mummified Russian president:

> One day a long black car with flags on it and motorcycles in front and behind came up our road and stopped at the cross. I caught a glimpse of a man in black with a long white face and a black hat leaning on a stick. He looked like he was dead and somebody had propped him up; beside him was a tiny doll of a woman who looked dead too, also in black. That was the president, Mr de Valera, and his wife. Both staring out different windows in the rain. We waved, but they didn't see us. He was blind as a bat, my mother said.[1]

That sums up a common view of the 1960s generation who believed that he had stayed around far too long. There was an irony, perhaps, in the fact that the highlight of his first term as president of Ireland (1959–66) was the visit of US President John F. Kennedy, in that this was an event that, particularly when the two men were pictured alongside each other, seemed to symbolise the past and the future, and left de Valera looking like he belonged to a different era.

Fintan O'Toole suggested, 'In a sense, de Valera's resignation had happened long before he resigned. He had become resigned to the failure of his policies and believed that there was nothing for his people to do but endure.'[2] Likewise, Tim Pat Coogan's critical biography of de Valera has a chapter entitled 'Dev clings on, and on' and refers to the fact that 'he rarely showed either the ability or the inclination to confront the great challenges of Irish life',[3] particularly in terms of unemployment, partition and emigration. These are perfectly valid criticisms, but they tell only part of the story. In a sense, de Valera became a convenient scapegoat for those frustrated with the failures of Irish independence, but to reduce him to the emotional, one-dimensional embodiment of such failures is somewhat short-sighted. There were plenty of his colleagues who were in a similar position in politics in the 1950s, as 1916 veterans, and they too were seemingly bereft of new ideas on how to improve the economy.

The constant use of the words 'restless' and 'vigour' alongside the name Seán Lemass imply that he was a Fianna Fáil dam waiting to burst throughout the 1950s, and that de Valera was being unusually stubborn in not relinquishing control of his party. But the reality was that, in all political parties, those prominent in the 1920s and 1930s had significant staying powers. Richard Mulcahy did not give up the leadership of Fine Gael until 1959, and William Norton did not step down as leader of the Labour Party until 1960. De Valera also sought in the 1950s to introduce younger members to the Fianna Fáil cabinet, including, in 1957, Neil Blaney, Jack Lynch and Kevin Boland, then aged 40, 35 and 35 respectively.

While it is true that Lemass was 17 years younger than de Valera, he was still a 1916 veteran; more crucial, perhaps, was the perception that, although he had this lineage, he did in some respects seem to belong to another generation, and clearly, there were temperamental and psychological differences between the two men.[4] But it should not be assumed that there were countless, restless Fianna Fáilers queuing up impatiently to take over the mantle as leader of Fianna Fáil. Surely if there had been, he might have gone sooner? Lemass was in some respects a reluctant Taoiseach; clearly, whatever about de Valera overstaying his welcome in the context of the failures of economic policies, he still had a political appetite, endurance and skill that were unique. Shortly after he became Taoiseach, Lemass wrote to de Valera:

Since I took over as Taoiseach, I have not ceased to wonder how
you carried the burden for so long without showing the strain. You
are a wonderful man and surely tough as teak.[5]

The two contributors to this programme were historian Pauric
Travers, President of St Patrick's College in Drumcondra, whose
published work includes a short study of the life of Eamon de
Valera, and David McCullagh, political correspondent with RTÉ
and author of *A Makeshift Majority*, a history of the first inter-
party government between 1948 and 1951.

I questioned McCullagh about the 1948 election. Fianna Fáil
had been in power for 16 years and one of the slogans the party
used was 'Better the Dev you know than the Devil you don't', but
it was not a message that swayed the electorate.

No, they were buying the alternative message which was particularly put forward by the new party—Clann na Poblachta—which
was 'put them out'. It was very simple and very effective. Fianna
Fáil had been in power for 16 years and Dev had succeeded in
establishing Irish sovereignty, particularly with the state of neutrality
during the Second World War, but the economic conditions after
the war were pretty parlous. There had been a long-running
teachers' strike, for instance, which had lost Fianna Fáil a lot of
support; the Republicans were turned off from Fianna Fáil by a
number of instances during the war—the execution of IRA
prisoners, hunger strikes and so on—and that led to the formation
of Clann na Poblachta which really swung the election away from
Fianna Fáil. Fianna Fáil lost six or seven seats, I think it was, and
ended up with 68 seats. They needed 74 for a majority, but it
looked as if they'd still stay in power because the other parties were
a complete ragbag. There was Fine Gael, there was Labour, there
was National Labour which had split from the main Labour Party,
there was Clann na Poblachta, and there was Clann na Talmhan—
the small farmers' party from the west. They had 67 seats between
them, one behind Fianna Fáil, and the balance of power rested
with independents, and to everyone's surprise—Dev's particularly
—they actually succeeded in putting together a coalition deal, or
an inter-party government . . . Fine Gael at that stage particularly
were extremely conservative, at least most of them in policy terms
were—they were seen as the Commonwealth Party and they were

getting into bed with Clann na Poblachta which I suppose could be compared with Sinn Féin today in that they'd only left the IRA, many of them just a short time before, and they were quite a left-wing party, certainly in terms of Ireland at the time. So it was an extraordinary wide range of policies, but 'put them out' was the over-riding concern.

Fianna Fáil's reaction to this seemed bitter; the actual title of McCullagh's book, *Makeshift Majority*, was a kind of slur that was cast on them by Seán Lemass, and de Valera suggested that it was as a result of a 'quirk' of the proportional representation electoral system. Was the truth that they were in complete shock that this could actually happen to them?

I think so, after 16 years in power, I suppose, you get used to it. Lemass made a speech in the Dáil which, when you read it back sounds fairly ok. He's sort of saying, 'We've handed the country over to you in a good state—remember to hand it back to us when we get back into power.' But I read one account of somebody who was actually in the chamber at the time and they said that it was extraordinary—that he was really, really bitter, that he was shouting the words across the Dáil chamber at Costello and his front bench. They really were completely shocked. And remember, after 16 years in power, 16 years of having a ministerial driver, and suddenly you have to go out and buy yourself a new car—not nice!

I queried Travers about the response of de Valera to this defeat. Was it the case that it liberated him to a certain extent, or were the foreign trips to promote an anti-partition message utterly cynical?

Dev spends a good deal of time between 1948 and 51 travelling. He travels to the USA, to Australia, to the Holy Land, to France; he goes to the Council of Europe, as we've heard from the opening clip. He's very interested in international affairs, but he also wants to sell the anti-partition message and it's interesting in talking about anti-communism to the Council of Europe in that clip we heard that he turns it very quickly into an attack on partition. The difficulty with that is that the 1948 election for the first time really begins to bring forward economic issues and all of the elections—the elections of 1948, 1951, 1954 and 1957—are fought largely on economic issues, and Fianna Fáil are rather slow to react to that. If you like, the Inchydoney moment [the venue for the Fianna Fáil party's 'think tank' in the autumn of 2004, where they attempted to create a more 'caring' image for the party after a disastrous performance in the previous summer's local elections] when they sit back and reflect on what is the message from the electorate in relation to the rebuff they've received—that comes much later. Seán Lemass suggested it was not really until 1954–57 that they sit down and seriously take stock. In the period 1948–51, they don't really present a strong opposition. The difficulties encountered by the inter-party government are very much of their own making, and really it's only Lemass who is a one-man opposition in the Dáil. Other than that, there isn't a coherent response, and the fall of the inter-party government is very much a product of the internal divisions within the inter-party government itself, rather than the effect of the opposition of Fianna Fáil between 1948 and 1951.

Have historians found evidence that there was an appetite for a new leader or a suggestion that de Valera should have considered his leadership position at that stage? According to McCullagh:

No, it never seemed to have occurred to anybody. Now, I suppose you could argue that the fact that he actually lost the 1948 election might have made him keener to stay on and to try and prove himself again with an election victory. Certainly there was no danger of him leaving office in 1948, despite the fact that he pretty much left the running of the opposition in Lemass's hands. Lemass seemed to lead for Fianna Fáil most times in the Dáil chamber. Dev was certainly a somewhat detached party leader, leaving it up to his deputy, and I don't think there's any suggestion that anybody seriously considered that he should step down in 1948.

Travers suggested:

It might have been a very sensible thing for him to do, given he had been 16 years as Taoiseach by 1948. He was 66; he had been 22 years as party leader; he was well over 30 years in active politics and that included 1916, a war of independence, and a civil war, so it would have been quite a natural thing by 1948 for him to step aside. The international situation had changed; the economic situation in

Ireland had changed; there was a sense in which the historic crossroads had arrived in Ireland. I think it was *The Bell* magazine in which it was suggested that the historic moment had arrived in Ireland and either the frozen pond, the ice that bound the feet of the Children of Lir, would be unfrozen, or else the story of the frozen pond would remain the same forever. There was a sense in which it was a crucial crossroads and that, at that crucial moment, Dev chose to stay on rather than to hand over to one of his colleagues. And it is interesting to speculate had he handed over at that moment what might have happened over the next few years.

Given the new emphasis on economics and a whole new discourse about managing the economy, did the inter-party government deserve praise for experimenting to a certain degree with its budgets and with Keynesian economic thinking? McCullagh suggested:

Yes, a very mild form of Keynesianism, and they really needed it, because in order for them to stay in power, they needed to satisfy each of the parties—Fine Gael wanted tax cuts, Labour wanted increases in welfare, and so on, and the only way they could do that was by a change in economic policy, and they were able to do that because of Marshall Aid, to a very limited extent, in fact, but still, it was quite significant in terms of the Irish investment at the time. They had access to that money and they spent it. Now, you could argue whether they spent it in the most effective way, because most of it went on agriculture, which was really just throwing it down the drain at the time, but it gave them a chance to invest in the economy, in housing as well, and keep all their constituent parties happy. But what happened then, when Fianna Fáil got back into power in 1951, is that they rowed back very sharply on that.

To demonstrate the sharpness of that, an archival clip of a very austere-sounding Seán MacEntee speaking about the 1952 budget was played, a reminder (this programme was broadcast during budget week in 2004) of the very limited choices that finance ministers then had:

The fevered spending of the Marshall Aid period is over. It is now a matter of urgent importance to arrange that where our expenditure is current expenditure, it will be financed from taxation or other normal sources of revenue, and that in so far as it is of a genuine capital nature, we shall endeavour to meet it out of the current savings of the Irish public. Onerous as it may be, we have done what is essential, but no more than is essential, to put the public finances in order and to revive confidence in the credit and stability of the state. On the solid basis thus laid, we can build a future worthy of the sacrifices of the past, worthy too of the men and women of this generation, the first to be born in freedom, but for that reason the more determined to preserve it.

Listening to that clip was also a reminder that Seán MacEntee could well have succeeded de Valera. The assumption is always that it was going to be Lemass but MacEntee was in a strong position in the party also. Travers took up this point by suggesting that if this budget had been different, the future of Fianna Fáil could have turned out very differently:

Well, MacEntee and Lemass would have been the two favoured candidates and Lemass, say in 1948, was, at the time of the election, 49, and MacEntee was 59. In some ways, MacEntee had very strong credentials, previously being Minister for Finance, and he's in a very pivotal position coming back in 1951 as the Minister for Finance. He has a tremendous opportunity in that budget in 1952 to make his name in terms of jockeying for the succession, to establish himself. In fact, it doesn't go that way; it goes quite the opposite, because it was a very controversial budget. It was highly deflationary; it posed significant cuts—a shilling in the pound on income tax—and increases in prices of petrol and tea and bread and butter and alcohol. It was reacting to a specific financial crisis in terms of the balance of payments, but arguably it was over-reacting and there was an argument, even within Fianna Fáil, that a different kind of budget was necessary. Lemass had argued in contrast for increased production to resist a deflationary policy, to encourage production, but the dominant view taken at the time of that budget was that there was a need to deal with the balance-of-payments issue and that if you reduce demand in Ireland, that that would in some mysterious way increase Irish exports. In fact, it had the opposite effect, and there's a significant economic crisis throughout the 1950s, so it was a poorly constructed, poorly devised, poorly directed budget, but I think you have to see it both in economic, but also in political terms, that in a sense it was the Department of Finance reasserting its control after the inter-party government period. There was also a sense in which there was a feeling that it would be possible to do this because you could blame the problems on the inter-party government. It did reflect, for the moment, the upper hand of MacEntee rather than Lemass, but if you stand back from it, it seems to me that that marks the end of the possibility of MacEntee succeeding because I think that budget dooms that Fianna Fáil government, and ultimately Lemass is the significant candidate for the future and it's simply a matter of time as to when he will succeed as Taoiseach.

Was there irony in the fact that eventually in the 1950s, when Fianna Fáil began to grapple with these economic questions, the party was effectively learning from what the inter-party government had done from 1948 to 1951? McCullough acknowledged that:

There is an element of that and, of course, they also had the personnel when it finally came to Lemass's time in office, as T. K. Whitaker had been appointed by the second inter-party government by Gerard Sweetman, Fine Gael's Minister for Finance. I think Pauric is right there. I think the 1952 budget was probably a mistake, and it's interesting to speculate what would have happened if Dev had stood down in 1948. I think it's probably most likely that Lemass would have been his successor, but there may well have been a leadership contest, but it's interesting to speculate what would have happened in the 1951 election, because there was no inevitability about Fianna Fáil coming back into power, despite the self-inflicted wound of the Mother and Child crisis. The government parties still won 64 seats; they had seven or eight independents who were willing to support them. Fianna Fáil only gained one extra seat, despite having Dev still in charge, so Lemass's electoral record when he finally became Taoiseach was somewhat indifferent. So it's interesting to speculate whether Fianna Fáil would have actually got back into power in 1951 and introduced a Keynesian deflationary budget in 1952, perhaps avoiding some of the problems that flowed from that MacEntee budget.

Travers elaborated:

> I think you can only speculate, but given that the inter-party government had self-destructed, I'm not sure it matters who was leading Fianna Fáil in 1951; that [inter-party] government would have had difficulty re-constituting itself. I think the wider issue is the more interesting one—given the 1950s, the crisis that engulfs the independent Irish state in the 1950s where, say between 1946 and 1961, more than half a million people emigrate from independent Ireland; where there's a sense in which the experiment of self-government is going down the drain, that 'this bloody country is finished' was the refrain on every lip. The issue is, could that crisis have been averted; could it have been dealt with in a more efficient or timely fashion? It seems to me, you can argue that it could have been dealt with more quickly—it still would have taken some time, but what you have to remember is that we manage an unusual accomplishment in the 1950s. It's very hard to buck the international trend, but internationally there's a boom in the 1950s and we managed to have a stagnant economy. That suggests to me that there's something wrong in terms of the policies and in terms of the political leadership. It takes a long time to come to grips with that and it's not until 1958 that that really happens.

According to McCullagh, 'Another interesting thing is that even if Lemass had become Taoiseach somewhat earlier, in 1951 or whatever, would he have actually pursued the policies that he did later on? And the answer is, probably not, because he wasn't advocating things like attracting in foreign investments or removing tariff walls until the mid-1950s.'

Travers agreed, and added:

> Garret FitzGerald has argued that if Lemass had become Taoiseach earlier, he would have been a good Taoiseach but that he couldn't have done in 1951 what he did in 1958. Having said that, Lemass was, from as early as 1942, arguing for economic planning. In 1951, he was arguing for promotion of production, and there's no doubt that the crisis as it develops in the 1950s might have been addressed in a more timely fashion had Lemass been in control of economic policy.

It's also the case that when Lemass stepped down in 1966, he actually told a press conference that he had never wanted to be Taoiseach and that this image of him as impatiently waiting in the wings was not accurate at all. Travers elaborated on this issue:

> Well, that's absolutely right. In fact, he tried to persuade Dev to stay on and, in a sense, perhaps it was irrelevant who was Taoiseach. The issue was, who was controlling economic policy, and there's no doubt that in the 1950s there are two views within Fianna Fáil, and it takes some time for that to play itself out, and there's no doubt the 1952 budget is significant in that.

How significant was it that de Valera began to make unusual comments in the 1950s about what you can actually practically achieve in politics, and the idea that you cannot achieve all that much? It seemed very unusual language for the leader of the main Irish political party to be using. According to Travers:

> Well, it's a confession of the limitations of what a politician can do, and I think we have to remember that. We talk about 'de Valera's Ireland' as if de Valera controlled everything and that all of the economy and all of social life were controlled by him, and that simply isn't the case. In 1948, during the election campaign, he confesses with a certain amount of frustration that, in relation to emigration for example, 'What can you do? You cannot say, "No, you cannot emigrate."' I think he's conscious of the extent to which things like the late age of marriage in rural Ireland, the resistance to sub-dividing land—that things like that are running counter to the things he would like to have pursued and certainly running counter to the ending of emigration.

Was the inter-party coalition very conscious of what de Valera was doing during those three years in opposition, in terms of his speeches on partition? Was there pressure on the coalition parties to be seen to be doing something about that, particularly people like Seán MacBride? According to McCullagh:

> There was a certain amount, and it certainly was a factor in the Declaration of the Republic in 1949. I mean, Dev was putting his

'anti-partition girdle' around the world, as it was termed, I think, in the *Irish Press*. He also, interestingly, when he arrived in New York on his American tour, featured in a Movietone newsreel, which started off: 'Eamon de Valera, the boy from Manhattan who made it big in Ireland!' But that publicity was one of the factors which was pushing the inter-party government towards making a change in the External Relations Act [which authorised the British monarch to sign letters of credence for Irish diplomats, and would need to be repealed for Ireland to be declared a republic] which was highly overdue and, probably, had Dev stayed in office in 1948, it might have been something he would have done himself anyway.

In this context, one of the ironies of the rise of Clann na Poblachta was that the party was using much of the same rhetoric that Fianna Fáil had used in the 1930s. An archival clip from 1982 was played, in which Charles Haughey was unveiling a memorial to mark the one hundredth anniversary of the birth of Eamon de Valera, and he talked about Fianna Fail in the 1930s, making the case for Fianna Fáil as the welfare party:

> These years were also years of enormous social advance. The first de Valera government took office in 1932 in the midst of a world-wide depression . . . It was a time when budget cuts were needed and they were made, but the new government did not narrow its initiatives to budget cuts alone. Within a few years of taking office, the de Valera government succeeded in increasing industrial output by 44 per cent and almost doubling the number of people in industrial employment. The Housing Act of 1932 began a great era of slum clearance, both urban and rural . . . In the decade after 1932, almost a quarter of the population were re-housed. It was an epoch-making achievement, but it was not all . . . unemployment assistance was introduced for the first time in Ireland in 1933. Old-age pensions were immediately increased and widows and orphans pensions were initiated in 1935. If he had done nothing else in all his long lifetime of service, de Valera's social achievements in these first years of office would ensure that his name should live on in honour as that of a great social reformer.

In terms of his own legacy, if de Valera had gone earlier, would it be the case that the assessments of his career would focus on the

1930s, when he was at his most creative in politics, and his most effective, instead of focusing excessively on the charge that he stalled modernisation?

Travers responded:

> I would be inclined to agree with that: that his achievements lie between 1923—the road back from the Civil War—to 1945; that they lie in the creation of Fianna Fáil, the contribution to political stability, the establishment of sovereignty, the establishment of a cohesive society in the 1930s, the demonstrations of that sovereignty with neutrality; and I think an area which increasingly will be seen as a significant is in terms of Irish foreign policy, which was a very sophisticated and quite moral foreign policy, which would have a relevance even today for a country seeking to negotiate a position in an international climate that isn't very favourable. I think in all of those areas there are significant achievements, but all of them lie before 1945. The situation, as I've suggested, has moved on. De Valera himself once advised Richard Mulcahy that if he was going to go into politics, he needed to study Machiavelli, and to study economics, and it's no criticism of de Valera to say that he mastered the Machiavelli better than the economics. By that I mean, he understood politics very well, but that his understanding of economics, particularly in the post-war period when the needs have changed, was less secure and certainly less secure, for example, than Lemass, who after all had an urban base. De Valera, in 1954 I think it was, said that Fianna Fáil needed to work on its urban base, and again it's one thing that worked very much in favour of Lemass rather than some of his other contemporaries.

Shortly before this programme was broadcast, historian Ronan Fanning had suggested that there had been many 'intemperate and unpersuasive hatchet jobs' on de Valera. There were question marks around the ethics of the shareholding issue in the *Irish Press* (see Chapter 12), and it was suggested that a large number of people educated in the 1950s onwards were very hostile and oblivious to his charisma. Did McCullagh think that these factors were still relevant to his legacy?

> Well, I think Pauric is right. I think the main work was done by the time of the 1948 election, the stuff that you could really look back

and say that he had achieved some truly extraordinary things—in terms of securing Irish independence, in terms of protection, which by the time of the 1950s was outdated and should have gone a bit earlier, but protection in the 1930s was a policy that led to great results. But I think the problem was that it's very difficult to say goodbye when you're on top, and I suppose you could compare it to our near neighbours in Winston Churchill, who stayed on too long but was quoted by his private secretary as, one night in the mid-1950s, sitting on the edge of his bed and saying, 'I just don't think Anthony is up to it', referring to Anthony Eden. He was right about that, as it turns out, but I think, like a lot of people, Dev simply stayed on too long.

Chapter 11

What if Donogh O'Malley had not introduced free secondary education in 1967?

B orn in Limerick in 1921, Donogh O'Malley was at the height of his career as Minister for Education, having already served as Minister for Health, when he died suddenly in 1968. He will forever be remembered for a speech he made in Dublin on 10 September 1966, when, in his address to the NUJ on the role of education in modern Ireland, he boldly announced that he was introducing free secondary education, with effect from September 1967. 'Every year,' he said, 'some 17,000 of our children finishing the primary school course do not receive any further education. This means that almost one in three of our future citizens are cut off at this stage from the opportunities of learning a skill and denied the cultural benefits that go with further education. This is a dark stain on the national conscience.'[1] His announcement was a surprise to the Minister for Finance, Jack Lynch, who had seen no costing, but also to the rest of the cabinet who had not authorised the announcement. It was arguably the most important development in the Republic's educational policy in the twentieth century. But what if there had been no such announcement?

O'Malley's initiative, and indeed achievement, should not be viewed in isolation. He was the third of three reforming ministers to hold the education brief, all appointed by Seán Lemass. John Horgan, the biographer of Lemass, makes the significant point that

Patrick Hillery's role in this regard may have been 'unfavourably overshadowed by O'Malley's more expansive political style'. Hillery had sent a lengthy memorandum to Lemass in January 1963 on the need for reform of the Irish education system and the need to confront vested interests. The barriers to implementation of reform, he suggested, were 'the accepted assumption of a very limited role for the state in education, the Department of Finance's fear of cost and its penny pinching attitude, and the church's proprietary attitude in the running of education'[2]—as good a summary as any of the problems in the Irish education system.

Hillery did manage to instigate a system of 'comprehensive schools', which would enrol children from ages 12–13 to ages 15–16, providing them with an opportunity to obtain the Intermediate Certificate, but they were not to rival existing secondary schools. Hillery also appointed a team of social scientists, in 1962, who published the seminal *Investment in Education* report in 1965. According to the historians of Irish education, this was significant because the authors approached the subject from a social and economic, not from a theo-philosophical point of view: 'behind all the tables and detailed recommendations was a single, obvious conclusion: That if the Republic were to compete in the emerging European market place, it would have to allocate more resources to education and would have to spend that money more effectively.'[3]

As Garret FitzGerald has observed, there are reasons for arguing that Irish governments in the 1960s were comparatively enlightened as a result of this acceptance that investment was a pressing need:

> This move was the outcome of early recognition within the Department of Education and also in political circles that education is, in fact, a key element in economic growth. Irish governments were among the first to grasp this reality and, in a country that in the 1960s was starting to emerge from economic stagnation, this realisation stimulated investment in education on a scale that before the end of the century had helped to transform the Irish economy. If that connection with economic growth had not been established 40 years ago, our education system would never have been developed at such a pace.[4]

Neither would many young Irish men and women have enjoyed the university experience. In September 2005, *Irish Times* journalist Patsy McGarry recalled:

> We were a blessed generation. A great majority of us would never have seen the inside of a university but for the culture created by the free education schemes introduced by Donogh O'Malley in 1967. Education was always a passion in rural and small-town Ireland, but few could afford it beyond primary level. By the time we came along, secondary schooling was free and the numbers going on to third level from our small town had risen from an average of about two a year to double figures. It was the early 1970s and, fully aware of the privilege, we took to university life with gusto. It helped that few of our parents had been to university so they generally assumed we were always bent over books in the library.[5]

The *Investment in Education* report provided the backdrop for O'Malley's speech, as did UNESCO figures which revealed that, in the Republic, only 36 per cent of children aged 14–19 were at secondary and technical schools, half the rate of some other European countries. The *Investment in Education* report also highlighted that in 1961, less than 10 per cent of the children aged 15–19 of unskilled or semi-skilled workers were in full-time education, compared to 46.5 per cent of the children of professional people.

But whatever about the achievements of Hillery, and his successor, George Colley, who sought the amalgamation of smaller primary schools, it was still the case that somebody had to challenge the Department of Finance and break a very significant ideological taboo. In doing this, O'Malley was also acutely conscious of having the public and indeed the media, who he cultivated so well, on his side. His speech on a Saturday evening was well timed to make the headlines of the Sunday papers.

This show opened with an archival clip of Taoiseach Jack Lynch paying tribute to O'Malley following his untimely death:

> He not only saw horizons that few of us dared to contemplate, but he reached out beyond them, impatient for the good that he would

find there; for the good that he wanted to bestow on his fellow man. For present and future generations of Irish children he broadened the horizons of knowledge and enhanced their prospects in life. It may be said that the work to which he dedicated himself had only started. The greatest tribute we can pay to him is to continue this great work at a pace and to the conclusion he would have wished.

Both of the guests on this programme were particularly interested in O'Malley and aware of the significance of his career: Joe O'Toole, an independent NUI Senator and former General Secretary of the INTO, has been immersed in education matters throughout his career; and Mary O'Rourke, leader of the Senate, is a former Minister for Education, TD and deputy leader of Fianna Fáil. I asked O'Toole about his memories of O'Malley:

I knew Donogh very well because he was married to my cousin and they spent every summer in Dingle. My mother was one of the Moriarty family in Dingle and her family are very strongly Fine Gael and my father's family were very strongly Fianna Fáil. My father bravely carried the Fianna Fáil line to the Moriarty family whose comfortable and cosy Fine Gael consensus was considerably unsettled when Hilda, my mother's first cousin, married Donogh. Much as they loved Donogh personally, accepting his political affiliation took a major swallow! I remember discussing education with him around that time; there was the formal opening of St Patrick's College in Drumcondra and he was there, and the President of Ireland, de Valera, was there, and because I knew Donogh from visiting the house at home, I was speaking with him, and he said—he looked over at Dev and said—'You'd better go over there and talk to that long f—er and keep him busy for a while!' But I remember at that stage he was talking about putting the two colleges together, and it was very interesting, in terms of what we are talking about this morning—because he was talking about merging UCD and Trinity. I mean, it probably made people weak at the knees even to think about it. He was talking about 'synergies'—using that word—you could have one medical school, one engineering school—works to the strengths of both colleges, and I said, 'Donogh, how are you going to get this done? I mean, I can't see these people changing after hundreds of years or 300 years in one case and 100 years in the other.' He said, 'Well, I'll just announce it and let's see how it works out!' and I think that he would have done all the homework on the free post-primary education. He was ably assisted by Seán O'Connor, another Dingle person and secretary of the Department of Education. With the *Investment in Education* report, they would have seen exactly the need for this and there's no doubt that it was time for it. In the last couple of weeks, I was reading a pamphlet written by Frances Devine about the life of Deputy Michael Moynihan of Killarney, and, as a councillor in 1966, Moynihan had made a speech at that time where he referred to what I consider the joke section of the Proclamation of the Republic—where there's a reference to cherishing the children of the nation equally, etc.—and he said that if we were ever going to bring that into being, the first thing we should do was to bring in free post-primary education. It must have been an issue that people were beginning to focus on, beginning to come towards. I think that's what Donogh's angle would have been, and he did seize the moment; he saw this was necessary and that this would run and, in fact, the big story then was did he have the approval of cabinet? Well, I think there are times in life when you know you can make a kind of statement and no one can afford to reject it because the issue is too big.

I asked O'Rourke about her own situation when the announcement was made:

I was teaching. I had just begun teaching. I had done my H.Dip. quite late, sort of—coming up to 30—and I had just started teaching and he came to Athlone. I would have known of him— read of him, followed him—and he came to Athlone to open a primary school which was run by the Sisters of Mercy where I taught in the secondary, and we were all there and the first thing that struck me about him was how good looking he was! Now, that might sound trite saying it when we're dealing with very big questions, but he was a stunner, and he spoke very well and his wife, Hilda, was in the car waiting for him, and I went over to her and she got out and we spoke for a few moments.

The two of them together, they were like a movie-star couple— so good looking, so talented, and of course the idea he espoused in that speech to the NUJ was a brilliant one, and it was something waiting to be said—all of the young people pouring out of Primary Cert, as it then was, and where to? What to do now? Their brains just half-tweaked, and all of the search in their minds left unanswered. So it was a brilliant speech.

But why did O'Rourke think it took so long? If you look at what Paddy Hillery was trying to do in the early 1960s, there seemed to be constant barriers put in his way as he was trying to push forward these ideas as well.

> Well, he was, and of course the big report, the OECD report a few years later, gave wings to all that. I wonder what kept it for so long coming to the forefront when you could only go to second level if you paid a fee—essentially that was it.

O'Toole suggested that there was 'a "class" thing at the time in parts of Ireland where education was something that was for the privileged'. O'Rourke agreed:

> Yes, and you could pay for it, or you went to boarding school or you paid in the local secondary school. Now, the nuns and brothers were great, and those who couldn't afford it were usually helped along but they would be a minority—an absolute minority. But it was such a terrific development—think of the change there was, and I know there was a rumpus because when I was in Education, I asked for some of the files—the schools couldn't be built in time to take them all in the following September.

There were, of course, criticisms from certain quarters. T. K. Whitaker, Secretary of the Department of Finance, made some and suggested that because of the suddenness of the announcement, it had not been particularly well planned and that would lead to problems. O'Rourke felt that O'Malley's logic was simple:

> But, you see, if you've a really big idea like that, there's no point in going into too much planning. You'd just better say it first and clear the decks. You'd better get it out and say it and do it and then mop up afterwards!

O'Toole added that, 'Whitaker was inclined to object to bold moves by ministers—he objected to free travel for pensioners; objected to the artists' tax exemption—he objected to many things. I think you're right what you say there, Mary, that it was such a big idea that its time maybe had come.'

His reputation as a hell raiser was another reason for there being a particular interest in O'Malley. Senior Fianna Fáil figures, including de Valera and Seán Lemass had warned him to curb his drinking if he was serious about being a minister, but there seems to be little evidence that he paid heed to them. Seán O'Connor, mentioned above, made the point that, 'he had a reputation as a hell raiser, as being impetuous and as having little respect for convention, which blinded many to his ability and his deep concerns and sympathy for the underdog.'[6] Was that an assessment O'Toole agreed with?

> Absolutely. There's no doubt about that. I would have known Donogh very well when I was growing up, and in one line I'll tell you what it was—he played hard and he worked hard. When he was playing, he was playing hard, and when he was working, he was working hard, and he had the intelligence to link both together. There's no question about that—he would take a direct line on the issues and it's interesting the point that Mary made there earlier, and she would have experienced the same—indeed, I saw her as Minister for Education many times: people trying to hold her back on proposals on the basis that they didn't have the infrastructure to put them together—and Paddy Lindsay at the time [Fine Gael spokesperson on education] challenged Donogh O'Malley in the Dáil, saying, 'How can you put this in place? You don't have enough schools; you don't have rooms; you don't have enough teachers; there'll be too many pupils', and I thought his answer was very telling. He said, 'Well, I'm not too sure about that end of the business but I'll look into it'—and he dismissed it!

O'Rourke made the point:

> . . . the audacity of the statement, the way it was made, the way it burst upon the people, so to speak, I think gave lie to the idea that if you were to bring forth great ideas, you had to be full of angst

and furrowed brows and all the rest of it. That wasn't Donogh
O'Malley's style. I would pick up on what Joe said, which was
correct—he played hard and he worked hard—but one didn't
mean that he had to be going around all the time as I said, full of
anxieties and with a bent back and deciding that if you were that
clever, you really had to show everyone you were that clever. He
didn't believe in that—that wasn't his way of doing things.

O'Toole saw this as the crucial issue:

> It was his method of management, of decision making. So many
> decisions are destroyed by people's discussion on problems about
> the implementation. He worked always on the basis of let's get the
> principle agreed first and then farm out the implementation to
> somebody else. If there had been a more cautious Minister for
> Education, this could well have been delayed till the 1970s. And the
> impact of that would have been quite extraordinary. If you look at
> what happened, and Mary will know this as well because Brian
> Lenihan [O'Rourke's brother] became Minister for Education, and
> it became necessary to move, to expand third level almost
> immediately, so you had the new third-level colleges, and Regional
> Technical Colleges, in Ballymun and in Limerick. I think it was
> Brian who put both of those together and, in an interesting
> symmetry, the then Minister for Education, Mary O'Rourke, some
> years later, gave them university status, so I think there's a nice
> family symmetry in that particular part of it.

Lenihan obviously knew Donogh very well in that they are often
mentioned together in the context of the young 'mohair-suit
brigade' of Fianna Fáil in the 1960s. O'Toole recounted that,
'When you [O'Rourke] were down in Athlone and I was a student
in Pat's, I regularly met and came across both of them drinking in
places like Groom's Hotel and what was great about both was they
were always interested in chats and discussions.' For O'Rourke,
'That was all part of a firmament of ideas which came about over
chats and pints when people came together.'

But just how significant was this new focus on investment, and
thinking about education in the context of the market place and
the economy? According to O'Rourke:

There's nothing wrong with that—of course, there's the two sides of education—the two layers of it. There is the economic layer, which equips people to move forward, to be developmental, to get jobs, to bring jobs, to be entrepreneurial—that's one side. But to my mind, and I'm sure that Joe would agree, the greater side is the fulfilment of a person, of your spirit and your mind, which can move forward because you're infused with knowledge, and the quest for knowledge which never leaves you because you have tasted the delights of books and further studies and education, so there is all of that, but there's no doubt that, in the 1970s, Ireland moved into—it wasn't called 'Tiger Boom' then or whatever, but we moved into good times, which we were only just ready for with the second-level education which had become so prevalent.

Is it an exaggeration to suggest that Donogh O'Malley in some senses can be seen as the father of the economic boom of the 1990s, precisely because of the introduction of free education? O'Rourke remarked: 'I don't think that's stretching it, no.'
O'Toole elaborated:

Well, what it did was it created the link between the First Programme for Economic Expansion and the Second Programme for Economic Expansion in the late 1950s going into the early 1960s, and it gave legs to that, but I have a view myself that one of the problems there was that Fianna Fáil had been in office for a long time, and I've always questioned Dev's commitment to education. I always felt that it in some way undermined his vision of the Gaelic Ireland and what might happen at crossroads and things like that, and I go back to the time when he did at one stage in his early career want to replace the Department of Education with 'Roinn na Gaolainne' [Department of Irish], and I often wonder did he grasp the relevance of change, because there's no doubt about it that in the mid-'60s, there were people in Fianna Fáil, like Haughey, like Brian, like Donogh who—whatever people's views on parties—they were, in terms of just looking at their own party, they were certainly trying to move it on and they weren't exactly the flavour of the month with Dev or with any of the others.

But was it not the case that Lemass essentially indulged O'Malley? And that Lemass had promised when he became leader in 1959 that he was going to make education a priority? O'Toole responded:

Yes, Seán Lemass always had at the base of all of his tenets, education, and therefore he was willing very much to indulge O'Malley in his ideas, and he was lucky that Seán Lemass was Taoiseach. I think if Lemass had not been Taoiseach, his dare-devilry wouldn't have got much further than that speech.

This raised the issue of authorisation, or lack of authorisation, and the question of what the reaction was behind the scenes in government to the announcement by O'Malley. Two letters from the archives, released in the late 1990s, were recorded for the programme by Joe Taylor, one from Seán Lemass to Donogh O'Malley after the announcement had been made. It was clear that Jack Lynch had been enraged in the Department of Finance, perhaps inevitably given how the announcement had been made:

> Dear Donogh,
> I think I should tell you straightaway that your speech regarding free secondary education on Saturday night last must not be considered by you to involve any commitment on the part of the government to any particular scheme or development in this regard, or to the provision of additional money for education services in the coming or any other year. While the giving of priority to educational development is government policy, the normal procedure of submitting detailed plans to the government for any changes that are desired, following on the process of circulation of the proposals to other interested departments and then detailed discussion with the Department of Finance, must be followed. You will I'm sure appreciate that if other ministers in respect of their own work were to seek to commit the government by making speeches in advance of the approval of the government of their plans, everything would become chaotic. In your case, you must expect to have an estimate of costs for any proposals submitted and subjected to meticulous examination, particularly as it now appears that this year's health estimates are falling short by almost £2 million of what the services are costing.
> Yours sincerely,
> Seán

O'Malley's response to Lemass, also recorded by Taylor for the show, was far from contrite; it is undoubtedly one of the best letters written by a government minister in twentieth-century Ireland:

Dear Taoiseach,

Thank you for your letter about the speech I made on Saturday night last. I appreciate that the normal procedures must be followed and government approval procured for new schemes involving the expenditure of public monies. I've no wish to circumvent this system and I shall in due course submit detailed plans, through the usual channels for the changes I wish to make in our education structure.

My speech on Sunday was made in the light of our discussion last week, when we went in detail through the memorandum I had prepared as the basis for the speech I told you I was going to make. It was my understanding that I had your agreement to outlining these lines of action, particularly in view of the fact that Fine Gael were planning to announce a comprehensive educational policy this week. It would have been disastrous for us, if, after your clear-cut policy of priority for education, you were left trailing after Fine Gael in this vital field.

That you are absolutely right in deciding a priority for education and that in doing so you are echoing a deep, fundamental desire in our people at this time is abundantly clear from the reaction to my speech. By now, I have received an unprecedented number of letters of commendation, particularly from parents. This is unique in my political experience and proves, I think, there is a widespread demand and support for what I wish to achieve.

I believe that it is essential for a government from time to time to propound bold new policies which both catch the imagination of the people and respond to some widespread, if not clearly formulated, demand on their part. I believe also that you have on a number of occasions done precisely this when it was needed.

I would be foolhardy enough to hope that my own policy statement of last Saturday was at least approaching this sort of thing. If I was under a misapprehension in believing that I had your support for my announcement, I must apologise. I would hope, however, that what I have said will persuade you that I was right in making it and that you will give me your full support in getting my plans approved by the government
Yours sincerely,
Donogh[7]

O'Rourke's response to hearing that letter dramatised was one of awe: 'That's just brilliant—isn't it? He stitched him in about ten times! There was no getting away.'

O'Toole suggested:

> There was probably a bit of table tennis there as well. Lemass was being very cagey—Lemass didn't say 'no'; he focused on the difficulties of implementation. And then Donogh came back and apologised, but didn't withdraw. It's a great example of the old Lyndon Johnston one—OK, let them deny it!

But O'Rourke thought it significant that, 'it's clear that Lemass did discuss it with O'Malley. In fact, the ploy—I'd say he actually discussed the ploy where he would go and make this speech—imagine, to journalists. And do you know what's interesting about that too? Health was short of money—what has changed? Plus ça change!'

O'Toole suggested:

> I suppose what would have happened there was that he sat down with his boss and he said, 'Look, we'll go along with this process—is this our thinking?' and Lemass would have said, 'Yes, this is our thinking', and once he gave that indication, all Donogh was doing was going along that line. So if his statement was overly previous, let's say, well, tough luck, you're still in line with what they both agreed and it was just a matter of pulling it back into the structural process.

O'Rourke, no stranger to cabinet meetings, added:

> And it meant when he went the next Tuesday or whenever they had cabinet meetings, when he went to cabinet, Lemass could say, 'Well, I've (to Jack Lynch) reprimanded that young Turk', and in turn O'Malley could say, 'Yes, well I was only putting into speech what we had already discussed.' And then he would be armed with all the letters in from the Mamas and Dadas in support of the proposal. Who would come out and say, 'NO, I don't want it—we don't want to give education!'

Reflecting generally on the question of a minister's relationship with the Department of Finance, O'Rourke added:

> There's nobody but Finance, and I think it's right that Finance are cautious. I mean, if you left it to ministers who had grandiose notions—not to put that one down to that—but if you did in general? Finance has to keep the purse strings. I remember when I was Minister for Education, you would get letters from, in their day, Ray MacSharry and Charlie McCreevy, telling you: 'Away with your notions; this is it and is it in the Programme for Government or is it in your Estimates, or can you do it?' But it meant when O'Malley would go the following week with his idea fleshed out in a government memorandum, I cannot see anybody around the table at that time, apart from Finance, saying, 'No, we're not going to do this.'

O'Toole surmised that that:

> . . . happened to every successive minister—particularly in areas like education. They would have always had to lodge their proposals and objections within the Programme for Government and then almost dare the Department of Finance to block it, because the Department of Finance always liked to have their fingers in every pie. I think the world doesn't realise that the Department of Finance have within it mirrored every single government department, and that there's an education department within the Department of Finance and a health department within the Department of Finance, etc., and that they do believe that they should run it, and particularly the Secretary of the Department of Finance at that time—Whitaker—felt that he was a sort of permanent Taoiseach!

Chapter 12

What if the *Irish Press* had not closed down in 1995?

T his programme was broadcast during the year of the tenth anniversary of the closure of the *Irish Press*, the demise of which had caused considerable distress and recrimination. The newspaper titles had been market leaders but were consigned to the dustbin, and the offices at Burgh Quay where, at one time, the three titles had employed 1,100 people, became the focus of a huge degree of emotion. Much of the emotion centred on who was to blame. Ronan Quinlan, a photographer and father of the chapel for the National Union of Journalists at Burgh Quay at the time of the closure, later observed that the controlling director of the Irish Press PLC, Dr Eamon de Valera, 'blamed the government . . . interference from politicians, the Supreme Court, The Competition Authority, the unions and the workers. If he wants somebody to blame he need only take a good look in the nearest mirror.'[1] This was an accurate summing up of the general feeling of the journalists about who was to blame, but also an indication of the many layers to the story of the company's demise and the degree of litigation involved.

This programme provided an opportunity not only to reflect on the possibility that the titles might have survived, or, indeed, closed at another time, but also to assess the impact and legacy of the papers.

The first edition of the *Irish Press* appeared on 5 November 1931, under the editorship of Frank Gallagher. Its inaugural editorial declared that the newspaper was not the organ of an individual, group or party, but a national organ 'in all that term conveys. We have given ourselves the motto—"truth in the news" and we shall be faithful to it.' The editorial was also utterly dismissive of the paper's competitors, the *Irish Independent* and the *Irish Times*:

> Until today the Irish people have no daily paper in which Irish issues were made predominant. There has been nothing comparable in Ireland to the great English, French and American dailies, which look naturally out upon the world from their national territories and speak authoritatively for their peoples. The *Irish Press* makes good that deficiency.

Initially, the *Irish Press* enjoyed huge success, and two further titles appeared: the *Sunday Press* in 1949 and the *Evening Press* in 1954. Getting the paper off the ground was a remarkable fundraising feat in the 1930s. Eamon de Valera skilfully managed to persuade holders of bonds sold by the first Dáil to transfer their investment to the *Irish Press*. Within five years, circulation of the paper had reached 100,000, even more significant given the fact that this was a new readership, and the paper was not dependent on winning readers from its rivals.[2]

However, the issue of shareholders for the 'men of no property' was more complex, and, indeed, cast a certain shadow over de Valera's retirement in 1959, when Noël Browne insisted on raising the issue in the Dáil, and demanded to know who exactly was benefiting from the company shares. Browne insisted that the paper was 'funded by one pound notes collected from rank and file republican supporters of the party. It was the intention that it should become a national newspaper and certainly not the political play thing and enormous financial asset of the de Valera family which it later became.'[3] In effect, Browne had publicised the financial structure of the Press company; having received a present of a share, he exercised his right to examine the company records.

In his autobiography, Browne recalled,

> It became clear that de Valera had systematically over a period of years become a majority shareholder of Irish Press newspapers.

Although he was controlling director of the newspapers, the share prices were not quoted publicly. The price paid by the de Valera family to shareholders was nominal. It was clear that de Valera was now a very wealthy newspaper tycoon.[4]

He revealed that since 1929, de Valera and his son, Vivion, had bought over 90,000 shares in the company. Browne eventually managed to table a motion in the Dáil in December 1958 on the inappropriateness of de Valera holding both positions, and his hypocrisy, given that he had previously suggested that holding paid company directorships was incompatible with ministerial office. De Valera's reply was that his position was merely 'a fiduciary one'; that he had not made any money from the paper, and profits had been used to expand and improve the paper.[5] In any case, de Valera's decision to seek presidential office knocked the story off the front pages.

The two guests on this programme were Michael Foley, a lecturer in journalism at the Dublin Institute of Technology and a former journalist with the *Irish Press* and the *Irish Times*, and Mark O'Brien, lecturer in the Department of Communications at Dublin City University, and author of the book, *De Valera, Fianna Fáil and the Irish Press*.

I put it to O'Brien that the assertion in the first editorial about independence was somewhat disingenuous, when it was quite clearly a propaganda tool for Fianna Fáil, at least in the early days. W. T. Cosgrave had also predicted that it would wither away relatively quickly.

Well, given where the paper came from, it was, I suppose, primarily set up to articulate the views of the anti-Treaty section. It was always going to be a de Valera-dominated paper. Nonetheless, to sustain itself in its existence and, I suppose, to attract advertising, the paper always would have to state that it was going to be an organ that would be independent of any party interest. They were probably disingenuous to say that it was impartial, but I don't think anybody who knew the media scene at the time would have thought that the paper was going to be independent in any way; de Valera's political opponents would certainly not view it as being independent and there are plenty of statements in the reports of the Oireachtas castigating the coming into existence of the paper. Cosgrave described it as a 'Republican rag' and his party at the time, Cumann na nGaedheal, put pressure on him to suppress the paper, and Cosgrave came back to say that there was no need to suppress this paper—in time, because of the propaganda rag he essentially thought it was, he thought that it would suppress itself.

But was it an exaggeration to suggest, as Frank Gallagher, who was the first editor, did, that it was a way of continuing the Civil War?

Not really. I think people perceived the paper as a mission, as a cause. Fianna Fáil had come into existence in 1926 and the existing press at the time weren't covering the Fianna Fáil message—de Valera was essentially a political pariah in terms of media coverage, so this paper was not only a newspaper, it was a mission; it was a cause to spread the anti-Treaty message and to drum up support for this new fledgling party at the time. Seán Lemass had remarked that the *Irish Independent* was increasingly hostile to the new Fianna Fáil party and that the party itself was, in Lemass's own words—'only beating the air without a press behind it'—it needed a newspaper to spread its message and, of course, the paper essentially acted as a rallying call to Fianna Fáil supporters and the anti-Treaty section.

Foley identified another role which the paper performed—the task of demonstrating

a commitment to constitutional politics, because constitutional politics in Ireland had always been associated with newspapers. The Irish Parliamentary Party was associated with newspapers such as the *Freeman's Journal*. The Parnell split had been mirrored by splits within newspapers as well. By 1931, de Valera is entering constitutional politics, so it is, I suppose, a natural progression of that—that you would have your newspaper, and, in a funny way, it is sort of looking back to the nineteenth century because the Irish newspapers at the time, the *Irish Times* and the *Irish Independent* and the *Freeman's Journal*, were becoming more commercial. They had lost, I suppose, the political slant that was necessary in the nineteenth century and the very early twentieth century, and they had become much more commercial, so here is a paper that was going to be like the *Freeman's Journal* had been—was going to be for a cause and also commercial. I don't think Frank Gallagher was being disingenuous because I think the view that Fianna Fáil would be a cause was there right from the very beginning, so the idea of being party political was to be a party newspaper like Sinn Féin had had in the sort of semi-underground papers that had existed. Now it was going to be out there and for a certain class of people.

This, of course, was crucial—the idea that the newspaper would appeal to those who did not feel they were being represented by the political status quo at the time. In an archival clip featuring Tim Pat Coogan, he observed:

> You want to cast your mind back to the scene and the time: there was no doubt that they all felt themselves on a national crusade. No hour was too long and there was no journey that was too long for them to undertake. There's a description of an awful lot of people, walking along the place in the early days, helping in some way, who were not even employed, taking off their coats, sitting down and parcelling up papers.

But to whom exactly did it appeal? What was within its pages in terms of coverage of sport, and would the GAA have been as successful without this paper? Aside from the obvious political affiliation, was the *Irish Press* doing things differently in that sense?

According to O'Brien, it was:

> The *Irish Press* was the first newspaper to carry news on its front page; up to that, the *Irish Independent* and *Irish Times* had devoted its front pages to advertising, so this was a new departure in Irish media, and of course the *Irish Press* is probably fondly remembered for devoting coverage to the GAA, which at that time wasn't being covered by the other press. I suppose the GAA owes a lot to the *Irish Press* in the sense that it forced the other newspapers—the *Irish Times* and the *Irish Independent*—to follow suit once they saw how popular this coverage was. And they certainly devoted a lot of attention to the Irish language as well.

The appeal to rural Ireland was also crucial, according to Foley, and getting to the intended reading constituency:

> It was being sold outside mass, and the *Press* had to hire its own train to get newspapers down to the west because the *Indo* wouldn't let them on the train to distribute the papers, and there was all sorts of stories. Tim Pat Coogan, in the introduction to Mark's book, talks about the postman or somebody else, or a Fianna Fáil activist even, getting the paper up the mountainside in the middle of Kerry, so there was this transport system that got the paper from Burgh Quay to Heuston Station—Kingsbridge as it was—down to Cork, from bus out to Bantry, from Bantry up a mountainside, and the final one would be an activist bringing the paper. Guinness actually talked to the *Irish Press* about distribution because they could distribute better than anybody else because they'd been forced to, and this was getting the paper out there to the remotest part of Ireland and I believe in a way it's what we would define as a public service—that the media has got to be accessible to all—and the *Irish Press* believed that that was the case because its voters . . . no, its purchasers . . . were small farmers living on the sides of mountains wherever. It also, by the way, had a very large working-class readership.

This was interesting, not because Fianna Fáil obviously had a lot of support in working-class areas partly as a result of its house-building programmes, but also because the *Irish Press* reporters did go into the slums and expose desperate living conditions when Fianna Fáil was in power. Clearly, there was serious journalistic investigation going on as well.

O'Brien remarked:

> There was, in the early days of the *Press* at least, a radical edge to its journalism. It certainly did try to expose a lot of the terrible conditions of the tenements in Dublin, so there was that radical edge that died off as Fianna Fáil attained power from 1932 onwards, but there was initially at least that radical edge to its journalism.

But just who exactly was controlling the paper? And was it true that de Valera, as he put it himself, did not give the orders?

According to Foley,

It has now become quite clear, because of research that has been done with regard to the question—was it a Fianna Fáil paper or was it a de Valera paper?—that it was, in fact, a de Valera paper, and to some extent when you start seeing it losing its way later on, part of that is because there isn't a de Valera in power to give it a focus. There is this difference between when de Valera is Taoiseach—then they know where they stand—and when, say, Charles Haughey is Taoiseach—then they're not entirely sure—and I suppose that might lead to the famous Haughey political obituary that appeared later on [in 1983, the *Irish Press* published a two-page political obituary, under the headline 'Haughey on the brink of resignation'. Tim Pat Coogan suggested that it was 'a cock-up rather than a conspiracy' and had been inserted by accident].'

O'Brien elaborated:

That's true. When Vivion took over, when his father went to the Park [to the Phoenix Park, as President, in 1959], I think Tim Pat Coogan recounted that on his very first day he was instructed, by Vivion de Valera that it wasn't a Fianna Fáil paper—it was a de Valera paper, and to bear that in mind in terms of news coverage, editorials, etc. And as Vivion's reign carried on, and the paper changed, journalists had a motto—the motto to be remembered was: 'to be fair to all, but friendly to Fianna Fáil'! So, at times of elections, the paper would always return to its roots and always support, and call for people to vote, Fianna Fáil. But Vivion certainly came under a lot of pressure. At parliamentary party meetings, people like Seán MacEntee and Frank Aiken couldn't understand what was happening with the paper, that it had, I suppose, slightly diluted its pro-Fianna Fáil bias. They couldn't understand that, because this was their paper—they had set it up; it was the Fianna Fáil paper—but in actual fact it wasn't; as we know, it was a de Valera paper.

Did this mean that it was increasingly difficult for people like William Sweetman, who took over after Frank Gallagher, to strike that balance between a certain degree of independence and remaining loyal to Fianna Fáil? As O'Brien observed, Eamon de Valera himself was responsible for appointing the editor:

He consulted Frank Gallagher and, after consultations with
Gallagher, de Valera came to the conclusion that Sweetman would
be an excellent editor because Sweetman could be moulded much
more than the other contenders for the post. And when Sweetman
was appointed, he was called to de Valera's office, and Dev outlined
what Fianna Fáil stood for, what its policies were, and asked
Sweetman was there anything in Fianna Fáil policies that conflicted
with his conscience or his beliefs, and Sweetman of course said,
'No', so Sweetman moved in as editor of the newspaper then.

On this subject, another archival clip was played, featuring an
interview with Tim Pat Coogan:

The hotline had gone cold by the time I became editor . . . De
Valera had gone to the Park [as President, in 1959] and was not
only above politics but also journalism. I would have thought that
what de Valera wanted would have had a very fair chance of 'fetching
up' in the paper, but one thing people, even his opponents, always
gave him was very high marks for courtesy, so whatever views he
would have put over, I think he would have done so that the
editor's integrity or his dignity had not been demeaned.

De Valera was also reputed to have told his biographers, Longford
and O'Neill, that he would rather have run the paper than run the
country. Is this one of the intriguing 'what ifs'—if de Valera had
been editor instead of Taoiseach?

Foley replied simply: 'He had the choice and he chose not to—
at the end of the day, Leinster House looked more appealing than
Burgh Quay!'

How important was the appearance of the *Sunday Press* in 1949
and then the *Evening Press* in 1954? Was it an exceptional
achievement to have this trinity of titles?

According to Foley:

Yes, it's absolutely extraordinary, especially when you, from this
distance, remember just how successful all three newspapers were.
They were the biggest selling newspapers in the country. Questions
about diversity might have been asked in those days about the *Irish
Press*. I mean, it's so hard to believe it—the *Sunday Press* and the
Evening Press were far less identified in a way with the party, so

they had a far freer range in that sense and they could do much. The *Evening Press*, of course, was in effect taking over from the *Evening Mail* and those other Dublin evening newspapers which were floundering then; there's no doubt about that. It emerges in 1954 and it becomes the biggest-selling evening paper. By the time the *Evening Press* closed, we were the last city in the English-speaking world that had two evening papers, so I mean it was quite significant. And the *Sunday Press*, as well, sort of built up a newspaper culture so that people remember the columnists—the Angela McNamaras [the paper's agony aunt] and all this sort of thing. It had a real place in a Sunday that was dominated by Irish newspapers and, again, in a world where such a huge amount of British media comes in, it's important to remember the columnists in the *Sunday Press* had this incredible sway within public life in Ireland. It knew what it was about, or we assumed it knew what it was about in terms of where it stood with de Valera, where it stood with Fianna Fáil. It could then be relatively free in other places which gave it a great journalistic tradition. Look at things like David Marcus's New Irish Writing. That was amazingly significant. You look at radical writers—some people like Douglas Gageby who went on to become a legendary editor of the *Irish Times*—he was a legendary editor of the *Evening Press* before that. It's always been called a great training ground for journalists in Ireland, and that in a way is a pity because it always paid lousy, so there was a lot of journalists who would then leave and go to the *Irish Times* or the *Irish Independent*, or in many cases went to Britain to work as well. It always had a very good newsroom. It was about getting news and, in a way, I've always felt there was an unspoken contract—'Yes, our editorials will be clearly biased. Yes, we will in a political sense be in favour of one political party. But on the other side, no one will interfere with our news gathering.' And it was always like that. I remember when I started in the *Irish Times*, it [the *Press*] was always considered the sharpest newsroom.

How significant a contribution did Tim Pat Coogan make to that sharpness?

O'Brien observed:

He did have a long reign; he was editor for over 20 years. He certainly allowed his journalists scope in their news collection.

There was one particular incident during the Arms Crisis of 1970 when Michael Mills came under pressure from both sides of the Fianna Fáil divide in that crisis, to make sure that their sides of the Arms Crisis events were portrayed in the newspaper. Coogan stood firm and allowed Mills the independence to write what he saw fit, or without any undue pressure from anyone—from either section of the political divide.

If there had been a less assertive editor at that stage, would they have caved in?

'Probably,' according to Foley:

One of the things the journalists have, I suppose, where you work in a paper that is so identified with one political cause, or whatever, is the defence that you are covering something well, and fairly, which is very difficult, I suppose. There might have been those in Fianna Fáil who might have thought with something like the Arms Crisis that there was only one way to cover that, or other issues, but of course the greatest defence somebody like Mills had was, 'I covered it well and therefore you can't criticise me. You might wish I didn't cover it as well, that I only gave one side.' So, in a way, that adherence to good journalistic practice was a way of defending what they did. If you went off and covered politics and you did a constituency profile and you covered Fianna Fáil well, you covered Fine Gael and Labour well, so no one can criticise you. You have shown that you are a good journalist and you are independent in that you will cover everything, and that's the best defence a journalist who works for a paper that, I suppose, is identified with one party can have, and in a way that's what Michael Mills did, and he was a very, very fine political correspondent.

By the 1970s, there was obviously a lot of nervousness in the Irish newspaper sector with Anthony O'Reilly taking control of the Independent group and the emergence of tabloids and diversification. If the Irish Press group had adapted sooner, would it have survived longer or was there still a fair degree of optimism that the Press titles could ride out this storm? O'Brien felt that there was:

Certainly. Vivion was still in control, although Coogan is on record as saying that throughout the 1970s as Vivion became increasingly

ill, the succession mechanisms weren't being put in place, and as
the *Independent* began to modernise and the *Sunday World* came
on stream [in 1973] with its colour and colour advertising, etc.,
there was very little movement or modernisation in the *Irish Press*.
The old plant was still there, so I suppose, as Coogan pointed out,
it was no way to run a railroad—there was no real modernisation
there. But having said that, the papers were still doing well and, I
suppose, the philosophy was, 'if it's not broken, don't fix it', but
ultimately, of course, it was broken.

Foley elaborated and suggested that the Press group could have
learnt much from what other newspapers were doing:

> Once you get to the 1970s, you can see O'Reilly buying into the
> *Independent* and things like the emergence of the *Sunday World*, but
> also what the *Irish Times* was doing—the *Irish Times* had modernised
> itself. In a way, the *Irish Times* should be a very fine thesis for
> marketing students to see what it did from the late 1960s onwards. I
> mean, it re-invented itself without losing its core, in a way that the
> *Irish Press* never managed to do, and, in a way, if you look at the *Irish
> Times* and look at the *Irish Press*, you can see it's like the right way and
> the wrong way. The *Irish Independent* is the same. It moves away from
> the sort of very craw-thumping Catholic conservatism that it had,
> which was simply incredible. I'm thinking of the sort of lead stories
> about a Catholic missionary dying. There is a story—I presume it's
> not true—about the dog of an Irish priest being run over in Lusaka
> or somewhere, and then becoming a story! That changed as well, and
> the *Irish Independent* begins to become what it has since become, but
> the *Irish Times*, I think, is really interesting to watch because, in fact,
> the *Irish Times* was taking the *Press's* readership. It was taking at least
> a section of it. The national school teachers, who were the backbone
> of organising Fianna Fáil down the country, were turning to the *Irish
> Times*—the *Irish Times* from the 1960s on was covering GAA. It had
> Irish language policies. It represented this new modern Ireland and
> a lot of very, very important influential readers of the *Irish Press*
> were beginning to slowly drift.

This, suggested O'Brien, threw up the question of whether those
who modernised the *Irish Times* could have done the same to the
Irish Press:

I remember, once, Douglas Gageby telling me that one of his life's unfulfilled ambitions was to have become editor of the *Irish Press* and to do to the *Irish Press* what he had done to the *Irish Times*. That's a huge 'what if'—what if Gageby had been appointed editor of the *Irish Press*?

Moving into the 1980s, things went from bad to worse, with a strike in 1983, and then a row over computerisation. Was this really the beginning of the end, or could things have been handled differently? O'Brien suggested:

It was in a way the beginning of the end. The *Irish Press* always had a fairly fractious industrial relations climate. It was the beginning of the end—that said, I suppose the new technology was really important and, in certain ways, the *Irish Press* actually led the way in the introduction of new technology. It was the first paper to bring in computerised technology, but it was the manner in which it was done which was problematic. The *Irish Times* and the *Irish Independent* followed suit, but they had learned, I suppose, from the mistakes of the *Irish Press*, in the sense that this technology wasn't forced on the workers. There was a greater process of consultation, and compensation for printers who were beginning to lose out. There was very little of that in the *Irish Press* and I suppose that did poison the industrial relations. But the *Evening Press* was still outselling the *Evening Herald* by up to 30,000 copies in the 1980s. I think as a result of the 1985 strike—the papers were off the streets for about 12–14 weeks or so, and it is very difficult to recover in terms of advertising and circulation, to come back again—people would have drifted off.

Foley felt particularly strongly about how management approached the issue of technology:

There is no doubt, in my view, that they used issues like new technology to try and reduce the staffing numbers rather than put in a redundancy scheme. They thought, 'We can do it cheap; we can actually force the people out', and I think that was their mistake, and the whole time I can remember working in the *Irish Times* before the *Press* closed, when you were covering stories with people from the *Irish Press*, they were always on some sort of union instruction not to work after certain hours or whatever. The industrial relations were appalling, and at the very end of the day, when the thing collapsed, I remember watching it, and you'd see the NUJ there trying to sort of keep the place open, trying to work out were there ways you could get in new investors, running the most amazingly imaginative dispute, going to the courts for the first time with SIPTU on the sideline screaming at the NUJ, being, as they saw it, elitist or whatever. They were saying, 'We can just go back to work if we settle', but of course there was no settlement.

In the 1980s, Dr Eamon de Valera and his associate, Vincent Jennings, were at the helm of the company. Ralph Ingersoll had taken a 50 per cent stake in the operating subsidiaries of the Irish Press PLC in 1989 and had advanced almost £10 million in share capital and loans to the Irish Press newspapers. But Ingersoll was then accused in the courts of oppressing his shareholding partners, Irish Press PLC. Years of hugely expensive (and, many thought, pointless) litigation followed. In 1994, de Valera and Jennings even sold a quarter share in two subsidiary companies to Independent News and Media (hardly suitable bedfellows!) for a pittance that was only enough to sustain the companies for six months in terms of cash flow and was the nail in the coffin of the Press group.

Perhaps most gallingly, at the time of the 1995 collapse, and after such vast amounts had been spent on litigation, journalists who were the target of libel actions in respect of material they had published in the Press titles were told that they would have to fend for themselves if the proceedings were processed. What did the journalists and the front-line staff make of it all? And, more crucially, could it have been avoided? How true is the contention of Damien Kiberd, when assessing the events ten years later, that, 'If the three titles had hit the wall in 1983 as opposed to 1995, it would have been better for all concerned: the owners, the workers, the readers. This is because the three bands still had massive value in 1983, or even 1985 or 1989, when Ingersoll arrived. The *Evening Press* sold 175,000 copies a day primarily to ABC1 east-coast readers in the early 1980s, the *Sunday Press* peaked at more than 400,000 copies, The *Irish Press* was also commercially robust.'[6]

According to Foley:

The interesting thing there was Colm Rapple was fired for writing about the Press finances in the *Irish Times* as de Valera and Jennings came back from the court where a settlement against Ingersoll was reversed, so that morning there was another £4 million put onto the debts of the *Irish Press*. That afternoon they walked back in and Colm Rapple was fired for the piece he had written, which was more or less about diversity in the Press. He got fired. It is hardly for us to ask what was in the mind of Jennings and de Valera.

But isn't it extraordinary that there are still people making money out of the Press titles when they ceased publication in 1995, and that to this day, Irish Press PLC continues to trade in Dublin? O'Brien remarked:

It is extraordinary, and there are people still making a lot of money. Whether it's moral or not, I suppose, isn't for us to judge; whether it's proper or not isn't for us to judge, but essentially when Ingersoll arrived on the scene in the late 1980s, the company was split up into roughly half a dozen different companies; assets were moved around so that when the ultimate collapse came in 1995, it was only the paper itself that collapsed. The parent company, Irish Press PLC, still survived, still had assets in the Isle of Man, etc., so it's those investments and that money that is still being used to pay the wages of the directors of the company. It should be stressed that when the *Press* closed in 1995, over 600 people lost their jobs— the only people who didn't lose their jobs were the directors.

But did it create openings for other newspapers, when it folded? If the *Press* had not folded, what would have been the experience of papers such as the *Sunday Business Post* or *Ireland on Sunday*—did it make success for those new titles more likely? Foley concluded:

Funnily enough, I think, by the time it closed, it had lost so much of its readership that I don't think there was a market left. Now there has been this sort of—ever since it closed, the last ten years— there has been this view that there is a market out there if only we could find it and you've all these little attempts to find it. The *Evening News* was one; *Ireland on Sunday*, I suppose, was another; and now there are stories that the *Andersonstown News* group is going to start a newspaper [*Daily Ireland*, which commenced publication in 2005]. I think that might have a chance actually, but it's looking for this elusive nationalist/republican audience that's somewhere out there, and I just think it's not there, and I think when you're talking about the Irish Press company, the paper which started off as a radical paper for a new Ireland—it's gone, and I just wish the company would fall on its sword and disappear so there was no half-life left.

Chapter 13

What if James Joyce and Samuel Beckett had stayed in Ireland?

This show opened with a rare archival clip of James Joyce reading from his book, *Finnegans Wake*. Considered by many to have been the greatest novelist of the twentieth century, Joyce was born in Rathgar in 1882, and ultimately left Ireland, choosing, it seemed, to be an exiled artist. He spent much of his life in Paris and Switzerland, and died in Zurich in 1941. Samuel Beckett, born in 1906 and considered a successor of Joyce in terms of fictional experiment, was also a native of Dublin. He grew up in the middle-class suburb of Foxrock, and left Ireland in the 1930s, travelled through Europe and eventually made Paris his home. He died in 1989.

Their lives and work raise questions, not just about language, writing and creative genius, but also the fundamental issue of where they considered home and the extent to which they rejected the country of their birth. This programme sought to reflect on some of these questions, and to pose the question: what if they had both stayed in Dublin? Terry Dolan from the School of English at UCD, and author of the revised and expanded edition of *A Dictionary of Hiberno-English*, and Éilís Ní Dhuibhne, novelist, short-story writer and an assistant keeper at the National Library of Ireland, were the guests who offered their perspectives on these questions.

It is interesting to trace the revision of accepted wisdoms about Joyce and Beckett's attitudes to their country of birth. In his assessment of Irish culture from the 1930s to the 1960s, Brian Fallon challenges the conventional wisdom about Joyce's negative view of his home place, drawing on the work of others to dispute the notion that Joyce's work was the medium through which all the shortcomings of an independent Ireland that was narrow-minded, puritanical, sexually repressed and censorious can be traced. Fallon points out that Joyce did not experience Ireland in the 1920s and 1930s first-hand—that he lived almost anonymously, a refugee from world conflict in Switzerland—spoke Italian at home to his wife and children, yet wrote in English, and that despite his being the symbol of a universalism and modernism, it was his native Dublin that was his literary obsession, even though he refused to revisit it. He elaborated:

> If he had returned, very possibly he would not have liked the reality of what he saw, and he might even have despised and detested it, but he never did return, as the world knows. For that decision, he scarcely deserves either praise or blame, yet apparently in the eyes of a large section of his commentators it somehow enhances his stature as a martyr-saint of literature. By the same logic, his voluntary exile also registers as an implicit indictment of a country and society with which he had long lost contact at first hand, and which he no longer knew except through the eyes of others. But does every emigrant who, for one reason or another, settles abroad necessarily hate and reject the country he has left behind? Joyce may have done so, or at least for some of the time, but the evidence seems contradictory and the man who wrote *Finnegans Wake* was plainly a very different Joyce from the one who spoke through the persona of Stephen Hero. There is a degree of acceptance, and even of celebration in his later work, which is very different from the narcissistic bitterness of his Dublin years. Shrewd critics such as Anthony Cronin have recently—and surely quite justifiably—tended to stress the celebratory and comic aspects of his writings, rather than the long-held view of the embittered exile cursing the memory of rabidly nationalist Ireland and the church.[1]

Beckett's disgust with his home country was perhaps more biting, but would he not have been the same no matter where he was?

Wouldn't he always have been a stranger? The protagonist in one of his earlier stories concludes that home is 'nowhere as far as I can see'. Beckett mercilessly lampooned the censors in Ireland but his book, *Murphy*, as pointed out by Declan Kiberd, is also harshly critical of 1930s England. The Beckett who had been well off in Foxrock is just another unemployed 'Paddy' in London. Kiberd sees this failure to settle, to identify a home, as an artistic blessing: 'it would make of Beckett the first truly Irish playwright . . . the first utterly free of factitious elements of Irishness. In the mid-1960s, his book, *All That Fall*, included the lines: "It is suicide to be abroad. But what is it to be at home, Mr Tyler. What is it to be at home? A lingering dissolution."'[2]

Despite the perception that he craved solitude, Beckett was an exceptionally sociable man, according to one of his biographers, James Knowlson. Undoubtedly he disliked the trappings of fame and eschewed self-promotion, which allowed the fostering of myths. Knowlson suggested:

> . . .the first and most natural of these myths was that he was a latter-day hermit, living a reclusive existence in his seventh-floor apartment in the Boulevard Saint-Jacques in Paris. Visiting Germany in 1936, he wrote in his personal diary of the 'absurd beauty of being alone', and after a long solitary walk in the Tiergarten in Berlin, he wrote 'How I ADORE solitude'. His social life in the city was, however, often exceptionally hectic . . . He had literally hundreds of friends or acquaintances from many professions and many countries—painters, musicians, directors, writers, academics—and a surprising number of really close friends . . . consulting his appointment diaries for the last 20 years of his life, while writing Beckett's authorized biography, I was amazed at how he managed to fit in as much work as he did, in view of the many distractions that he had.[3]

I asked Ní Dhuibhne about Joyce's relationship with Dublin, which dominated his writing life and, to a certain extent, his personal life also:

> Yes, he wrote mainly about Dublin. *Ulysses* is a novel which is really extolling the colourfulness and the interest of Dublin.

Dubliners, his first collection of short stories, on the contrary, is kind of condemning Dublin as sad—the overall pervasive mood of *Dubliners* is sadness, and the pervasive authorial feeling in *Dubliners* is compassion and pity for those who have the misfortune to live in Dublin. I mean, he was dying to get out of Dublin—Joyce as a young man in his twenties—and when he left in 1904, I think he had a complex relationship with Dublin and his home, partly because of his youthful experience. He had a terrible childhood, thanks to his profligate father who managed to lose the family fortune. The Joyces started off being fairly well to do— almost like the Becketts, really. His father owned a lot of property in Cork and, I found this extraordinary, but he managed to drink his way out of about ten houses—I don't know how you do that; it would be very hard to do it nowadays, but he was able to do that— and the result for the family was just disastrous and they constantly were running ahead of the landlord, flitting in the middle of the night, and they moved about 20 times I'd say during Joyce's childhood and adolescence, and went from being comfortable to sometimes not having any food. I think that might have affected the way Joyce looked at his native place.

Is there any evidence that his attitude to Dublin mellowed over the years—if he had been writing about Dublin in the 1920s or 1930s, would he have been kinder?

If he had stayed? I imagine if he had stayed that his attitude might *not* have mellowed. Many of the *Dubliners* stories were already written while he was in Dublin and then he wrote the rest of them in Trieste not too long after he had left. By the time he gets to the last story in *Dubliners*, and the most celebrated—'The Dead'—it is kinder to the city than the rest of them. I think the typical *Dubliners* story for me is 'Araby' where this little boy wants to go to a wonderful exotic exhibition or fair or something, but has to wait all day for his father, or his uncle (can't quite remember which) to come home with a shilling, and he doesn't come—he's out drinking or that—and finally he comes and the boy goes to the fair and it's all closing up—there's about one stall left. I think that conveys the kind of feeling Joyce had about Dublin as a place full of disappointment. By the time he wrote 'The Dead', he'd been away for three or four years—he'd been in Trieste which he liked very much. Indeed, then he went to Rome; he didn't like Rome so much—he felt he was being ripped off all the time by people—and he began to think a little more positively about the good aspects of Dublin, the hospitality and so on and, I mean, even though 'The Dead' is what it's called and it's known in general all over Ireland and all the rest of it, I would often have thought it was a very negative sort of story: there is a party—everyone comes on time, they get plenty to eat and drink, and hospitality is mentioned as kind of one of the good qualities of Dubliners, so already there is a mellowing attitude there and I think that came about as it does in most emigrants and exiles once they get to a certain stage when they've been away from the place for long enough, so would that have happened if he'd stayed? I think not.

Dolan elaborated on this question of his relationship with Dublin city, and on Joyce's extraordinary ability to master the Dublin accent:

There is a case where Joyce at one stage did say that with Ireland getting a little bit richer after 1920, he says—'Do you think I should be disappointed now that Ireland is changing so much that I'm going to lose my shape and my destiny?' So he did have a sense, you see, that Ireland was changing and there is some evidence too that later on in his life, there was a kind of nostalgia for Dublin, but in many ways he needed Dublin to be that continuous, vexatious point which stimulated him—to look at it and to try to get to the sense of it and to externalise Dublin into the horrors of the whole world. It was a literary obsession. Well, you see, Homer did it for the great cities of Troy and Greece, and he wanted to do it for Dublin. Paris already had great people to write about it. Dante had written about Florence, so Joyce was going to do for Dublin what these other great writers had done for other cities, and he did it brilliantly, not least through the brilliant language which he uses. There are so many cases in *Ulysses* and also *Dubliners* where we can see pure Dublinism and even the younger Dubliners today can just about recognise it, though some of them despise it because they see in Dublin 4 from their grand vantage point that that is old Ireland, culture Ireland, blarney Ireland and that kind of Ireland!

Ní Dhuibhne continued:

He did, and I often think that Joyce in one sense never left Dublin—he kind of brought Dublin with him in various ways wherever he went. He was only over in Trieste a year or two and his brother was over and his little sister and his older sister, and there was constant coming and going, and of course he didn't go alone. I think there's a big difference actually between somebody setting off alone for abroad at that sort of age and somebody setting off with their partner or spouse, which he did, so, you know, he had Ireland there with him all the time.

I wondered was there much evidence that he cared about what Dublin thought of him. Was he conscious of that? There was a reference in one book to Pádraic Colum talking about him having a kind of persecution complex, but at the same time he was very conscious about how he was received in his own city. Dolan asserted that 'He was, very, very much so', and Ní Dhuibhne offered suggestions as to why:

> And by his family. I'm the kind of writer who never shows anybody anything—I just don't want to show people my stuff before it's out there and they're buying it or whatever, but he sent *Dubliners* to his Aunt Josephine and he sent her chapters of *Ulysses* before it was published and everything. He always got an awful lot of affirmation from his terrible dad as a child—that was one good thing about his childhood and he kind of went on seeking this kind of approval. He was such a family man, he wanted them all to approve and to like what he was doing, and they didn't—I mean, they didn't like *Ulysses*; that would have been a very negative thing for him if he'd had to kind of live among the people he was writing about.

Dolan added:

> He also wanted them to check his accuracy as well. If you go back to a native Dubliner, that native Dubliner can tell you whether something has the right rhythm in whatever words he is using at all—say words like 'barm brack', 'Jock' and 'Doris'—and so many other words he uses all the time—'Ráiméis' as a citizen in the Cyclops chapter. So, over and over again, he uses the rhythms of Dublin. But one interesting thing is, too, at one stage he did try to get back to Dublin. He did try to get a job with Corriere della Sera in Italy and

was turned down—he didn't get the job, so he did have that slight intention to come back maybe for a short professional stint.

But wasn't there a tendency for people like Joyce to live anonymously when they were abroad? Is it the case that even if writers like Beckett and Joyce were in Ireland or were in Dublin, they would still, to a certain extent, be exiles because of their craft? Dolan observed:

> Well, there's their craft, but also there's an element of jealousy as well because, you see, we had Yeats and we also had Shaw—both of them got a Nobel Prize, and Joyce in *Finnegans Wake* has quite an 'iffy' reference to the fact that he did not get the Nobel Prize, so I think he would see himself as overshadowed. I think he was a little bit jealous as well. We must remember that he preferred Ben Jonson to Shakespeare, and I think because in his heart of hearts he might have recognised Shakespeare as a bigger star, whereas I think Ben Jonson is B-list and he knew he was beyond being—was pretty A-list himself.

Ní Dhuibhne added:

> He seems to have been fairly arrogant—T. S. Eliot found him arrogant when he met him—but I don't think Joyce ever lived anonymously; he was very unlike Beckett—he was always surrounded by people and he was a socialite really, wasn't he?

Dolan had no doubt about that: 'Oh, he was—he liked parties and dancing, singing and drank an awful lot of wine.'

Is it true that Beckett committed a distinctive Irish voice to paper as well? Dolan responded:

> Well, he did it too in some of the work. *Waiting for Godot* is so much of an Irish play. As soon as we begin to read him, we see— even the word dúidín (little pipe), and also in other words that he used—Hiberno English right the way through. There is no question, he retained Hiberno English, did Beckett, as did Joyce.

A clip was played from one of Beckett's pieces in which Dolan identified:

Many examples there of Hiberno English; there is the 'r' in Sir, 'blāst' you, not blast you—we have the 'betther', not better, as I would say, as a Londoner. The strange syntax of 'and you an orphan' which is directly from 'agus' in Irish. 'Stravagin', a very old-fashioned word used in Hiberno English; 'turen around'—between the 'r' and the 'n' there is almost another vowel there—as we would say—'Colm', 'elm', 'fern'—called the 'epenthetic' vowel, and 'witcha' rather than 'with you'—so right the way through, especially the 't's, the 's's, the epenthetic vowels and the syntax—all Hiberno English.

And what of his writing in French—can Beckett's Irishness be detected there also? According to Ní Dhuibhne:

Well, both Beckett and Joyce had a great ear for language and they were great linguists. I mean, Beckett was a wonderful French speaker even before he ever went to France, and Joyce learnt Italian perfectly and he learnt Danish before he left Dublin because he admired Ibsen so much, and so on, so they were linguistically gifted people. I think they would have had a special ear for dialect and that all along. *Waiting for Godot* was of course originally written in French—*En attendant Godot*. Beckett didn't think much of it—it was something that he tossed off while he was plodding away on one of the novels which he had enormous difficulty getting anyone to publish. He never, according to Deirdre Bair, his biographer, considered it one of his favourite works, by any means—he said he didn't really know where it came from; but anyway, one of the reasons that it was a hit once he finally got it on—which took a considerable amount of time, he was never lucky until *Godot* with getting his stuff produced or published or that—one of the reasons that the French, the audience in Paris liked it was that it was one of the first times that they had heard ordinary French as spoken on the street corners on the stage, the 'Comédie Française'. There was a literary language which was used in drama; there was a type of language which was considered appropriate for drama that just wasn't the same as the language of ordinary people. So Beckett would have had that from Joyce, I think—the idea that you should use that kind of language—because Joyce was one of the first also to take the language of ordinary people and use it.

Dolan added: 'And use it in the drama too—you get, "*ah! maladroit que je suis*"—"how maladroit . . . how clumsy I am"— but Beckett translates that himself as, "ah, what ails me, all bloody thumbs", so he brings in the pure Dublinism into something which is quite a grand piece of French argot, so there is no question about that.'

It is perhaps open to debate as to where Beckett picked up the Dublinisms. He did move from the leafy suburbs of Foxrock to study at Trinity College, and he said that the students there were the cream of the country—rich and thick—and he left after four terms. But what Joyce and Beckett obviously shared was exile and it does raise this question of how they defined their own identity. There are an interesting few lines from *More Pricks than Kicks*, which is one of Beckett's earliest pieces, in which it is asserted: 'what I am on the lookout for is nowhere'. And yet when Beckett was asked if his French domicile meant that he had rejected his Irish citizenship, he said '*au contraire*'. So, in that sense, did they think of him as someone who was not seeking to let go of his Irish identity?

Dolan suggested:

Joyce did too, because if you think of that great scene in *Portrait of the Artist as a Young Man*, when Stephen is talking to the Dean of Studies and Stephen begins to think the words 'home/Christ/Hail Master'. Now, they are different in his mouth than in my mouth, but the first word Joyce chooses to determine who is Irish and who isn't is the word 'home'. I think that's quite significant.

Ní Dhuibhne added:

I think Beckett had a difficult personality; he suffered from depressions and he was, I think it is reasonable to say, fairly neurotic, especially when he lived in Ireland. He had a very comfortable lifestyle in comparison with poor old Joyce—I mean, he was out in Foxrock, he was well off, he was nurtured, he was kind of offered a job in Trinity as soon as he graduated, which Joyce would probably have jumped at if he'd got it, but he didn't. Beckett was a brilliant student, but Beckett, I think, had to get away from his mother. He had a very complicated relationship with his mother, May, who seems to have been okay really, but they were always quarrelling and they didn't get along.

So mothers and fathers have a lot to answer for when it comes to assessing the personalities of Joyce and Beckett?

And with everyone! Yes, as a mother, I know that. I think Beckett seemed to be much more relaxed and happy as soon as he got to Paris and he kind of had a more youthful perspective. I don't think it's just artists ... maybe it is—I mean, I was always dying to get away abroad and the bright lights and everything is going to be more cultured and civilised and Bohemian, and it was like that. When Beckett went to Paris first, he went in a very ordinary kind of way, on a scholarship—it wasn't kind of some big gesture really—he stopped wearing his Foxrock tweeds and because they were all very sporty, he was always hiking in the Dublin mountains with his dad and all the rest of it, but he kind of came back with a French beret and a tight black suit and everything, so I think he just liked the difference—'*Vive la différence*' I suppose it was—the glamour and the exoticism of abroad, which of course was much more intense then than it is now where everyone is going to Paris for the weekend.

There was also the question of publication: if Dublin had been more author-friendly, might they have stayed? Dolan observed:

From a practical point of view, Paris was full of little publishing presses all over the place, and if you really wanted to become an exile in the mind, you'd want to publish something. In Dublin, it was very difficult because of censorship and because there were fewer publishing houses. In Paris, there were lots of these little places where you could get things published, so it was much more open for the possibility of making your voice heard.

Ní Dhuibhne added:

Beckett did say when asked why did he go that it was for the usual reasons—censorship, theocracy and so on—and that was an aspect of Dublin life. I'll just read a tiny extract from this piece by Seán O'Faoláin—one of the ones who did stay: 'No Irish writer living in a country where circumstances are particularly complicated and difficult for every type of artist, complicated by religion, politics, peasant unsophistication, lack of stimulus, lack of variety, pervasive poverty, censorship, social compression and so on, can fail to want to do something about it.'

The conditions of life for artists just were not good.

Irish artists were also influenced by Ireland's relative isolation and neutrality during the war, a conflict that had a huge effect on Beckett. Joe Taylor, who did a marvellous job on Beckett's difficult-to-master accent, read the original script of a broadcast which Beckett delivered after he had returned to Paris in 1946 from Normandy, where he had worked for the Irish Red Cross in what became known as the Irish Hospital. He made observations, not just about those in Normandy, but also about the Irish people who were helping them. There also seems to be an implicit criticism of Irish neutrality:

> One may thus be excused if one expresses the opinion generally received, that ten years will be sufficient for the total reconstruction of Saint Lô, but no matter what period of time must still be endured before the town begins to resemble the pleasant administrative and agricultural centre that it was, the hospital and wooden huts will continue to discharge their function and their cures . . . long after the Irish are gone and their names forgotten, but I think at the end of its hospital days it will be called the Irish hospital, and after that, the huts when they've been turned into dwellings, the Irish huts. I mention this in the hope that it will give general satisfaction and, having done so, I may perhaps venture to mention another, more remote but perhaps of greater importance in certain quarters. I mean the possibility, the possibility that some of those in Saint Lô will come, realising that they have got at least as good as they gave; that they got indeed what they could hardly give—a vision and a sense of a time-honoured conception of humanity in ruins, and perhaps even an inkling of the terms in which our condition is to be thought again. These will have been in France.

The resentment at Irish neutrality was understandable, according to Dolan, as 'When Beckett himself won the *Croix de Guerre*, he was a fighter himself, and he could see no point in not being active in some way.' Ní Dhuibhne concurred, and suggested that if it had not been for the war, he might have been a very different artist:

> Yes, I think he might have been slightly disgruntled with the Irish. I think Beckett who was the sort of person who, like Joyce, would have been fairly apolitical, found himself sort of firmed up by the whole experience of being in France during the occupation and the war. He joined the Resistance for the kind of reason that actually is always significant for soldiers in armies—because of having seen what happened to his friends, his Jewish friends being murdered by the Nazis and brought off to Concentration Camps and all the rest—so suddenly politics became very real and personal for him and he was brave. He found himself, in a way, and he found his voice too. I mean, he says he doesn't know where *Waiting for Godot* came from but obviously it came out of that whole experience of the war, and even in quite a literal sense it replicates to some extent the kind of banter and conversation that he and his partner, Suzanne, had when they had to flee from Paris in 1942—somebody informed on them as Resistance fighters and they walked to the south-east of France to a village in the mountains called Roussillon, and they slept out and all the rest of it, so the *Godot* landscape came from that. I suppose his very bleak nihilistic vision of the world would have come from that experience.

Dolan added:

> And also not knowing. Because the word *Godot* is a middle-English word—God-Ot—it means 'God Knows'. So waiting for God knows, waiting for God knows what, so I think that's part of his English heritage there.

Is he also at this stage, in the aftermath of the death of Joyce, shaking off Joyce's influence to a certain extent, with his writing becoming much more pared down?

Dolan saw it as 'becoming much more austere, much more paralysed', and Ní Dhuibhne pointed out that 'the *Murphy* image is not exactly exuberant, but the language is so much richer and it's all about language really, but at this stage he is withdrawing from language, isn't he?' Dolan suggested, 'as Joyce tried to do a little bit in *Finnegans Wake*, didn't he?'

Ní Dhuibhne felt that the most interesting 'what if' was what if Joyce had immersed himself more deeply in the Irish language:

> Well, I think both of them found that language was so important to them, but the language became inadequate, Joyce had to invent his own language and that kind of goes. My personal regret is that Joyce didn't go back to Irish. I feel if he'd taken the language more seriously—if he'd learnt it, which he clearly could have done. He did have lessons from Patrick Pearse and he didn't like them—I don't know very much about that but obviously it didn't work out. In *Dubliners*, he takes a cut at Miss Ivers who is a real middle-class Gaeilgeoir. I mean, he was positively enough disposed towards Irish and he must have met Irish speakers when he went back to Galway, and he went to the Aran Islands for a brief visit with Nora at one stage on one of his visits to Ireland after they had emigrated, but he never really met enough ordinary Irish speakers—because Joyce loved the ordinary person. I mean that's what *Ulysses* and *Dubliners* is all about—he was interested in the real thing and he didn't get it; instead, he got the kind of politicised nationalistic Gaeilgeoirí that he would have met in the Gaelic League to some extent—

Dolan agreed:

> Exactly. One very big 'if' is—if Beckett had never gone to France, he might have never met Joyce, because he was teaching in the École des Langues, and this Jewish uncle that I mentioned knew Joyce in Dublin and gave him the introduction to Joyce, so, had he never left Ireland, he might never have met Joyce. The relationship between the two men was a very complicated one, because Beckett, I think, absolutely idolised Joyce, and sixty years afterwards, he still remembered Joyce's phone number which was 'Segeur, 95.20'! That shows adulation and great friendship, but what is funny too is he never got on with Nora at all. And Nora didn't like him because I think he regarded her as not important in his friendship with Joyce. Of course, that was a fatal mistake. This was no doubt complicated by Beckett's relationship with Joyce's daughter, Lucia. It complicated things between Beckett and Joyce himself, but, from

very early on, Beckett did have this superior attitude to Nora, which, of course, she, being a brilliant, brilliant woman, was very sensitive to.

Ní Dhuibhne added:

It was, of course, complicated by poor Lucia falling in love with him really, and there was a rift in the relationship with Joyce himself at some stage but they mended that, and, in fact, Samuel Beckett was good to Lucia and wrote to her right up to the end really, so he was very loyal—he was a curmudgeonly, difficult, taciturn person, but you'd have a sense that he had strong loyalties.

Dolan concluded:

He was kind and he also believed in tradition, so he always smoked every day and he always had two glasses of whiskey every day. And he lived to a very ripe old age, unlike Joyce who died at 59.

Chapter 14

What if Frank Duff had not established the Legion of Mary in 1921?

This programme opened with an archival clip of Frank Duff speaking about the early years of the Legion of Mary, known until 1925 as the Association of Our Lady of Mercy:

I saw that we were dealing with something completely out of the ordinary. It is true that within three months of its work I did tell them that they were destined to cover the whole world. They thought it so funny that they must have spent the best part of five minutes in extraordinary laughter! But I said to myself, 'this is remarkable'—ordinary simple people showing a degree of spirit which seemed to be limitless.

Duff was a civil servant in the Department of Finance when he established the Legion in 1921. It went on to become the largest such organisation in the Catholic world, claiming more than three million members by the end of the twentieth century. Despite this, Duff does not feature prominently in the history books—an omission all the more surprising when you consider some of the tributes that have been paid to him. Pope John XXIII suggested that the Legion represented the 'true face' of the Catholic Church, and, in the 1980s, an American bishop referred to the handbook of the Legion of Mary as 'one book that has changed the face of the earth'. At home, the late Cardinal Ó Fiaich wondered would the day come when the church would declare him Irishman of the twentieth century.[1] The contributors to this programme were Finola Kennedy, an economist and historian who has done extensive research into the life of Duff, and suggested that he 'is the great absentee from twentieth-century Irish history,'[2] and historian and Dominican sister, Margaret MacCurtain, who has looked closely at the life and times of Edel Quinn, one of the best known of the Legion's missionaries.

One of the striking things about the development of history writing in Ireland has been the gulf between the public perception of individuals and institutions that had such influence in twentieth-century Ireland, and the space afforded them in the history books. Despite its national and international impact, the Legion of Mary does not merit a single mention in Joe Lee's *Ireland 1912–85* or in the long-awaited *New History of Ireland VII, Ireland 1921–84*, a tome of over 1,000 pages. It was striking too that, in June 2005, when Marian Finucane devoted the last week of her RTÉ Radio One morning programme to the search for Ireland's greatest woman, Edel Quinn was a name that featured prominently, and she was nominated by both young and old—though, again, she does not feature in the recorded surveys of twentieth-century Ireland.

Duff had huge difficulties in trying to obtain official endorsement from the Catholic hierarchy for his work, despite the pace and scale of his achievement and activities in the 1920s and 1930s—the opening of the Sancta Maria, Morning Star and Regina Coeli hostels, the beginning of the Legion's global spread after the Eucharistic Congress in 1932, which had been attended by many Catholics from outside Ireland who sought to establish the Legion in their home places, and Duff's visit to Rome where he was received by Pope Pius XI in 1931, a visit that was made possible by the intervention of William Cosgrave, President of the Executive Council of the Irish Free State, rather than by the Irish hierarchy.

During all of this, Duff had to wait eight years, until 1940, for a personal interview with Edward Byrne, Archbishop of Dublin, to discuss the work of the Legion; clearly, the attitude emanating from the archbishop's house in the early years was one of overwhelming negativity.

In the event, the hierarchy did not approve the Constitution of the Legion until 1935, and the first edition of the handbook of the Legion with the imprimatur of the hierarchy was published in 1937. Perhaps what jarred with the authorities was the emphasis on the role of the laity; as Duff saw it, they were the true measure of the Catholic spirit. There may have been a simple snobbery about the concept of high-profile lay activity, or a feeling that they represented a threat of some kind—the truth was that many of the clergy wanted nothing to do with the Legion.

Duff was also an ecumenist before his time, which did little to help his relationship with John Charles McQuaid. In 1942, he had to acquiesce as McQuaid banned him from involvement in the Mercier Society, which encouraged dialogue between members of different faiths. Duff's account of his work with the prostitutes of Monto was also censored by the Catholic Church, though by the 1960s, the hierarchy had a much more benign view of the work of the Legion. Duff's reflections on the difficulties he had included the observation: 'anyone who wants to work in Ireland will be cribbed, cabined and confined . . . even when the world has more or less taken up the Legion, Ireland looks on it suspiciously.'[3] It has also been suggested by some historians that the work of such organisations 'narrowed the ground' available to those who wanted to galvanise poor communities into left-wing politics,[4] though this assessment should not detract from the heroic work being done by individuals. According to the *Irish Catholic Directory* of 1945, the Legion of Mary was about 'the careful selection of men whose inadequate moral and material equipment causes them to live on a level below that which is compatible with decency and who are accordingly undergoing a process of degradation.'[5]

Another archival clip featured the recollections of Kieran Kennedy, who was actively involved in the Legion; it gave a good overview of Duff's personality:

> He wouldn't pull any punches about people whom he wouldn't have agreed with, even if these were members of the hierarchy. He deplored the fact that the hierarchy and the priests hadn't always given as much support as they could to the Legion and he was

particularly impatient of those who wanted to rewrite the Legion Handbook even when they'd never worked the Legion system. He was certainly a very forgiving man—some of the people who criticised the Legion and whom he would criticise in private conversation, if they then made a gesture towards the Legion, they were received with absolutely open arms. I think that was true, for instance, in the case of Eamon de Valera, who, for a long time, didn't see much in the Legion, but towards the end of his life did come to see the value of it and they became very close friends. He told us once he thought de Valera had spoken his heart more freely to him than he would have done to anybody else. Duff was the least status-conscious of men. He treated them all the same; it didn't matter if they were a cardinal or a beggar. He tried to see in all of them the person of Christ.

What exactly prompted Duff to undertake this work in 1921, when the War of Independence convulsed Ireland?
Finola Kennedy suggested:

You have to go back a little before 1921. Duff was a very successful, brilliant young man when, in 1913, the year of the lockout and the tremendous associated suffering and poverty in Dublin, he was invited by a friend, J. J. O'Callaghan, to join the Vincent de Paul Society. Now, up until that moment, he hadn't been conspicuously interested in, if you like, social or religious issues, and when he joined the Vincent de Paul, he joined in Whitefriar Street, and he began to see the awful poverty and neglect of the poorest of the poor, and he persisted with his Vincent de Paul work, and then, in 1918, he transferred as president to a group of the Vincent de Paul in Francis Street, and there were other groups meeting in Myra House which was then the house owned by the Vincent de Paul Society. The groups included the Pioneers and various other groups, and, on one occasion, a man called Matt Murray was recounting his visits to the old Dublin Union, and a group of women who were there—young girls, aged about 18 to 20—were quite moved by this account. They went to Frank Duff who was present and Fr Michael Toher, who was a curate in the parish in Francis Street, and said, 'Why couldn't we do that?' and of course at the time the Vincent de Paul was restricted entirely to men, so a date was set for the following Wednesday and that, as it transpired,

Eoin O'Duffy: unbridled fascist or defender of free speech? Blueshirts give the salute, Charleville, County Cork, April 1934. 'It's very hard to be a charismatic leader and have a strong Monaghan accent!' (Maurice Manning) (*Irish Examiner*)

The handover, 1959: Seán Lemass takes over from Eamon de Valera. End of an era and start of a new dawn? 'Dev simply stayed on too long' (David McCullagh). (*Irish Times*)

Donogh O'Malley, May 1965. 'I believe that it is essential for a government from time to time to propound bold new policies.' (*Lensmen Press*)

Editor Tim Pat Coogan launches the new tabloid style *Irish Press*, 1985. Bigger and better or last chance? 'I wish the company would fall on its sword and disappear so there was no half-life left' (Michael Foley). (*Photocall Ireland*)

Playwright Samuel Beckett in May 1970. 'How I ADORE solitude.' (*Hulton-Deutsch Collection/Corbis*)

Author James Joyce with publisher Sylvia Beach in Paris. 'The first word Joyce chooses to determine who is Irish and who isn't is the word "home"' (Terry Dolan). (*Bettman/Corbis*)

Frank Duff, founder of the Legion of Mary, with Cardinal William Conway, at a session of the Ecumenical Council, September 1965. 'The great absentee from twentieth-century Irish history' (Finola Kennedy). (*Topfoto*)

President-elect Mary Robinson takes the bouquet while a forlorn Brian Lenihan looks on. Election count, 9 November 1990. 'It was an extraordinary accident in a way, but I suppose it was an accident waiting to happen' (Tom Garvin). (*Derek Speirs*)

A well-practised voter casting the beloved ballot in November 1982. Where did his 7th preference end up? (*Derek Speirs*)

T. K. Whitaker, newly appointed Secretary of the Department of Finance, 29 May 1956. 'In many ways, Ireland had the moral basis of a backward society' (John FitzGerald). (*Lensmen Press*)

U2, early promotional photograph, 1981. 'You don't join a band to save the world, but to save your own arse' (Bono). (*Topfoto*)

Members of the Dublin Unemployed Association, protesting outside Leinster House, 22 July 1953. 'Is it Communism to protest for three meals a day?' asked one of their leaders, in response to the 'red scare'. (*Lensmen Press*)

Drinking buddies: a Jamaican carpenter and a group of Irish labourers in the Coach and Horses, a London pub, easing their lonely hearts. 'I took drink to make me fit in, to make me feel that I belonged' (Joe McGarry). (*Hulton Archive/Getty Images*)

Noel Browne in February 1957. 'How many people are remembered for fifty-seven years having been three years as a minister?' (David Neligan). (*Lensmen Press*)

became the first meeting of the Legion of Mary. Frank Duff always claimed that he really wasn't the founder—that it was something beyond him. He believed that it was really Our Lady who had founded the Legion, and it was something that he was an instrument in the founding—that was the way he looked at it, because it was completely unplanned, and when he went that first evening, one of the members, Rose Donnelly, had set up a little altar with a statue of Mary and two vases of flowers and two candles, and that is the Legion altar, which is replicated at every Legion of Mary meeting throughout the world to this day, and it was unplanned.

At what stage was there mention of prostitution, or the Montgomery Street region? People do associate the Legion with a crackdown on vice in Dublin in the 'Monto' region in the 1920s—was that the main thing on their agenda?

Kennedy observed:

The first thing they did was visit the cancer wards of the old Union Hospital, and then, because of the location of their meeting, they were in an area where there were a lot of lodging houses for prostitutes off Newmarket, and these sort of areas, and they began to call there, and it was kind of daring in those days, and they really discovered—Duff's immediate insight was—that these girls were absolutely lovely girls up from the country, that they were in this for economic reasons, that they had very little alternative ways of surviving, so how the Monto initiative occurred was that one of the girls they were visiting in that area moved to the lodging houses round the Pro-Cathedral and Montgomery Street, which is where the Monto name comes from, and Railway Street and Elliot Place and that sort of area where you had on-street brothels, the ones that are described by Joyce in *Ulysses*, and one of the girls they were visiting moved there, and they followed her and they befriended her, and eventually that whole area (where no priest had entered, and it was in the parish of the Pro-Cathedral!) was closed down, and he opened a hostel in 76 Harcourt Street, which was given to him by W. T. Cosgrave. It had been one of the safe houses for Michael Collins, and he installed the girls there and he gave them a home, and two women moved in full time. One was Josephine Plunkett and one was a Miss Scrattan whose father,

Thomas Scrattan, had come to Dublin with Newman, and they were the two women who lived there and looked after the girls with the assistance of many others who gave a number of hours during the day. So he saw the economic reality. He was completely concerned with their eternal welfare.

Significantly, given the culture that prevailed with regard to women having children outside of marriage, Duff was also concerned that these women keep their babies, and if it hadn't been for Duff, wouldn't many of those women have been forced to hand their babies over to institutions?

Well, this was really one of the most remarkable things. When in 1930 he opened the Regina Coeli Hostel for women, he had already opened the Morning Star Hostel for down-and-out men in 1927. The first person to present was a pregnant woman—a mother and her unborn child—and he welcomed her with open arms, and from that developed a unique system, I think, where mothers were encouraged to keep their babies and they lived in units of three or four, and one woman stayed at home, as it were, and acted as a kind of mother to the others, and the other three would get jobs. Now, they weren't terrific jobs—they might have been domestics in the Richmond Hospital which was nearby—but he was adamant that a woman should have the option to keep her child and that was so far ahead of its time. I've seen material in the Diocesan Archives where he wrote to the Archbishop complaining about a particular social worker and the phrase he used was, 'She is shovelling children into these orphanages', and he was trying to provide an alternative.

What was MacCurtain's assessment of the difficulties Duff had in getting the bishops to acknowledge the work of the Legion?

That was the surprising thing—that the hierarchy were cool towards it. Now the perception was that it was just the Dublin hierarchy. I come from the experience of Cork in the early 1940s, both as a schoolgirl and later as an undergraduate in University College Cork in the 1940s. At that stage, we never saw Bishop Lucey, but Frank Duff actually came to the university to speak on ecology—marvellous, marvellous stuff, I still remember it, and it was packed with students. I don't think we noticed it at the time that there was this kind of chasm—well maybe that's a bit strong— this gap, frostiness, between the hierarchy and Frank Duff, because of course we were lay students ourselves, but, you see, in between, there were these priests who were really very, very good when they took the position of spiritual director to a presidium. We had Father Valdenburg, the Dominican scholar, and his talks were gems in Irish, so you had a very high standard of curates basically, and then you had—it didn't seem to matter very much, but you were aware that the local hierarchy did not take a part in the Legion— maybe this was a very good thing.

If the hierarchy had looked at the Legion of Mary initially and decided it was acceptable as long as it included only women—the idea that you could bracket it off into some kind of charitable female endeavour—would that have made a difference?

I don't think it would have attracted the kind of young person that came along to it. There was a certain social element to the Legion, where the mixed socials were very interesting, because you had this common background of involvement—it wasn't so much social work; it was actually in the appreciation that the kind of society that you were dealing with was hungry for something more than just a handout, and I think that's why a number who were in the Vincent de Paul were happy to move over also into the Legion, so I think it was brilliant that he had this movement for the laity. I think that's one of the reasons why it went worldwide. I think that's why it attracted Cardinal Suenens who was responsible for the whole insertion of the element of lay ministry in Vatican II.

Did Kennedy, too, see it as a movement that was emancipating the lay people?

I think he saw their basic role in the church which had been neglected. I think he saw the church as Aquinas did, as the Body of Christ, and he saw, as Newman saw, that the church would look funny without the laity—that it wasn't purely a hierarchical structure run by the Pope and bishops, but that every single member had a role and every single person who called themselves a Christian or a follower of Christ had really an obligation to care

for their fellow human being in the fullest sense, and I think that
that was one of his great insights; that, at a time in Ireland when
the church was very heavily clerically oriented, that he saw the role
for the most ordinary individual member of the church.

This also involved a daunting administrative challenge—was it the case
that Duff was particularly adept in this regard, particularly when you
consider the fact that it became such an extensive organisation?
MacCurtain suggested:

He was great, I think, at spotting people. When I say 'spotting
people', it wasn't that he recruited them; he just saw their potential.
I mean there was León Ó Broin [writer, historian and Secretary of
the Department of Posts and Telegraphs], there were the Moynihan
Brothers [Seán, who was secretary of the Executive Council of the
Government in 1932, and Maurice, who in 1937 was appointed
Secretary to the Department of the Taoiseach], and there was, of
course, Edel Quinn, the Cork lay missionary who joined the
Legion and volunteered for Legion work in East Africa. I mean,
there was the situation where, in 1927, I think, he saw the potential
of this young woman, but observed her for about three or four
years before he actually decided that she was the person.

On that subject, an archival clip was played where Duff talked
about the decision to send Edel Quinn to Africa:

She wanted a difficult assignment and then she said the famous
phrase, 'I don't want to be sent off on any picnic!' So there was a
laugh at this which was vitally important because it relieved a
super-charged atmosphere, and then Dr McGuinness's sense of
humour destroyed him because he used the first breath that came
to him to say, 'Picnic? Picnic? You'll be a picnic for somebody!' So
the whole place dissolved into merriment and that's what was
wanted—sanity returned to the picture.

Quinn contracted TB, which seems to have ended her hopes of
entering religious life, but she was determined to travel to East
Africa, despite, as Duff acknowledged, strong objection to her
preferred course of action. She responded to Duff by insisting, 'I
am going with my eyes open.' She died in Nairobi in 1944, having

made, from 1936 onwards, hugely courageous trips (and all the while nursing ill-health) into the interior of Africa, even more of an achievement given her gender, and she provided great help to missionary priests. Did MacCurtain see her as a legend in her own lifetime?

> It was amazing. She died at the age of 37 and she had travelled the whole of interior Africa at a most interesting time—the development of Africa was only just beginning; roads were opening up; many times, her old car got stuck in a forest; her driver had to go and look for help; she was at the mercy of any wild beast that came along; she just used her typewriter and wrote these marvellous letters home . . . Edel could not have done that on charisma or a kind of personal aura alone. There was actually a wonderful administrative type of programme for establishing the Legion and appointing as leaders and speakers the local community. This was wonderful for Africa; this was the first time that Kenyans particularly—whom I saw in action—got a chance to be leaders in the local presidia, who were able to speak and learnt to speak and to listen to each other. It was a fantastic mechanism, and the bishops, I can tell you—the missionary bishops—they knew immediately that they had a treasure, not just in Edel Quinn, but in the whole administrative side of the Legion of Mary.

Wasn't it significant as well that Edel Quinn seemed to be stepping outside the parochial role that was ascribed to women at that stage in Ireland?

> She was such a liberated young woman that, truly, thinking about her over quite a long time, I am continually amazed at both her ability to work outside the structure and at the same time to keep in touch with the authorities of the structure that she was working for. But it was her sheer ability—it was a kind of a genius that she had to establish foundations and keep them moving and keep in touch with them even when she was very, very ill. And, of course, her travel right through Central Africa was truly phenomenal, because when she came back to where she might have been staying in one of the convents, she went up, showered, came down and, for about an hour, played a hard game of tennis!

But what did membership mean for the ordinary, less adventurous rank and file? What was the attraction—particularly, say, for those getting involved at schools?

Kennedy responded:

> I'd say a lot of people were initially drawn into it just because somebody asked them—they had a friend or somebody. And then, I suppose, there was a certain sense of the group—being associated with other people in some kind of a joint endeavour, which has its own kind of inspirational impact when you're bonded together with other people. I think there's a basic spirituality about the Legion that is essential for its survival, that somebody like Edel Quinn or Alfie Lambe in South America or Michael E. Cong who was the first South African legionary (and, I think, a freed slave, if I am correct) represented; that they really had a depth of spiritual life which implied a value system which motivated them in a very different way, and I think that young people particularly were affected by that. The first time I was recruited into the Legion, I was actually in Switzerland. I was studying there, and I think young people at an idealistic stage are attracted to something which makes demands on them. There's quite a commitment and then, as you say, there's this organisational genius that Duff possessed, so there's a structure where you're actually given a task to do. The first task I did as a young student in Switzerland was bringing blind children for walks, and I remember two of us used to do that, and I can still hear the echo of their laughter, and the impact it had on me as a person who could see was—how could these children be so happy and apparently so joyful? So I think there's something very attractive about the Legion as a system. It's inspirational, but also it's practical.

If there had not been such strong organisations like this in the twentieth century and beyond, wouldn't it have been the case that ordinary Catholics would not have had that sense of participation; that, despite the focus on bishops and the hierarchical nature of the Catholic Church, this actually had a huge impact on the reality of people's lives?

> I think that's absolutely right and I think that this is what Duff saw, that his definition of a Christian was someone who cared for their fellow human being, and how did you ensure that this happened?

And while as individuals people can, of course, do a great deal, there are many situations that individuals are relatively helpless and an organisational structure gives support and gives discipline and, after all, Duff did base the Legion on the nomenclature of the old Roman Legion, and the standard of the Legion is a carbon copy of the standard of the Roman Legion, except that the Holy Spirit replaces the eagle, and an image of Mary replaces the image of the emperor, so it's a very disciplined organisation, and it works.

I questioned MacCurtain as to what would have happened if Frank Duff had become a priest. Was it something he considered, given his obviously deeply held beliefs?

One of the Moynihan brothers told me this—that Frank Duff was very much a lay man, and he pointed out that Duff loved young women as well as young men. He was very obviously heterosexual, and I think the question should have been framed differently in the sense of—Why was Frank Duff not married? But he actually committed himself totally to the Legion, but he was the kind of man—when I met him, he was in middle years—who was very attractive in his own way, and his charisma was that of a lay man, of a very spiritual, magnetic, endearing lay man who could chuckle!

His interest in women was also relevant to the idea of the feminine side of God, and the whole cult of Marianism which was extraordinarily popular in Ireland. MacCurtain observed:

It was, and I think that was the attraction, as was the emphasis on community. When Finola was talking there about what attracted her or how she was recruited to the Legion, I think for a lot of us of that generation who came right through the early decades of the twentieth century and into the 1960s, this was the only form of community service that was available to us. But it wasn't just an emptying out of oneself in a community service; you also were replenished yourself in the weekly meetings. There was a wonderful balance in the way that it was structured.

Another clip was played of Duff talking about the deliberations of the Second Vatican Council, to which he had been invited. In the clip, he was somewhat self-effacing:

The debates and discussions were almost exclusively in Latin. I have a reading knowledge of that language but it was completely inadequate to follow what was said. I stuck it out resolutely, partly as a matter of duty and partly in the hope, which proved to be in vain, that custom would work me into the understanding. Alas! It did not, and, to the final day, I remained as innocent as I was in the earliest stages of what was going on—you'd get bits and then you wouldn't be able to follow the lot.

But it did seem entirely appropriate that he was there given that, as far back as the 1920s, he had been implementing what the Vatican II decree on the laity was offering.

Kennedy believed:

Well, there's no doubt about that and it was interesting that when he arrived at the Council, it was Cardinal Heenan who pointed out to the assembled bishops that he was there, and they broke into a spontaneous ovation. I think that clip is delightful because it shows the complete honesty of the man. He could have easily said, 'Oh yes, of course I was lapping up all these documents and footnotes and so on', but his work in Rome during the months that he was there involved many, many talks to heads in religious houses. He gave many talks there and he actually started a Legion presidium also—the Legion was already in Italy. Never miss an opportunity— he was very proud of that! But you're absolutely right that the role for the laity envisaged in Vatican II was, in fact, what he had been putting into practice from the 1920s and he was so overjoyed by what he saw as his complete endorsement and also the place of Mary—people had said afterwards that there was no separate document, but he was absolutely delighted that she was put in the *De Ecclesia* Decree [Mary features in Chapter VIII of *Lumen Gentium* which is the Dogmatic Constitution of the church— documents were issued as Decrees] in the central document on the church, if you like, as distinct from some kind of 'add-on', because he saw her essential role. And just to come back to a point which was made about the feminine side of God and so on, he also wrote many, many articles, some of which are quite extraordinary, and one of the most striking ones that I read was one on Mary and the Holy Spirit in which he explores the relationship between the Godhead and, in particular, the Holy Spirit and Mary. He was not in any sense elevating Mary to the Godhead, but saying that the Holy Spirit so identified with Mary that she was almost like a human representation of this feminine side of God, and it really adds up to a lot of sense and it's very deeply rooted in the Eastern church, whereas the Western church has been slower to come to this insight. Although it was there with the early fathers, I think it has been somewhat lost and was probably re-discovered also by Paul VI in his encyclical, *Marialis Cultus* [The Right Ordering and development of devotion to the Blessed Virgin Mary (1974)], where he speaks of this intimate union between—I think the words are, 'The Holy Spirit and the Virgin of Nazareth', which Duff also had.

Chapter 15

What if the Jim Duffy tape had not been released during the 1990 presidential election?

This show opened with a clip of Taoiseach Charles Haughey introducing Mary Robinson as President of Ireland in December 1990, and her inaugural speech:

> Citizens of Ireland, you have chosen me to represent you and I am humbled and grateful for your trust. The Ireland I will be representing is a new Ireland: open, tolerant, inclusive. Many of you who voted for me did so without sharing all my views. This, I believe, is a significant signal of change, a sign, however modest, that we have already passed the threshold to a new, pluralist Ireland.

Six months previously, virtually no one would have predicted that either Robinson or Haughey would find themselves in such a position. The 1990 presidential election was unusual for all sorts of reasons—the perceived outsider won, reputations were on the line, and party leaderships were enhanced in some cases and threatened in others. Considerable debate was created around the issue of the possibility of 'extending the parameters' of the office of President. Robinson was suggesting the possibility of banishing the 'sleepy president' stereotype. If successful, she could perhaps make the Irish people care about the presidency and the person who held it, despite the legitimate contention of some that she was running for an office that does not exist—after all, the Irish Constitution did not envisage an 'active' presidency.

The creation of the office of President followed on the removal, in 1936, of the ceremonial office of Governor General, who, under the terms of the Anglo-Irish Treaty, was the British Crown's representative in the Irish Free State. But the new office, too, was largely ceremonial, and the Constitution, as the late John Kelly pointed out, 'is extremely sparing in its attribution of any independent functions of the office at all'.[1]

Prior to 1990, the presidency was little debated or discussed. In June 1983, Gene Kerrigan, then a pioneering investigative reporter with *Magill* magazine, penned an amusing (if unfair) portrait of President Patrick Hillery. Hillery had reputedly said, on taking up office in 1976, 'At the moment I'm going into a vacuum that's hard to explain'. A former EEC Commissioner, within two weeks of the resignation of his predecessor, Cearbhall Ó Dálaigh, he found himself an agreed presidential candidate; within six weeks, he was installed. He did not really want the job, but stayed 14 years, attending functions—tidy towns competitions, garden parties, and the like. Mischievously, Kerrigan traced the evolution in Hillery's golfing prowess to a handicap of seven, giving him the lowest handicap of any European head of state, and was emphatic that the presidency was an irrelevance:

> The first President, Douglas Hyde [1938–45] was useful because he was a Protestant and his election (unopposed) showed that the south was not sectarian. In things that didn't matter. Like the presidency. Seán T. O'Kelly [1945–1959] looked nice in a top hat. De Valera [1959–73] was great at impressing Americans and was something of a tourist attraction. Ó Dálaigh [1973–76] provoked an interesting row with the coalition [over his decision to refer the Emergency Powers Bill to the Supreme Court to test its constitutionality]. Hillery got his golf handicap back in shape.[2]

The key issue of the 1990 campaign was the extent to which Robinson could create a new debate and discourse about the presidency, while also dispelling fears that she was too radical in her views to hold such high office, particularly as the front-runner was a long-established and popular Fianna Fáil minister, Brian Lenihan, who many believed deserved the position as a reward for long service. Robinson's campaign was exceptionally clever and skilful in this regard. John Waters perceptively observed, in his book, *Jiving at the Crossroads*, that the key to Robinson's success in 1990 was her contention that, in moving towards a 'new Ireland', it was neither necessary nor advisable to leave 'the old Ireland' behind. One thing she said to him, in an unpublished interview,

> . . . made sense of all the seemingly contradictory things she had said elsewhere, about Catholicism, about socialism, about progressive politics, about the view Irish people need to have of themselves. 'I'm a Catholic from Mayo,' she said. 'There's nothing about that Ireland that I don't know. So it's me. I understand it from within and I want to develop it on, but in the way one would want to develop oneself, almost. I don't repudiate so much as want to coax along into a different world'.

In this statement, Waters was convinced, 'lay the key not just to Mary Robinson's chance of being elected, but to the future of Irish politics.'[3]

Also in this statement was the influence of Eoghan Harris, in many respects the mastermind of her initial campaign. But it was also the case that different people had different notions of what the Robinson candidacy meant. She was, in fact, appealing to all sorts of constituencies for all sorts of reasons. She had a particular appeal for women—vocal feminists and quiet feminists, mothers and daughters, Catholics and agnostics.

The discrepancy between perception and constitutional reality concerning the office of President was only one aspect of this campaign; the other was the cut and thrust of contemporary party politics. The campaign resulted in the sacking of Brian Lenihan from government, at the behest of the Progressive Democrats, after tapes revealed by a UCD politics student, Jim Duffy, contradicted Lenihan's assertion that he had never phoned President Hillery in January 1982 to persuade him to exercise his right not to dissolve the Dáil, necessitating a general election, but instead to invite Haughey to form a government. But what if the tapes had not been released? Would Haughey have been introducing his fellow party man as President Lenihan in December 1990?

The two guests on this programme were Tom Garvin, Professor of Politics at UCD, the department under whose supervision Jim Duffy did his thesis on the presidency, and Ivana Bacik, Reid Professor of Criminal Law at Trinity College Dublin, who stood for the Labour Party in the 2004 European elections. I queried Garvin as to the prevailing cynicism about the office prior to 1990 and the significance of what happened during the election:

> Well, in effect, what happened was that Fianna Fáil's grip on the nomination, and the almost automatic election of whoever Fianna Fáil nominated, was broken by Mary Robinson. In effect, she imposed herself, if you like, on Fianna Fáil, in a way that had never happened before, and which was not imagined or even imaginable. Fianna Fáil had behaved as though the presidency were its private property and, in effect, it was—the whole way from Douglas Hyde through to the 14 years of Paddy Hillery and, before him, the 14 years of Eamon de Valera. It was an extraordinary accident in a way, but I suppose it was an accident waiting to happen—the kind of monolithic character of Irish society had been breaking up in the 1980s; there were cultural wars about abortion, contraception, divorce and everything else right through the 1980s. The Catholic Church seemed to be winning all the battles, but actually it was losing. What had happened, however, was a new liberal majority had not been really mobilised and what Robinson did—and I think it's the most important thing she did—was to mobilise that majority for the first time.

Bacik had been involved in some of the cultural wars that Garvin mentioned and was an active supporter of Robinson:

> I'd experienced them very directly, and I'm listening to Tom and I think he's absolutely right, but I think that the reason why Mary Robinson's election was so significant was because up until then that hadn't become apparent to anybody. It really wasn't apparent until December 1990 that there was that shift. I mean, I remember Mary Robinson stepping in and defending us—I was a student in 1989, and being taken to court for distributing abortion information along with a number of other students, and she stepped in to defend us in court and we became her clients at a time when very few politicians and very few public figures would come out on

our side and when it really seemed as if that liberal group in Irish society, that liberal view, was very much a minority view. I must say I couldn't believe that within a year she had been elected President—it just seemed unreal, that that shift had been occurring all the time . . . I really didn't think she had a hope. I mean, we had been really knocked back by so many campaigns in the 1980s. I remember us as students in the 1980s going on all of those sort of liberal campaigning issues, but always feeling that we were up against the establishment, and I remember people would come up and spit in the street at us—at those of us who were identifiably student leaders, or who were identified with that liberal agenda. So we really didn't feel as if we had any sort of power in society, and Mary Robinson's campaign was a sort of thrust against the establishment, but I didn't think it was going to be effective. I couldn't believe it when she was elected. Looking back now, you can see there are many reasons as to why it was so effective— perhaps the most important one being that the shift was already occurring and that this was the marker of it.

Mary Robinson began her campaign well before the other candidates, and visited more remote parts of the country at the beginning of a very long campaign, in order to extend her profile—how significant was that?

According to Bacik:

That was a huge strength. She reached out to people beyond the Dublin middle-class vote that she might have been expected to get. She went down to Allihies in West Cork and, I think, started her campaigning there, but she had already been campaigning all around the west of Ireland. She reminded people that she herself, of course, is from the west, and she had already got a great deal of popular support, and there was a real momentum behind her campaign. I mean, friends of mine—my mother, in particular—were very active in that campaign, and they could feel the support was building.

Did Garvin attach much significance to debates about the relevance of the office of President, and talk of an open and active presidency, or did he share the view of the office as largely ceremonial?

Well, the President is actually quite an important person. He or she is not just ceremonial. He or she is the guardian of the Constitution. He or she can refer any Bill he or she wants to the Supreme Court and have a ruling on its constitutionality—that's an extraordinarily big power for one person to have. It's been used very, very rarely and, interestingly enough, one time it was used, the government treated the President as though he was impertinent—back in the time of Cearbhall Ó Dálaigh in 1976, and Ó Dálaigh felt he had to resign over it. That is the other big crisis of the presidency, by the way, and it is rather interesting that, at least twice, this apparently innocuous office has been the centre of a huge political shift in Irish life—in 1976 and again in 1990.

As a student and researcher, Jim Duffy was breaking new ground, in the sense that nobody had looked at this seriously as a thesis option. Some were quick to point out that what Jim Duffy had done in revealing private research tapes was unethical and damaging to research students, but there was also a belief that other people were using him. Garvin recalled:

He was an excellent student. He actually got first-class honours afterwards, but we didn't have strict ground rules nailed down about confidentiality at that time. We have now.

An archival clip was played of Jim Duffy speaking at a press conference in 1990, in which he talks about the dilemma of what to do on discovering that Lenihan was lying, and being in possession of the evidence to expose that:

I wish to make it clear that the decision to make available the text of a portion of the interview was taken with great reluctance. I was left with no option in view of the political pressure I was subjected to when it was made known that I had conducted the interview with the Tánaiste who I respect and who was of enormous assistance to me in my research. The recording of the interview has been placed in safe custody.

But did it create a dilemma for politics departments and supervisors of theses generally? There were suggestions that some told him he was morally obliged to release the tape. In her book, *Candidate*, Emily O'Reilly noted that the student chaplain in UCD assured him that he had done the right thing and that he had had a 'moral responsibility' to do it.[4] What if he had not taken that advice, and was it/is it a black and white issue?

'No, it's not', according to Garvin.

> I spoke to Jim at the time and more or less told him to be very careful before he released anything that was supposed to be confidential. I can't remember what else I said but that was the general tenor of what I said. Brian Farrell, my colleague, I think, told him bluntly not to and I think several other academics advised him more or less the same way.

Bacik suggested:

> It's very difficult—just thinking about the ethics of the research and so on—obviously normally one wouldn't ever want to disclose that sort of material. I would really empathise with Jim's position though because he knew that a lie had been told; he knew that he had this material and, I suppose, it's a different situation when you're talking about exposing hypocrisy in that way, and I think he probably felt himself—quite apart from the advice he was getting from others—that he might have had a moral duty, but I do also think that, after the initial shock about the phone call and about Brian Lenihan's denial and so on, that there was a shift, and people started feeling very sympathetic towards Brian Lenihan because he was such an ill man as well, and because he was a very much-liked and respected figure even among people who weren't pro Fianna Fáil, so I'm not sure that that tape in itself had the biggest effect on the campaign. And, of course, Brian Lenihan still went on to get more first-preference votes.

This was a significant point—the strategists behind the Mary Robinson campaign were looking at this golden figure of 34 per cent first-preference votes. If they could creep over 34 per cent, Currie's transfers would elect her. Did Bacik feel that the momentum was there to reach that goal, regardless of the tape?

I do, actually. I think that the momentum was building because of the dynamic of Mary Robinson's campaign. People were flocking to campaign for her; we hadn't had a presidential election in 17 years. I mean, it was a thing that a whole generation of us had never known—a presidential election—so I think it galvanised a whole lot of people. And because she wasn't running as a Labour Party candidate alone—even though it gave credit to Dick Spring and it gave great credit to the Labour Party, she wasn't a Labour Party candidate alone; she made that quite clear from the beginning. There was this sort of shift in public opinion that had not been discerned until then and also, of course, then there was finally the Pádraig Flynn intervention that shifted public opinion away from Brian Lenihan and back towards Mary Robinson, and I think those were probably more significant in the end than the Jim Duffy tape, however sort of cataclysmic that was for Brian Lenihan personally.

This was perhaps the more significant 'what if'—What if Pádraig Flynn had not got so carried away when bellowing down the phone from Castlebar to a Dublin RTÉ studio on the *Saturday View* programme. The vintage clip was played in which he asserted:

> She was pretty well constructed in this campaign by her handlers, the Labour Party and the Workers Party. Of course, it doesn't always suit if you get labelled a socialist, because that's a very narrow focus in this country. So, she has to try and have it both ways. She has to have new clothes and her new look and her new hairdo . . . and she has the new interest in her family, being a mother and all that kind of thing. But none of, you know, none of us who knew Mary Robinson very well in previous incarnations ever heard her claiming to be a great wife and mother.

In the Dublin studio, an enraged Brendan Howlin of the Labour Party ('That's outrageous and desperate') and then Michael McDowell of the Progressive Democrats ('You're a disgrace. It's about time you had manners. It's disgusting') castigated him, and Flynn later apologised, but the damage had been done. Most people remember where they were when they heard it. Tom Garvin recalled:

I nearly crashed my car. I was on my way to Naas to give a lecture. Yes, it was a defining moment; it was one of several defining moments. My own memory of that campaign is actually watching Brian Lenihan saying that he hadn't phoned the President while the tape was being played behind him, so his voice saying one thing was matched by his voice saying the complete opposite— I knew he'd lost the election then.

So, in Garvin's view, was the Flynn intervention an even more significant 'what if'?

I'm not dead sure, but it certainly accelerated things. I don't know how crucial it is, I don't think any of us can say . . . there was a certain degree of sympathy for Brian Lenihan after [the Duffy tapes affair], the opinion polls more or less indicate that had the election been held ten days later, Brian would have been absolved and he would have become President of Ireland, but as it was, Mary Robinson made it.

Bacik felt that the Flynn debacle, because of the nerve it struck regarding the comments about her personal life,

. . . sort of hit deeper if you like than the Brian Lenihan/Jim Duffy intervention, because I suppose a lot of people didn't remember perhaps what had happened—the whole sequence with President Hillery and so on—or it didn't matter so much to people who hadn't been politically active then, whereas this sort of just hit people. He was so insulting of somebody on this very personal level—suggesting that she had somehow never cared for her family before—I mean, that was the implication, and I think that really angered people and it generated a great deal of public sympathy towards Mary Robinson. Brian Lenihan, of course, had nothing to do with it, but, I mean, Pádraig Flynn is not unknown for putting his foot in it, and Michael McDowell's response did capture what most people felt, and that's why I think it actually might have been more significant.

Garvin agreed:

I think you're absolutely right, Ivana, but I think we must remember that Flynn was on a landline from Mayo; he was on his own, perhaps without any handler or advisor or whatever, and all the others are in Dublin and the atmosphere is quite different and people's attitudes were rather different. In other words, it was 1990 talking to 1984, so to speak, or one half of the decade talking to the other half of the decade, and so it's a very peculiar interview, and I think it's one of the most fascinating anthropological snatches that RTÉ has ever produced!

There were other implications of this election also, particularly the question of Alan Dukes's position as leader of Fine Gael and the difficulty they had in coming up with a convincing candidate, given that senior party members like Garret FitzGerald had made it clear that they were not interested. His party leadership was essentially on the line. What was the significance of that? Garvin responded:

Well, Dukes had been doing another heroic thing: he had been backing Fianna Fáil strategy on the economy over the previous four years—the Tallaght strategy, and his leadership *was* on the line and he was in a rather weak position politically; and Austin Currie—though he's a fine man—was not all that strong a presidential candidate . . . he certainly was not box office in quite the way that either Robinson or Lenihan were, if you like to put it that way. But he was good enough for his transfers to help Mary Robinson over the bar.

Bacik reflected on the fact that the 'liberal' candidate was pushed over the finishing line by what some considered traditional conservative Fine Gael transfers:

That's right. I mean, it *was* Austin Currie's transfers—Brian Lenihan was still 80,000 first preferences ahead on the first count, and it was the Fine Gael vote, and, I suppose, that's why things like the Pádraig Flynn intervention did make a big difference: that it might have made people who wouldn't normally agree with Mary Robinson—as she said on that clip you played at the start, 'the people voted for me who did not agree with my views'—and she was seen as a radical figure at the time; I mean, her defence of us, her championing of contraception legislation, of gay rights and so on made her quite a radical figure. But clearly there were lots of people who voted for her who would never have shared her views on those issues, and lots of conservative Fine Gaelers. But I think that when it came down to it, they wanted her rather than Lenihan or they felt that she would make a better President than Brian Lenihan, and I think Pádraig Flynn may have helped them to feel that in a personal way.

For Alan Dukes, perhaps one of the great 'what ifs' was what if Garret FitzGerald had agreed to be a candidate, which would have created a very interesting campaign as well. But there was also the question of the influence of the Progressive Democrats, which was central to the whole sacking of Brian Lenihan, and the significance of his relationship with Charles Haughey. Archival clips were played of Haughey speaking about his friendship with Lenihan, his determination to stick by him ('I will not be asking for the Tánaiste's resignation from the cabinet. I will not be putting him under any pressure to resign, nor will his cabinet colleagues. It is entirely a matter for my old friend of 30 years') and then his Dáil announcement that he had sacked him, along with Dick Spring's general haranguing of Haughey:

> For the last week or more, we have been in a virtual tail spin of lies and mismanagement, with the situation daily becoming more out of control. The corrupting effect of the political cynicism we have been watching cannot be overstated.

Bacik observed that the question of Haughey suggested another 'what if'—what if Haughey had not been leader of Fianna Fáil at that time? Could that have influenced the election?

> It's so dramatic to listen to it now and I suppose it does bring back the mood of the time, and something we haven't mentioned is the feeling about Haughey—I mean, Charles Haughey himself generated hugely strong feelings of opposition, which Dick Spring had tapped into, and just listening to Dick Spring talking there, you remember the huge strength of support he got for his very strong and very coherent attacks on Fianna Fáil over that period. He was regarded as the effective leader of the opposition and that led to the Spring tide of 1992, and we can see Mary Robinson's

election as the start of that. But the anti-Haughey feeling must also have contributed to Mary Robinson's election in a huge way, even though Haughey was seen to have shafted Brian Lenihan, yet at the same time, for Fine Gaelers to support a Fianna Fáil that had Charlie Haughey as leader, I think, must have stuck in their throats. I suppose when we look at the Austin Currie vote, a lot of Fine Gael people must have switched to Mary Robinson, knowing—in a tactical way—that she was their best hope of beating Fianna Fáil. I think that must have been at least partly because of strong opposition to Charles Haughey.

In terms of the actual legacy of Robinson's election and her presidency, did it lead to the breakthrough for women in Irish politics that some predicted, or was it a false dawn? Bacik suggested:

> Well, I think it should have done, and I think at the time it did mark a huge shift in attitude towards women's rights as much as towards other issues that we might describe as 'liberal' issues, and I think Mary Robinson was always very clear that she had won a women's vote in particular, as well as obviously winning lots of men, but she had won a women's vote—she made a very strong position on that and she had a lot of very strong women working on her campaign. I think it did lead to a great change in the position of women and so on—a lot of changes in legislation following her election. Maybe they'd have happened anyway, but certainly her election was a sign that these things could be brought in—that Haughey could bring in contraception legislation, for example; that we could have a divorce referendum, and so on. But why didn't it lead to more women coming into the Dáil? You know, it should have done, but I suppose the reality is that for the majority of women, nothing really changed; we changed some of the legislation, we certainly have some very strong women in politics, but we never made that huge change that we needed to. I think, in particular, to bring in things like childcare and to really put money behind the promotion of women was what was needed and it didn't happen.

Did Garvin, wearing his political scientist's hat, believe that it did not lead to a breakthrough in the number of female deputies because people were looking at the presidency as a different issue, a different vote? People who voted for Mary Robinson may well have gone back to their political parties in a general election, for example.

> Yes—the idea of having a woman President must have seemed impossible in 1988, and then in 1990 we got one, and we got a very, very good candidate. She was a terrific candidate—we have to remember that. It wasn't just that Mary Robinson was a woman. She was a woman of a very respectable—if you like, bourgeois— family, with very strong west of Ireland connections—an extremely able group of people, as far as I can make out—brilliant young woman, Reid Professor in Trinity and all the rest of it. Also, I think there was a breakthrough. If you remember, back in the 1950s and 1960s, which I remember, believe it or not, the only women in the Dáil were the relatives of dead men—that is literally the case—the widow got the seat, almost like the married women's property act or something like that; there were just no women in politics. All right, they don't dominate politics, they don't flood the Dáil. I don't know how many women TDS there are now, but there are an unprecedented number of women TDS compared to 30 years ago.

Bacik added:

> And I think 1992 marked a big increase in women TDS certainly, but I suppose, looking at other countries where you have a big increase of women in politics, it's generally due to some sort of positive action.

Garvin suggested, 'Part of that is mechanical—part of that is proportional representation by list. In the Scandinavian countries, for example, you get very large numbers of women TDS because the nominators can put them at the top of the list.'

Bacik interjected: 'But also there's a policy about positively nominating them, which we don't have. The British Labour Party, to great effect, managed to do that where they had effectively gender equality.'

But Garvin demurred: 'Yes, but that's a different electoral system again. With our electoral system, the marginal voter is so important that they will tend to favour a man because they think he will get a few more votes than any woman no matter how good she is. I mean, it's not fair, but there it is.'

This programme was broadcast in October 2004, just before Mary McAleese put herself forward for a second term as President. Is it the case now that you have to be a woman to be President of Ireland? And did Bacik want to follow in the footsteps of Robinson and McAleese (both formerly Reid Professors of Criminal Law in Trinity) by becoming President?

Garvin was intrigued: 'Now, that's a fair question! It's almost working the other way now!'

Bacik responded:

No, I don't! But there is an interesting thesis about the President having been feminised now because we've had two women in and it's seen as sort of a woman's job because it's not as much hard politics as being a TD or being a minister and so on. So there is an interesting thesis about that—it having been unthinkable prior to 1990 to have a woman President, it would now be almost beneath a man to go for President! I don't buy that thesis, I have to say, but I think it's an interesting one that we talk about it that way. I think that what happened in 1997 is that people did try to emulate what had happened in 1990, but you can never go back and do that again, and Mary McAleese has been a very different President.

But is it a good thing for the presidency that there was no contest in 2004? Are we going to witness an exciting presidential campaign in the future?

Garvin admitted, 'I would rather like to have seen an election campaign actually, just in the interests of democracy—there is a point there. But McAleese has been a marvellous President. She knows the job; she is doing it very well. I think a lot of people think that as well. In other words, if there were an election, I think she'd romp home, unless another Jim Duffy was lurking in the wings somewhere with another tape!'

As was reported in *Magill* magazine in 1997, Jim Duffy met Brian Lenihan a few times after the controversy, and Lenihan shook his hand—'he was that kind of man'.[5]

Chapter 16

What if Proportional Representation had been abolished in 1959 or 1968?

This show opened with an archival clip featuring former Taoiseach Seán Lemass speaking about proportional representation in 1968, the second time the Fianna Fáil party had proposed its abolition through a constitutional referendum:

> A discussion on the Constitution of 1937 was had . . . not on whether we have PR or not, but whether the Constitution should establish PR as a constitutional requirement rather than leave the electoral system to be determined by law. I would have been prepared, in the framing of the Constitution, to have left it to be determined by law . . . I would say that de Valera came to the conclusion that PR was not suitable to Irish circumstances long before he actually proposed to the Dáil legislation to actually change the system, but there was always the political question as to whether it was feasible to make the change, and when it was desirable.

In 1959, and again in 1968, Fianna Fáil governments proposed the abolition of a very distinctive Irish electoral system: multi-seat constituencies by means of a single transferable vote. The electorate rejected the proposals on both occasions. The result was very close in 1959: 48 per cent in favour of abolition, 52 per cent against. By 1968, the gap had widened considerably, the figures being 39 per cent and 61 per cent respectively.

But if the proposed abolition had been accepted by the electorate and the first-past-the-post/straight vote system had come to pass in Ireland, what would the state of the Irish political parties be? One of the striking things about the assessment of political scientists and historians on the Republic's relationship with PR is the impression that they can never quite make up their minds. In 2004, Tom Garvin suggested that the system 'handed extraordinary power to the marginal voter in the sense of the voter just capable of changing his mind because of a personal inducement in the form of a personal promise by an ambitious candidate. The effect was to generate a sometimes pathological personalism and a disregard of the public interest'. And yet Irish voters have been praised for twice rejecting the attempt to abolish it, particularly in 1968, when, suggested Garvin, the amendment of that year was 'clearly designed by the sea-green republicans Neil Blaney and Kevin Boland to shore up declining electoral strongholds in the West for the Soldiers of Destiny, rather than to improve the quality of democracy in Ireland.'[1]

The general consensus has been that the voters were right to be sceptical about the abolition of PR; it has been maintained that the fact that they voted against it in 1959, but also endorsed de Valera as president 'were a comment on the political sophistication of the Irish voter'.[2] Historian Joe Lee suggested that the arguments against it were not convincing enough—he pointed out that its abolition in Northern Ireland in 1929 did not improve the quality of the representatives, alter the 'localism' of Northern politics, or alter the standards of parliamentary debate. In the Republic, he argued, it has been something of a stabilising influence, by satisfying voters' requirements, preventing the kind of very large majorities that could lead to splits and factionalism, and that, in doing so, 'it has probably forced parties to close ranks more firmly than would have been the case with the straight vote.'[3]

Each time it was proposed, it certainly succeeded in uniting the opposition parties in horror and fear. The initial proposal in 1959 was followed by a parliamentary battle that resulted in the Seanad rejecting a government bill for the first time since the 1937 Constitution was adopted (under its powers, the Seanad could

delay it for only 90 days). Garret FitzGerald recalls in his autobiography how the proposal in 1968 led to serious discussions
between the Labour and Fine Gael parties about a possible merger
to counteract the threat of Fianna Fáil dominance in the event of
the straight vote. With the assistance of Jim Dooge, they prepared
a report on the impact it would have on Fianna Fáil's strength and
suggested that Fianna Fáil could win up to 96 seats in a Dáil of 144
if the straight vote were introduced (based on the vote they received
in the 1965 election). The talks did not lead to agreement, but
FitzGerald makes the point that, had they succeeded, 'the political
history of the succeeding years would surely have been very
different.'[4]

The two guests on this programme represented, in a sense, the
academic expert and the practitioner: Richard Sinnott of the
Department of Politics at UCD who has written extensively on
Irish electoral behaviour, and Frank Flannery who was director of
elections for Fine Gael in the local elections of 2004.

In 1959, one of the arguments that was used by Fianna Fáil was
that the abolition of PR would result in strong government .The
argument against was that it would entrench Fianna Fáil in power
forever. Did Sinnott believe that it was as simple (or as cynical) as
that?

> No, I think Fianna Fáil had come through the 1950s in a state of
> some shock. Having ruled for 16 years non-stop after 1932, they
> suddenly found themselves out of government, in briefly, and then
> out again, and that was the partisan reaction. They said: 'What can
> we do about this?' and they looked across the water and they saw
> that 'We get 40+ per cent of the vote; if we were in Britain, we'd
> have a 20–40-seat majority.' So there's no doubt about it that there
> was a partisan motivation. On the other hand, you must also
> remember that the 1950s was a period of considerable crisis. The
> beginning of a systematic governmental response to that crisis in
> the form of the Whitaker paper on Economic Development and
> the move to free trade and all that, so I suppose the government
> could maintain they were also looking at the national interest and
> could at least make the argument that a system that gave a single-
> party majority would be a better system for the times that were

ahead and for the changes that were being made. So I think there was both a national interest and there was the partisan factor and I suppose the national interest can always be interpreted in ways that suit a particular party!

What did Flannery think of Fine Gael's reaction at the time?

Well, I think the rule at the time was that if Fianna Fáil was proposing something, well then Fine Gael at the time would have had a very questioning approach as to what their motivation was. It was a time of still fairly bitter politics. Civil War politics was fading away but even in the debates in 1968, let alone 1959, the old Civil War politics were still there and, you know, abuse was being fairly readily hurled across the table and so forth, so you would have had those factors. But politics had come out of a period of a real multi-party phase throughout the late 1940s and 1950s into a phase in the 1960s and 1970s where you just had a two-and-a-half party system. There was just Fianna Fáil, Fine Gael and Labour, and for about seven elections in a row, beginning in 1965, there was very few independents, very few others. Sinn Féin made an odd fleeting appearance, virtually nothing, and interestingly we've moved back into a fully-fledged multi-party system again now. Now, in that period of time, there's no doubt in my mind that a straight-vote system would at least initially have led to a huge plurality of seats for Fianna Fáil. I think *Seven Days* [an RTÉ television current affairs programme] did an analysis in 1968 which was quite decisive, which analysed the voting patterns then and showed that 40 per cent of the vote would have delivered 70 per cent of the seats. Happy days for Fianna Fáil! And it's interesting to note that if you look at the history of Irish voting from 1927 forward, starting in 1932, Fianna Fáil have only dipped below 40 per cent twice, and they were in 1992 and 1997—quite recently, and that's interesting. Their vote tended to be around the mid- to high 40s in very many of those elections, which in a straight-vote system would have been overwhelming. Now, the 'what if' is if you had a straight-vote system, would people have changed their minds? If I were on a Fine Gael bench there or a Labour Party bench, caution would suggest that you may as well stick with the system you have, so I think that's why the existing system was vigorously defended, and, indeed if you read the arguments of the day, the arguments

for retaining the system were far more powerful; there were virtually no good arguments for getting rid of it.

Flannery had done a trawl through the archives to give examples
of the arguments and the advertisements that were being used
during these referenda—he read them out, and added his own
comments:

> The argument for change in 1968 put forward by the government
> advertisement of the day was that if you adopt the straight-vote
> system, you will get these benefits:
>
>> 'You will have a deputy who is known to you and is easily
>> accessible to you' (probably didn't add anything new to the
>> circumstances)
>> 'You will be sure that your vote is used to elect the candidate
>> you want instead of benefiting a man you do not want as has
>> happened with PR' (a little patronising to the voter—the idea
>> that they didn't know what they were doing with their vote)
>> 'You will be able to clearly show your disapproval of a government
>> you don't want' (under PR you can do that anyway)
>> 'You will have a strong opposition ready to take up office if you
>> want a change' (now, if they didn't have any seats in the House
>> it would be hard to see just how strong they might be!)
>> 'You will help to avoid the danger of weak coalition governments
>> making policy by compromise.' (This reflected the very strong
>> arguments against coalition governments which came out of
>> the 1950s and which was a big issue then. It was a Fianna Fáil
>> thesis then that coalitions don't work.)

Frank Aiken had insisted in 1959 that coalitions were built on
betrayals and broken promises. According to Flannery:

> Yes, that's the problem they had with compromise. They didn't
> believe in compromise at the time. There was the strong one-party
> government, almost one-party state view. One of the other
> arguments they used was that with the straight vote you could
> ensure that the small compact constituency represented by deputies
> living in your area will be substituted for the present large un-
> manageable ones. So that was it: keep it all cosy with one deputy. I
> wouldn't have thought it was a very imposing argument—and the

arguments against were much more simple—with the straight vote, 40 per cent of the vote gives 70 per cent of the seats; you'll end up with Fianna Fáil forever, an effective dictatorship in Ireland, instead of the democratic system we currently have, and that's why the people voted no in 1968 in huge numbers.

In 1959, 120,000 people who voted for de Valera as President voted against the proposed abolition of PR: what was the significance of that, from the perspective of someone who has looked so closely at voting behaviour? Sinnott noted:

De Valera was voted in on a vote of 56 per cent, which, in terms of first-preference votes, is a very decisive vote in a presidential election, and at the same time only 48 per cent voted for the proposal that was on the same day and, quite clearly, people did distinguish between the issue with a good deal of sophistication. On the 'what if' question though, I think you do have to broaden it out to ask not only what would have happened immediately but also what would have happened on the assumption that, as Frank said, the voters would adapt their behaviour to the new system. And, I think, let's say the 1968 one had been passed—that's the simpler case—supposing Fianna Fáil got it right and the straight vote was introduced? In a sense they were maybe a bit arrogant and a bit bold in going for the very same proposal that had been defeated. I think it was because it was so close; if they had modified PR rather than going for the British system, they might have got away with it. But let's suppose they had got away with it in 1968, you'd have had a Fianna Fáil majority in 1969; let's take the same elections again, you'd probably have had a Fianna Fáil majority again in 1973—that would have taken us up to 1977; and let's suppose they would still have been entrenched in 1977; but then, taking the economic circumstances at the time, by 1981, there would have been a strong reaction to the political dominance of a single party in a period where, if you cast your mind back to the early 1980s, we were in a period of considerable economic crisis and, I think, you could then have had a conservative swing to Fine Gael. I think you have to consider also the dimensions in terms of which party competition occurs, and I think it could have actually led to a moderate Left–Right alignment of the political system in which, I think, Fianna Fáil would have actually been left of centre and Fine Gael, in the circumstances, would have been right of centre, and a lot of things could have panned out very differently.

So it certainly would have altered the political spectrum in a very significant way?

> I think it sort of has to—the Progressive Democrats would never have been founded because the big difference that PR introduces— I know there's some debate about this—is that if you have one seat in a constituency, then 50 per cent of the vote guarantees you the seat, but depending on the number of candidates, you can get that seat in a straight-vote system for much less, but if you have five seats in a constituency, then you're guaranteed a seat if you have one-sixth or 16.6 per cent of the vote, and that does not allow for the growth of small parties, so there would have been an inhibition on the formation of the Progressive Democrats, on the emergence of Sinn Féin/the Workers Party (subsequently the Workers Party), an inhibition on the Green Party, so you wouldn't have had the multi-party system that Frank referred to a few moments ago—it would simply not have occurred. Now there are pros and cons there. There are people who will say, 'Well, it's a better system because you know beforehand what government you're going to get when you cast your vote'—that's the big defence of the British system. It presents a clear government versus opposition, in/out choice to the electorate.

Was there a sense that the voters were being patronised as well, by being told in effect that they did not really understand their electoral system? Seán Lemass, for example, suggested that the electorate didn't really know where its number three preferences went. The idea he seemed to put forward was that everybody could understand the first part of the system, in terms of voting in order of his or her preference, but that, after that, it gets quite complicated.

Flannery responded:

> I don't actually agree with that myself at all. I think the Irish people have always been relatively sophisticated. It's a typical point a politician might make which is somewhat patronising to the public, but staying with what Richard was saying there, I mean, Garret FitzGerald was arguing in 1968 against the straight vote

which he was very much against at the time. He argued that it was a primitive form of the democratic preference and it effectively enshrined minority government as opposed to majority government. In Britain, you always had minority governments, whereas in Ireland a government will tend to represent a majority of the electorate. And he pointed out that most advanced European democracies, by even the 1920s, had abandoned what he would have seen as, I think—I don't want to misquote Garret FitzGerald—but a fairly primitive approach to the exercise of a franchise, and that the systems we have obviously are more European and they envisage government by compromise and coalition government and, I think, history has proved that coalition government can work very well in Ireland because all governments are now coalitions. And at the time, in 1968, as well, Noël Browne made some very interesting points in that debate. The Labour Party was against changing the PR system, but at the same time they were against going into coalition with either Fine Gael or Fianna Fáil, and they sustained this position throughout the 1960s and only changed in 1973. Noël Browne cogently argued for the people to reject the proposed change in the voting system; he said the logic of it is that then you use the transferable vote to create an alternative government, so that if you're going to have the transferable vote and not use it strategically to create a new government, it defeats itself, and he was the only one in the Labour Party who was arguing cogently on that account. In effect, Fianna Fáil got the result they wanted for several elections because of the fact that the other two parties did not combine their forces against them.

Several Fianna Fáil ministers were sent out to bat for the government's proposal in 1968. An archival clip from the *Seven Days* programme was played, in which Charles Haughey was interviewed about the issue by Ted Nealon:

No deputy should suppose that he won't retain his seat under the new dispensation. I think at this stage the Irish people haven't quite come to grips with the situation in their minds. I don't think the issues have been put fully before them; I don't think they've been asked positively to decide and I think as the campaign gets going, that will change . . . Party loyalty won't have a great part to play in the campaign. I think there will be lots of people, and I don't want to enter into merit at this stage, or issues, but there will be lots of people voting differently from what they might ordinarily vote at general and other elections . . . The overall picture last time was a majority of 45,000 in favour of change in rural constituencies, counteracted in Dublin with a net of 33,000 against, but you must remember there were 39,000 spoilt votes in the last election.

The distinct impression was that Haughey, though articulating the government line, was hardly bubbling with enthusiasm, and certainly was not putting forward many cogent arguments, beyond the reference to how close the vote had been in 1959. Did Sinnott think that was a fair assessment to make?

Well, certainly in that particular case. Now, he did say, 'it's early days in the campaign' and, I suppose, for a government at the time, it was a campaign that had to be handled carefully and gingerly, because if they were overenthusiastic, it would fuel the suspicion of the electorate and the accusations of the opposition that this was all purely to manipulate the system for partisan advantage, so it was a delicate kind of issue.

But why were there so many spoiled votes? Sinnott suggested:

If you take the 1959 one, probably what you got was people going in to vote for the presidential election and simply not filling in the one on the referendum, so when there are things paired together like that, you get something of an increase in spoiled votes. There's also an element of protest voting in elections; the spoiled vote is a bit higher because people can actually make mistakes in filling out their vote—but I think the point that Haughey made there illustrates precisely the temptation that was there in the late 1960s to have another go when they said, 'Oh, you know it was so narrow that it was outnumbered by the spoiled votes—the margin was less than the number of spoiled votes.' That temptation must have been there throughout the 1960s to Fianna Fáil to have another go at the system.

How relevant at this stage was discussion about clientelism and the amount of time TDs have to spend in their constituencies doing local work, sorting out local problems, rather than being, in effect, national parliamentarians? According to Sinnott:

There were three phases of the debate really about PRSTV. There was the 1950s debate, and then there was the 1960s debate, and then in the 1980s a number of senior political figures began to make noises, to put it that way, about the disadvantages of the system, but this time the argument was quite different. The argument tended to focus on the alleged effect that PRSTV had on encouraging or nurturing or fermenting clientelism in the role of the Dáil deputy in the constituency. The way the argument works is this—that because it's a multi-seat constituency system, you get as much or greater competition within parties, between candidates of the same party as between candidates of opposite parties, and the only way in which a candidate can then fight his or her corner is to refer to their role of constituency service or quote/unquote 'clientelism', rather than to say, 'We have policy difference', because they're both in the same party and they can't have policy differences.

As someone who would have observed that at close quarters when directing elections, did Flannery notice candidates spending more time looking at people in their own party rather than the actual opposition?

Well, not necessarily all the time, but of course they have to because it is just a permanent fact of life that an elected representative is looking at opposition from all quarters and can be defeated from an up-and-coming, very bright person from within their own party, so it is a source of continual tension. It's interesting that in 1968 there was an all-party committee—I know Michael O'Kennedy, a young Fianna Fáil man at the time, was on it. I was speaking to him recently, and he said that committee which also included people like Declan Costello, and a lot of very bright young politicians, proposed that the referendum in 1968 should have been about the single transferable vote being retained within single-seat constituencies to tackle this very issue we're discussing, and, for some reason, the government decided to re-run the 1959 one and ignored their recommendations. That is a possible system. The multi-seat constituency, though is what gives our system its proportional representativity bit; the single transferable vote doesn't guarantee any proportional representation, but the multi-seat constituency does give a bit of it, so that if you take out the multi-seat constituency, then you will by and large make life extremely difficult for small parties and for independents because there will be only one seat per constituency, and it will tend to go to the candidates that can head the poll in the constituencies which, by and large, tend to be those from the bigger parties.

In his political memoir, former Labour Party Minister Barry Desmond drew attention to the following: 'Charlie McCreevy tells the story of a local supporter calling to the house on Christmas morning: "I thought I would get you in! Will you ever fill in this form for me." Charlie duly did the needful, but pointed out that the form needed to be signed by a doctor. He pointed out his constituent should go nearby to the GP's residence to "finish the job". "Ah Charlie, I could never do that, it's Christmas morning!" exclaimed the beloved voter'.[5] Is the Irish electorate also attached to the system because it gives voters a unique access to their politicians and, in a sense, keeps the politicians on their toes?

I think they do. That Fianna Fáil advertisement in 1968 said, 'You'll have your deputy near you', but in effect, nowadays, the Irish people are used to having more than one deputy near them, and if they don't get what they want from their Fianna Fáil representative, they can try their Fine Gael representative, or they can try their Labour Party representative, and they can put pressure on them. The Irish people like the system that we have, but having said that, I personally think there are arguments in favour of single-seat constituencies and I do think it could work in Ireland, but it would work mainly for the larger parties. If you took away your multi-seat constituency, you would probably need to bring in an element of the list system, so that if a party got a percentage of the vote, it could be reflected in giving them seats. In Parliament in Scotland, they give half of the seats, as far as I recall, to the result of the vote and then the other half are distributed from a list, and that also gives parties an opportunity to do what used to be an argument for bringing in some excellent candidates—say a person of unbelievable distinction, like Richard here, could be put on a list and put in Parliament without having to have the hard work maintaining the system on the ground. They do that in other countries. In Ireland, people expect their government ministers to work for it.

Sinnott elaborated on some of the different political cultures:

> In Germany, party canvassers don't knock on doors either during elections, so there are different political cultures there, but there is no doubt that there is an expectation of a degree of availability by the TD, by the elected representatives. In my view, I think this clientelism would have been there anyway even with a single-seat system. I think it's part of the political culture. It's part of the fact that we're a very small society. The competition would still have been there because you would have had these ambitious people emerging to threaten the seat; threaten the incumbent's hold on the seat via local government, so all of that, I think, would still have been an undercurrent, and I think if you'd had single-seat constituencies, you'd still have had a good deal of this. I mean, it is a growing phenomenon in Britain. Interestingly, for a long time, MPs didn't have to go back and forth—they could live hundreds of miles from their constituency and visit it occasionally. That's no longer the case, but the debate has been more sophisticated in the 1980s and 1990s, but I think it has faded. Noel Dempsey made a very strong push [when Minister for the Environment from 1997 to 2002], and Noel Dempsey was in favour of this hybrid system whereby effectively either you have two votes, as in the German system, or there are two parallel systems running off the one vote: one system to elect individuals per constituency and the other to make sure that the overall outcome is proportional. I think that's probably the strongest candidate. It is certainly the favourite form of electoral reform.

So why was there so little progress made with that proposal?

> Interestingly, because Dempsey didn't manage to get enough support within the Dáil. I think the decisive blow against it was actually a poll of Dáil deputies that was conducted by the All-Party Committee on the Constitution, and they got quite a high response rate in that poll but it was decisively against change, and one of the problems with electoral change is that the people who have to make the change are the people who, by definition, have benefited from the existing system, so there's an inherent conservatism in terms of resistance to change.

Chapter 17

What if T. K. Whitaker had not been appointed Secretary of the Department of Finance in 1956?

The name T. K. Whitaker evokes a relatively rare consensus on the part of historians and economists of twentieth-century Ireland. It is generally accepted that May 1958 marked a watershed in Irish economic thinking, when Whitaker's proposals for economic development were delivered to the government. Six months later, the White Paper derived from his proposals was published as *The Programme for Economic Expansion*, with an emphasis on free trade, export-oriented expansion of the economy and investment in public capital budgets. A period of economic expansion and growth followed, and it seemed the ghosts of economic protectionism and the failed policies of three decades of independence had been laid to rest; it was now accepted that a small population with low spending power could not thrive in a protected economy.

A native of Rostrevor, Co. Down, who grew up in Drogheda, Whitaker joined the civil service where his rise through the ranks was meteoric, and he became secretary of the Department of Finance at the age of just 39, appointed by the Fine Gael Minister for Finance, Gerard Sweetman. He held this position for 13 years and went on to become Governor of the Central Bank, Chancellor of the National University of Ireland, a Senator and chairman of various review groups and committees. He was also actively involved in North/South co-operation.

Whitaker might well not have been appointed to such a senior position in the civil service in 1956; he was appointed instead of Sarsfield Hogan, who had more seniority in the Department of Finance. Most senior officials could safely assume that they were guaranteed to be promoted, so for Whitaker to be appointed over Hogan was unprecedented. Notwithstanding that fact, it has been observed that Hogan accepted Whitaker's promotion 'with a gentlemanly generosity'.[1] Whitaker, of course, was not alone in challenging the conventional orthodoxy about economic policy in Ireland. Seán Lemass had been signalling that he was anxious for a change in direction, and Whitaker needed his drive, alongside the blessing of Eamon de Valera. Younger economists like Garret FitzGerald were using the pages of the *Irish Times* newspaper to argue the merits of opening up the economy, and urging policy-makers to learn from the experiences of the newly formed European Economic Community which seemed to be delivering substantial benefits and profits to the six member states.

What Whitaker was adamant about was the need for the Department of Finance to become creative and to assert a leadership role. In May 1957, in correspondence with his assistant secretaries, he insisted that it was necessary and desirable 'that this department should do some independent thinking and not simply wait for [the Department of] Industry and Commerce or the Industrial Development Authority to produce ideas',[2] the articulation of a clear desire to see his department take the initiative in planning. Later in the same year, he prepared a memorandum entitled *Has Ireland a Future?* in which he listed twenty-one proposals for change, and alluded to the psychological importance of a new initiative: 'the Irish people are falling into a mood of despondency. After 35 years of native government can it be, they are asking, that economic independence achieved with such sacrifice must wither away?'[3]

One of the greatest sacrifices in that context was emigration—a contemporary *Irish Times* editorial suggested that the success or failure of the *Programme for Economic Expansion* would be measured by emigration figures, and it was here that the impact of the new policies became apparent. Average net emigration fell from 43,000 per annum in the years 1956–61 to 16,000 in the years

1961–66 and 11,000 from 1966 to 1971.[4] Whitaker's skill was widely recognised, at home and abroad, as was his lack of arrogance; John Horgan has recorded that in 1963, a British delegation preparing for trade talks with its Irish counterparts was informed in a memorandum that he was 'brilliantly able, but with a quiet and unassuming but pleasant manner'.[5]

The archival clip that opened this show featured Whitaker being interviewed about the situation he found himself in, in the 1950s:

> A number of us felt that things were going so badly wrong—that there was so much despondency and despair around that we ought to try and do something positive; if there was any prospect of development to find out what was the way towards it and what ways previously followed ought to be abandoned. We were a young generation, a new generation of Irish well-trained, well-educated people and we were at the heart of things in the public service and there was a certain responsibility on us to do anything we could to pull ourselves out of the rut we were in. There was a kind of Wordsworthian feeling about it: 'this dawn it was, and that to be alive, but to be young was very heaven'. All my collaborators worked extremely hard with no hope of reward during the period we were working on *Economic Development*.

The contributors to this programme were Professor John FitzGerald, an economist with the Economic and Social Research Institute, and Professor Tom Garvin of the Politics Department at UCD whose most recent book went to the heart of this discussion: *Preventing the Future: Why was Ireland so poor for so long?*

I asked Garvin about the appearance of this document with the name of Whitaker attached, which was unprecedented in the civil service:

> Yes, Irish civil servants are always anonymous. They are instruments, theoretically speaking, of their minister, and all the rest. Of course, this is just a fiction. In fact, policy was often articulated, invented and even implemented by civil servants rather than by the minister involved. Whitaker in 1956, for example, writes to Sweetman [Minister for Finance] about the economic crisis of that

year, the fiscal crisis of that year: 'You are the only person in the Cabinet who understands this problem, or is capable of understanding this problem'—you know, it's quite an extraordinary remark for a civil servant to make! But it also tells you of the presence Whitaker had—he was able to say things like that in a way that nobody else could to his own minister, but of course then Sweetman was a highly intelligent guy who knew some economics and I think he was the chap who bumped Whitaker up into the secretary-ship at around that time. So Whitaker was not only, if you like, a dominant intellect in many ways, he was also favoured. They knew they needed him and people like him. But I think the key in that little piece from Whitaker that you just quoted is that for many of us, or a group of us, he was part of a movement—he wasn't just one man sort of standing against an obscurantist multitude or something like that. A whole generation of them decided this had to stop, that the swamp of despond that Ireland had worked its way into in the years after the Second World War would have to stop, have to be drained. 'We are living on our capital, we have been living on our capital for the last seven or eight years,' Whitaker says, in, I think, 1954. He's very direct, he's very brilliant and he uses the word 'failure' again and again—'we cannot go on like this.'

When Garvin wrote about this core group of individuals, he mentioned 'the developmentalists', as he termed them, and also observed that they were often outsiders within an elite. What did he mean by that? Rather defensively, he replied:

> That is a sociological observation—that there are often people who didn't have a conventional southern background, if you like. They were city boys or they were Northerners—that's all I meant.

I asked FitzGerald about the economic boom going on in the rest of Europe at this time in the context of the dividends of post-war reconstruction. If Ireland had been bombed relentlessly during the Second World War, might the pressure to reconsider economic policies have built up at a much earlier stage than the late 1950s? Is that a fair question to ask or assumption to make?

> Yes, I think the rest of Europe was sort of destroyed and had to pick itself up, where, in Ireland, Rip Van Winkle-like, we'd fallen

asleep and it was 'great'—we'd survived the Second World War and there were no changes forced on us in that we had to bring about the changes ourselves, and it wasn't until the late 1950s that Whitaker won through, and really the story of Ireland's economic success in the last decade I think is not the success, but how did Ireland fail for so long? Part of that was the 1950s, that it wasn't until the end of the 1950s, rather than 1945, that we started changing, in terms of moving for free trade, saying globalisation is good for you, which the rest of Europe knew in 1945, and also investing in education. I think education is one of the keys. In 1966, long after the Whitaker era, if you like, the OECD reported that 50 per cent of Irish kids left school before aged 12, and in fact the education administration had no record of them—they were just thrown out of the system with roughly the three 'R's—if that. They were semi-literate, they went to England to build the roads or to be chambermaids, and they were just thrown away. There seemed to be no idea whatsoever that education is not just something to make you a virtuous citizen or a pious person; it's to make you somebody who can earn your own living. If you want to be a plumber in Ireland, you make sure your father was a plumber—it was as simple as that. Also if you wanted to be a tradesman, you couldn't get a Leaving Cert because the age for apprenticeship was too young. Again, the banks only hired you at age 18, making sure that graduates couldn't get jobs in the banks. The whole place was tied up, very, very tight. It was like a series of monopolies designed to stop any change, to stop any disadvantage. Everybody was playing a zero sum game. In many ways, Ireland had the moral basis of a backward society.

Garvin elaborated:

In a sense, that's what *Economic Development* and the changes were about. The ideas in it, well, first of all, free trade and opening up— that forced people to change; the people, businesses that had been doing rotten jobs and were incredibly inefficient saw the writing was going to be on the wall, but actually if you look at *Economic Development*, the first programme, the economic ideas in them aren't great, but it was the fact that people felt, 'This can't go on— we've got to change', it was the decision to change, try anything— education wasn't big—that it was the *Investment in Education Report* in 1966 which I think was written by Martin O'Donoghue,

Paddy Lynch and Bill Hyland from the Department of Education, but there was a process set in train of: 'We can do better' and part of it is free trade; part of it is urbanisation. Actually another thing is that a lot of the development would seem to come—or be expected to come—from agriculture. Of course, agriculture wasn't going well; it was going to be manufacturing, it was going to be the urbanisation of Ireland which was going to bring success, so it's not that the ideas were great, but they were pretty good for their time in the Irish context, but there was a feeling: 'we can do better'.

But wasn't it also the case that it took outside individuals to come to Ireland to articulate some of the home truths, or elaborate more frankly on the state of the Irish economy, particularly in the context of Marshall Aid Funding and the post-war reconstruction plans: that American economic advisers were using very direct language about Ireland in the late 1940s, highlighting, for example, the fact that less than 45 per cent of houses had electricity, and that there were very few telephones in Ireland.

FitzGerald responded:

But we were very little exposed to ideas from the outside world. When I joined the Department of Finance in 1972, I put away all the files on Ireland's external economic relations; I put them all away—they were about going to London, or hiring British academics coming over to tell us how to do things. And suddenly the world changed, and we were exposed—within months, I was off to meetings in Brussels, and you were exposed to a much wider range of ideas. I think it was through a meeting of the World Bank, I think in India, that Whitaker, through the World Bank, had contacts with the outside world, but really it's only in the 1960s you have the Organisation for European Community Development which was very important, and they brought investment in education and then of course in the 1970s the EEC, so that we were very little exposed and if you look—I haven't gone back to look at the files in the Department of Finance—but I'm sure you'll find it's all about going to London. Remember the Treasury in 1922—that six people came over from the Treasury to the Department of Finance to bring ideas and help them do the job, and I think there was still one of them left in the job in the 1950s, but we were very caught up in the British Isles way of thinking, and that only began to change at a very late stage.

Garvin felt that this was an exaggeration:

> That's not completely true. Seán Lemass as a very young man back in 1929 wrote a position paper for the Fianna Fáil party in which he recommends free trade. He recommends a united Europe, but he knows he's not going to get it. He says that the old free-trade Europe of 1914 had broken down because of the First World War and there were, if you like, 22 or 24, or whatever it was, protected areas in Europe, and we were going to have to be another one. In other words, we have to go for protection to survive. The real tragedy is that, after 1945, they held on to protection after it ceased to be necessary. It made some sense in the depression, it made a lot of sense during the war, but it made no sense whatsoever after that.

There were some seriously depressing budget speeches during the 1950s in which ministers for finance spoke in grave terms about the prevailing economic difficulties. An archival clip was played of Gerard Sweetman in 1956, in which a journalist referred to what was 'the beginning of what became known as "the Sweetman squeeze" but it was only the beginning, because the Minister had to harden his taxes three months later and spread them over an even wider range of goods.' The emphasis in these speeches seemed to be very much on survival, as opposed to any creative thinking. Was that a fair assessment?

Garvin commented:

> Oh well, '56 was a crash. You must remember it is Suez/Hungary. I only vaguely remember it myself—I was 13 years of age. What seems to have happened was there was a panic. I think there was a panic at an elite level, and Whitaker and his pals were able to take advantage of that and shift everything around. Also, Lemass changed sides. Lemass seems to have remembered his younger self and come back to the theory of anti-protectionism and abandoned, if you like, his love for Industry and Commerce and decided to become Taoiseach. I think Lemass didn't believe in protectionism. I mean, that is quite obvious. He didn't philosophically believe in protectionism, but presumably he had been so long in Industry and

Commerce, you know, building factories and all this sort of thing, and being in power, that he just was enjoying himself, I suspect. He always said that he hated being Taoiseach, but he loved being Minister for Industry and Commerce, and I suspect there's some truth in that.

FitzGerald suggested:

If you look at some of the ideas he had in the immediate post-war period, Lemass's ideas were quite mad, and the Department of Finance quite rightly stopped him doing some of these things.

Garvin interjected: 'fertiliser factories!'

Yeah, he was going to sort of develop Ireland by state industry and it would have been a disaster. Now, it's interesting—the process, how he went back to maybe his old ideas, and also to what extent was de Valera the problem in that? It's interesting that you have *Economic Development* and the *First Programme* while de Valera was still Taoiseach, that—all right, it's Lemass, but Lemass was still Minister for Industry and Commerce at the time—so how did that changeover happen without de Valera stopping it?

Garvin believed that even if de Valera had wanted to stop it, he would not have been in a position to do so:

I think de Valera actually was agnostic about economics—he was much more worried about culture and identity and religion than he was about economics. Economics to him was something he didn't fully understand and I think he realised after a while that he didn't understand it. He delegated that to Lemass. So if Lemass was changing his mind on economics, de Valera would go along. De Valera always said there was never any problem between Lemass and himself—they were like chalk and cheese, but they worked very well together.

Was it that Lemass simply decided to go with a younger generation of people, and was this a measure of just how influenced by Whitaker he was? This seemed a fundamental question. At a later stage, Whitaker authored his own book, *Interests*, and he wrote about the duty of a civil servant and the importance of a good relationship with their minister but that ultimately a civil servant had to accept the decision the minister made. At the same time, he also suggested that it was often up to civil servants to make sure that they were not prisoners of outmoded policies. Where is the line there in terms of the kind of influence that he had? And how significant was the talk of the psychological value of setting targets, which was common in places like Russia and Germany?

According to Garvin:

> They were worried about that—it sounded vaguely Nazi. The Nazis had a four-year plan, so when they started talking about plans, that appealed to the left, whereas free trade appealed to the centre and the right, so by and large it was a psychological mechanism which appealed to everybody, and the fact that they only targeted 2 per cent per year GNP growth and they got 4 per cent—that was magic, absolute magic.

Did FitzGerald believe that was a deliberate underestimation?

> No, I don't think so, but I think also James Dillon, in the Dáil on behalf of Fine Gael, was very opposed to this and saw it as sort of left-wing ideology. One of the interesting things, I think, is how Lemass relied on Whitaker and Whitaker was Secretary of the Department of Finance when Lemass was Taoiseach from 1959 onwards. Now, that would be unheard of today, and I think it reflects the fact that you had—and Whitaker himself mentioned it—a small number of educated, skilled people. It was a much smaller world, and also the Minister of the Department of Finance must have been happy about this relationship to have developed it, and it obviously developed over the course of the 1960s because the idea that you would have the Secretary of the Department of Finance beside Bertie Ahern when he is negotiating with Blair on Northern Ireland would seem crazy today, whereas it was Whitaker who went with Lemass to Stormont [in 1965, for the meeting with Terence O'Neill, the first time the leaders of Northern Ireland and the Irish Republic had met].

Garvin developed this point about the unique status of the man:

Whitaker was more than Secretary to the Department of Finance—
he was a kind of leader in his own right. But they were an extraordinary generation of civil servants. My dad [John Garvin, Secretary
of the Department of Local Government and Public Health] was one
of them. James Deeney [Chief Medical Officer], Whitaker, obviously,
Charlie Murray [Secretary of the Department of Finance, 1969–76],
John Leydon in Industry and Commerce, Tom Barrington
[Director of the Institute of Public Administration], the civil
servants—they were extraordinary people. They were distrusted
very much by the politicians at the very beginning because they
were regarded as 'hold-overs' and 'Free-Staters' and 'West Britons',
all this kind of thing, by people like Seán MacBride notoriously,
and others as well, and then they realised after ten years they were
very lucky to have them, to have these people to do their thinking
for them. I seriously think that that was the relationship.

But whatever was going on at an elite level, there was also the issue
of the growing disquiet on the streets. An archival clip was played
of Sam Nolan and Johnny Mooney talking about their situation in
1957 as members of an unemployed protest movement:

If you lived in the 1950s, you'd understand the poverty levels in this
country that are not imaginable by people of a later generation.
The level of unemployment had been rising in the previous year—
that was 1956—and there had been cutbacks in public sector
employment. Assistance or benefit in those days in monetary terms
was really, really on the poverty line and people's ability to survive
was very limited indeed, so people were more susceptible to saying,
'Well, what the hell, we'll have to do something, we'll have to
agitate, we'll have to protest.' The very first meeting was held
outside Werburgh Street Labour Exchange. At that particular time,
there was the TB van outside the labour exchange, asking people to
go along and find out if they had TB. One fella jumped up on the
platform and said, 'The only thing I can say is that they found
nothing in my stomach', and another fella got up and said, 'I've
been unemployed so long that if I got a feed now, I wouldn't have
the energy to eat it.'

Whatever about civil servants and policy-makers, would Whitaker
have been regarded as somebody who would have been very

much in tune with the public mood as well? FitzGerald remembered:

> He left the Department of Finance when I was there but what was interesting was that everybody spoke well of him, and normally with people in Ireland there's a begrudgery, which Joe Lee talks about in his book, and that everybody had huge respect for him, both in the civil service and outside, so he obviously did hear and listen; people felt that he was in tune with what was going on, and I think that was unusual.

Garvin added:

> That's interesting. I was 16 when Dev went to the Park [to become President in 1959] and Lemass became Taoiseach, and it's something I wonder do other people of my generation remember the same way. It was as though the light went on. I really mean that—in 1959, the light went on—I don't know what it was exactly. Lemass himself actually talks about it and complains about it. 'Don't be too despondent and don't be too optimistic'—that's real Lemass—'Well, we don't need all this despair, we don't need too much optimism either, we need to go to work'—all this sort of stuff, and it was just wonderful; it was such a difference from the preaching and ranting of the previous generation.

FitzGerald elaborated on this perception of a cultural and generational shift:

> The previous generation were out of touch. The younger generation were all leaving—they were all emigrating. The number to emigrate in 1957 was equal to the number born in that year. And the younger people knew they could have a much better life by going to Britain—that Ireland was an economic failure—and the older generation, they felt de Valera was living in cloud cuckoo land. Maybe he wasn't, but he certainly—looking back—doesn't seem to be aware of the fact that people wanted a completely different lifestyle. They could have it in the rest of Europe, and Ireland was this isolated bastion where we'd managed to create a disaster all of our own, and the changes in the 1950s—and it took a very long time for them to mature—made a younger generation

say, 'Look, we can do better.' They weren't quite clear on *how* they were going to do better. Looking back on it, they weren't sort of wonderful documents, looking at it from today's point of view, but you've got to read them in the context of the time and it was hope following on despair.

Garvin also reflected on those who were asking the difficult questions and making the necessary criticisms:

A lot of the dissidents who came out in public were—I use my own word, 'outsiders'. Tuairim ['Opinion'—a think tank that published many papers critical of Irish society, economics and politics in the 1950s and 1960s]—their London Branch, and I emphasise London—actually excoriated the Irish education system around 1959. J. P. Kelleher, an Irish-American academic wrote a brilliant piece for *Foreign Affairs* [an academic journal] in 1957 about the intellectual vacuousness of the public mind in Ireland. It was quite brilliant and it angered people enormously, and McQuaid actually—in his private papers—says, 'I was terribly hurt'! Sad as that, really. They were just talking to themselves for a long, long time. There was no real public debate. In many ways, Gay Byrne had not happened! Gay Byrne and the 1960s and the opening of public debate on all kinds of issues that were not talked about— economic issues, sexual issues, family issues, psychological issues, spiritual issues and all the rest of it—that had not happened. There was this great silence in the 1950s. I can't describe it any other way.

If Donogh O'Malley had been Minister for Education in the 1950s at the same time that Ken Whitaker was Secretary of the Department of Finance, could the silence have been challenged at an earlier stage?

'I think it might have happened earlier if it weren't for electoral politics—that's my own belief,' was Garvin's response. 'The real disaster in many ways—though it was good for Irish democracy—was the 1948 election where de Valera and the boys are thrown out in favour of a weird coalition of Republicans and Fine Gael. Lemass is the key. I mean, Lemass might have got going earlier.'

FitzGerald wasn't quite convinced:

But I don't think you would have seen the changes occurring earlier if Donogh O'Malley had been there—I don't think that is a 'what if' that would have happened. If you read the documents at the time, people didn't see education as being so absolutely crucially important and there's a process beginning in the late 1950s through investment in education where people came out and said, 'Look, we have watched 20 years in the rest of Europe from Siberia through to Snowdonia the investment in education and it's working—we'd better do the same.' So, I think that, in the late 50s, you see the beginning of a learning process but they didn't have the answers.

Garvin added:

> I think actually that Northern Ireland is crucial here—the spend on education in Northern Ireland in the 1950s was four times per head per child what it was in the Republic of Ireland. This is absolutely terrifying—you know that Northern Ireland is getting educated and the Republic was remaining half-illiterate.

How significant was Whitaker's Northern Ireland background?

'My sense of it is that he knew the North—he explained the North to Lemass and Lynch,' offered Garvin. 'And apparently they had to have it explained to them—that's what I find fascinating: that they didn't know the dynamics of Northern Ireland. The first time I ever went north was 1964 and I now realise I didn't understand what I was looking at. I was looking at a relatively prosperous advanced society that was in crisis.'

Did FitzGerald as an economist believe that, in light of the Celtic Tiger of the 1990s, the achievements of the *Programme for Economic Expansion* would be reassessed, or accept the suggestion that some of the achievements may have been exaggerated?

> No, I don't think we have to do that. Nothing happened or nothing changed until the late 1950s and then you see a gradual process of change. Now, you don't get revolutions in economics; it's a process which was started then which takes very long, and very possibly it could have been done better—we could all do better—but looking back on it, the 1960s is a successful time where we were beginning

to learn lessons and, along the way since, we've made a lot of mistakes, and finally we've got to the situation that we should have been in, probably in the 1950s. If you look back, Ireland was one of the wealthiest countries in Europe in 1922, and things went downhill from the time we became independent. Probably looking at the 1950s and blaming it all on the 1950s is wrong, but one should go back and, as Tom said earlier, Seán Lemass's ideas in 1929 were quite interesting.

Garvin concluded:

There's one codicil I'd make. There was this kind of silence—I can't describe it as anything else but the great silence of the 1950s—but actually culturally Ireland was quite dynamic, particularly on the stage. The theatre, as far as I can remember in the 1950s, was very dynamic, and theatre was free—you had free speech in the theatre. Plays were put on and were quite subversive in all sorts of ways.

FitzGerald finished by adding:

But there was an anger, if you read Synge, Brendan Behan, Dónall Mac Amhlaigh [author of *Dialann Deoraí*—an account of his emigrant experience in London, translated into English in 1964 as *An Irish Navvy*], and they're all people who emigrated. There may have been great Irish writing, but a lot was taking place—either people who had experienced emigration or had emigrated and published in England. And you must see the reaction—Irish society finally woke up to the fact that their young people were angry and they had left.

Chapter 18

What if the members of U2 had gone to different schools in the 1970s?

This show opened with an archival clip of a young Bono describing what the band was all about, with a suggestion that if they had been better at imitating other people, they might never have had the success that came their way:

> U2 is a rock group. Some people call us a punk rock group. We'd like to think of ourselves as a modern rock group, be it new wave or whatever. We set out to try and use rock music in an inventive sort of way, and, rather than follow other bands or other people's formulas, try and do something on our own account. I've said before that I think we were probably the worst garage band in the country. I mean, there were a lot better groups than us—it was just our inability to play other people's songs that led us to write our own songs and that's actually when U2 began or U2 was born. I think if you sat down and actually tried to—you got your calculator out and started to compute, you know, on what you are worth and what you are owed—I think you wouldn't be able to write a song or write the sort of songs you write about. I try not to think about that sort of thing as much, as I am certainly flattered that such large amounts of people are buying our records.

U2 came together as a band in the 1970s, at a time when the Irish music scene was vibrant, innovative and noisy. The youth of the Irish population and the ability of its musicians to absorb historical musical influences while creating something new sparked much originality. Within a year of U2's formation, Fr Brian D'Arcy appeared on the RTÉ television programme, *Radharc*, declaring with a mixture of pride and bemusement, 'This is the pop generation.' He went on to assert that young unemployed Irish people could identify with punk music more than anything else. But it was not just about punk; this was also a time when Thin Lizzy were dancing in the moonlight; the Boomtown Rats were looking after number one (because, in the words of Bob Geldof, 'we could trust no one else'); across the water, the Sex Pistols were helping God save the Queen; and (God save us) three-chord Status Quo were rocking all over the world, while Niall Stokes was putting the finishing touches to his new music magazine, *Hot Press*.

The longevity of U2 has been exceptional; 2004 saw the release of the album, *How to Dismantle an Atomic Bomb*; the following summer, the band played three successive nights at Croke Park, a stadium as magnificent as the band that it hosted. The story of the band, sometimes described as Ireland's greatest living artists, raises intriguing 'what ifs' which were teased out with Dave Fanning, making a rare appearance in the studios of Radio One (and warned to behave himself accordingly) and Barry Devlin of Horslips, who at that stage were reinvigorated and touring to promote their greatest hits album.

Various—some might argue, extravagant—claims, have been and continue to be made about the significance of U2. Some observers in the 1980s suggested that as a band, U2 were there to remind us of our mortality and vulnerability and dislocation, while John Waters suggested, 'It's easy to mistake U2 for a normal rock band, albeit a hugely successful one, but they are much more than that. I believe that U2 are among Ireland's greatest living artists', though this was an assessment he was later to revise. In 2005, he suggested that the band was now doing things just to 'tread water' and that the members lacked 'distinctive creative identities within the collective ... there is this contradiction about rock 'n' roll that, while it can survive for a while in a state of ironic self-referentialism, it needs at least the promise of a further purpose. U2 have lost that—they are what they are and seemingly for no other reason.'[1]

In his book, *The Unforgettable Fire*, published in 1987, Eamon Dunphy suggested that U2, two years after they had appeared on the front of *Rolling Stone* magazine under the heading 'Band of the '80s', had the courage to be known at a time when mystique may well have served them better. He observed that prior to their appearance at the Live Aid concert in Wembley Stadium in 1985, they 'were not a stadium band', but that afterwards, manager Paul McGuinness 'knew that his band could play anywhere'. Their rise to global stardom may have been gradual, but it was brilliantly planned.[2]

The following year, 1986, concert promoter Jim Aiken suggested 'not only is rock music in Ireland as good as any in the world, it's for rock music, as a result of U2 mainly, that Ireland is best known abroad now. It's not for Guinness or leprechauns: It's for rock.'[3]

The fact that U2 have lasted so long means that their impact and influence are continually being revised; Bono, after all, had said in 1998, 'You don't join a band to save the world but to save your own arse and get off the street', but ten years later, it was clear that saving the world had indeed become part of his, if not the rest of the band's, mission. Bono also acknowledged at various stages that confusion over his own identity and the group's identity is part of the reason why they experimented so much, re-invented and explored all sorts of musical influences. Perhaps what is most intriguing is their closeness, which has survived through personal loss, rows and alcohol. In November 2004, in an interview with the *Sunday Times*, they revealed that it was this closeness that has allowed them to survive. Despite the rows about Bono's appetite for politics, their love for each other 'is a very elegant co-dependency'. As Larry Mullen, the most direct of the band, pointed out, 'in the end we want the same thing; we want to be on the radio, have big singles. We don't want to be thought of as a veteran band.'[4] It appeared that as long as they were agreed on that, they were able to work out all the other issues. Quite clearly, there is a fundamental respect between the four of them, because they are all outsiders to a certain degree and, as The Edge puts it, 'There's nowhere else to go.'

I asked both guests to go back to the very beginning and the school in which these four putative members of U2 found themselves—Mount Temple. It was an unusual school for the Ireland of the early 1970s. Fanning suggested:

> You could file it under progressive and the other schools also to be in that file would also be—well, nothing actually! Certainly looking back, when you read about that school now, because you read about it in the context of U2, and there's so much written about U2, you do see that it was out there and that they were encouraged to do things that many other schools maybe didn't encourage one to do, and they encouraged them to do it together and they encouraged them to follow music if that's what they wanted to follow, so, absolutely they got a leg-up big time.

Was there a sense that they were being drawn together in this school because of various family issues, various re-location issues?

> I don't know the answer to that question necessarily but I would guess at an answer and say No—not necessarily at all. I mean, sometimes the school that a lot of people go to is the school often that is nearest to your house for (a) because a lot of people from that area are going to go, and (b) because of the commutes these days. Now, maybe not back in 1976, but it still makes a lot of sense, so I wouldn't have thought so—no, not necessarily.

Both Devlin and Fanning agreed. 'There was a re-location issue for Adam. Adam was a different kettle of fish,' Devlin suggested. 'Talking of "what ifs"—what if Adam Clayton had gone to a different school. He would certainly have been fecked out of that!' How important did Devlin believe the influence of what was going on in the traditional and folk music scene was for U2, with the Bothy Band, and then the sense of rock with an Irish sensibility—Thin Lizzy, and, of course, Horslips (with whom Devlin played the bass guitar).

> Well, you know, they're always kind enough to go—'Yeah, these guys laid the ground work for us.' But, I mean, as we'll probably discuss later on, they're such a unique and compelling and self-

contained phenomenon that it's kind of slightly irrelevant what went before. I suppose what was most interesting from their point of view was the fact that they made the decision that they would stay in Ireland and work out of Ireland, which is something they've continued to do, and so maybe that was something that they learned—maybe learned from us—because Michael Deeney and Paul McGuinness actually had a promotion company together at one stage called Headland Promotions, and Paul has always said that he watched what Michael Deeney did with us, and I suppose had we delivered in the way that U2 eventually delivered, that those structures would have worked that way. So, in terms of straight musical legacy, U2 do, I think, have a uniquely Irish sensibility—I don't think it could be from anywhere else, but to be truthful, although I'd love to say that they did, I don't think that they borrowed their legacy from anyone else.

Fanning interrupted to suggest:

No, but I think it's important to remember—and Barry is being a little bit unfair to himself there—that when you think of a bunch of bands there like Planxty, and Paul Brady and the Bothy Band and all the rest of it—and I can be in the middle of all this because I soaked up every single one of them mainly because my older brother played the uilleann pipes and I got into all this. Whoever would have thought that a lot of good folk music would be soaked up by so many students of the 1970s when the Led Zeppelins and Palmers and all this seem to be ruling the roost in terms of alternative music or something else to get into the charts. Along came Horslips, and, to be honest, I'd say a lot of the bands I've just mentioned didn't like Horslips at all—they wouldn't have liked what Horslips were doing to pure traditional Irish music by rocking it up and also, don't forget, 'glamming' it up. So, I mean, the Horslips thing was the one that was flamboyant; the Horslips was also the one that was reflecting what was in the charts in terms of the T Rexes and Garry Glitters—all those kind of things—and also they were revving up and rocking up the old 'trad' stuff that was in our blood that we didn't even know was necessarily in our blood from the age of two! What Horslips did was it opened as many doors in the 1970s, more so than U2 ever did in many ways. I mean, U2 went on to do something else—you can be nice about

U2, Barry, but before all that what Horslips did was absolutely phenomenal. A lot of doors that were opened, a lot of people didn't want them opened at all.

What about the significance of the emergence of Paul McGuinness who met U2 first in the Project Arts Centre in 1978. Is that one of the great 'what ifs'—if McGuinness hadn't seen that future for U2? According to Devlin:

> It's very interesting that there's a kind of an analogy here. There's a question that's often asked about The Beatles—'What if they hadn't met George Martin?'—and although Paul's relationship and his place is very different from Martin's, in the sense that he wasn't their musical mentor, I think that, had they not met Paul, they would certainly have evolved in a very different way. I think what Paul taught them most was to be outrageously demanding of everyone, in terms of what they expected people to deliver for them, and to be outrageously demanding of themselves in terms of what they could do—they already had an aspiration to be extraordinarily good—but I think Paul put a structure, not just a management structure, but a conceptual structure of 'you can, and you should'. Paul takes a high moral ground about this, you know. He goes—'You should be the best, you really shouldn't be shuffling around going "ah, we're Irish and it'll do"', and I think that's the thing that he most gave them, but there is a real 'what if' there.

Fanning added:

> The whole thing about that is there's 'what ifs' all along the way, you know. I mean, you know, could you say, 'What if at least Bono and Edge had met, but they hadn't met Adam and Larry?' And is that being incredibly cruel? I mean, it possibly is, but there's a possible point about that kind of thing, but then you could say, 'The Beatles were the Beatles, because Ringo gave them the heart and soul, George was the quiet one and the other two were what they were', but in terms of the Paul McGuinness thing, just remember what bands did in the 1970s. Again, Horslips were different there, but an awful lot of the bands floundered on the rock called London—they all went over to London, and, if you went over to London for a certain amount of time—three months,

six months, a year or whatever—it was a question of how long you'll last; it was a question of the measure of your success. I remember going to see U2's first, or was it their second gig in London—in a place called the National Rooms. There was A Secret Affair—yes, you can laugh all right—there was five people watching U2 and, when I walked in, McGuinness was—'Oh God, great, there's somebody here.' There was a mad revival at the time for about ten minutes and A Secret Affair were the ones that were heading, and I can't remember who were second and U2 were on first. In other words, they were third on that bill, and we went back to some party that night with Rudy (a man from Northern Ireland) in some flat and I remember meeting Bono on Grafton Street and him saying he was going to go to London and I was saying, 'Oh, God Almighty, when a band goes there, it ruins them.' The funny thing is that within two months or three months, London was out of the picture completely because McGuinness said, 'Look, I'll tell you what, let's just do America, let's just go for it' and didn't he sign on with this thing Premier Talent which had Bruce Springsteen at the time. McGuinness made no bones about it whatever, and there was a ladder there—there was a rung each time, and he was saying, 'That rung is mine next month . . . that next rung is mine next month' and he just climbed the damn thing.

U2's earlier material in the late 1970s and early 1980s was well received critically but did not do well commercially. Is this something that is forgotten now?

Fanning observed, 'Actually there were ten times better bands in Dublin than U2 at the beginning.' Devlin added:

> . . . and ten times more loved bands—they weren't that loved in the beginning. I remember bands like The Blades and Paul Cleary, who of course was a very good song-writer. Bands like The Blades were seen as bands that tied in much more with the movement, with The Specials and the two-tone thing that was going on in Britain.

Fanning added, 'But even more than that, they were the people's band—they were the cool band, the street band, and their first five singles would knock anybody's first five singles out of the water—they were absolutely brilliant.'

Another archival clip was played of an interview Pat Kenny had conducted with Bono in the early days, in which he talked about the importance of believing in 'the lies' about the band's ability. Clearly, it was very important to believe in them, particularly if you wanted to conquer the United States. Fanning suggested:

> This is about what Barry was saying there—the old Irish thing of, which I have part of it still, and will have for the rest of my life— you know how you go into a restaurant and the food isn't good and you don't complain. Barry just said there, 'Be the best, just demand the best, expect the best, and don't do the old—"ah sure we're Irish and we'll do".' That's really what you're talking about there.

Another important development in the growth of U2's appeal was the idea that they were phenomenal live performers. How important was that in terms of their appeal becoming more and more widespread? Devlin thought that it was hugely significant:

> I mean, they have always believed hugely in the value of touring. Bono has always said a record is just a record until you bring it to somebody's home town and so they just tour. When they tour, it's relentless. The other thing about them is they are a phenomenal live band. If you heard Dave's session with them or the session that Dave was at down in Hanover Quay, or if you heard the Jonathan Ross live tracks—the three tracks they did—they're fantastic [the band had appeared on the BBC television programme, *Friday Night with Jonathan Ross*, early in December 2004]; they can manage a stadium, or they can manage a studio set-up with 50 or 100 people with equal aplomb. They've become, by some way, I think, the best live band in the world. I mean, the Rolling Stones, for instance, can be a very shambolic live band; they can have good nights and they can have bad nights. U2 are always on it and they don't do watered-down versions of their recordings—their live versions are versions in their own right, with their own dynamic and their own drive. By some way they're the best live band I have ever seen.

In terms of that ability to perform live, the LiveAid concert in 1985 also threw up an interesting 'what if', not just in terms of the global audience, but the gamble that Bono took. They were told they had 15 minutes to perform three songs, but Bono chose to play just two and indulge in a slow dance with a member of the audience. Fanning remembers:

> I know that when they went back into the dressing room afterwards, they were all crying into their beers, saying, 'We've completely and absolutely blown our career', because this was an absolutely huge gig; it kept building up, week by week, beforehand. This LiveAid thing suddenly became the biggest thing ever, even beforehand. Don't think it just suddenly happened on the day. And when it did shambolically happen on the day, all the shambolic parts of it were just as good as the great parts. And the U2 thing—they did blow it in some ways, but just remember where Bono's head was at that stage. You're talking July 1985, and before that, for the three previous years, they'd got a number 1 album in Britain with *War* which is the third album, and the *October* and *Boy* albums before that had done very well obviously. But now they were kind of big and they'd gone to Red Rocks in America and they'd brought out *Under a Blood Red Sky* from that, and that had gone down really well in the bad weather, and it just worked. Something came out of the sky for pyrotechnics, and the lighting and everything worked, and Bono was on a real high around that time. It was just before the *Wide Awake in America* EP and therefore two years before one of the greatest moments of rock, *The Joshua Tree*. So it was all happening really well, and one of the things he was famous for—and was getting away with—was climbing stacks and steeples and waving things, these stupid white flags and pathetic T-shirts on him, and then big leather jackets and then the mullet, which really is inexcusable. All that combines to go to *LiveAid*. Hilariously, they were supposed to do three numbers, and 'Bad' being a number which is on *The Unforgettable Fire*, which is a damn fine song—but it came out a year later on *Wide Awake in America*, the live version. It's still one of the greatest things they've done ever, and they were kind of honing it at that stage, so there he goes and does his long version of 'Bad' and brings somebody up out of the audience because he thinks at that moment that he is God. I mean, you know, if you're going to be as big as U2 are now, there has to be a stage in your career when you genuinely thought you were, and it was in those six months that he thought he was, so therefore no wonder he thought he blew it when he got off the stage. Needless to say, for every single person who played at LiveAid, within the next six months, all their albums are

back in the charts; their current album went up the charts. The only band for which every single previous album, all six albums, went straight into the top 10, or whatever it was, was U2—it actually worked completely in their favour.

A clip was played of the live performance of 'Bad'. Devlin added:

> Funnily enough it's still my favourite U2 song. When the Edge does that funny jangly thing with echo on, it . . . it's a chilling moment and, everybody goes, that's 'Bad'!—it is a fantastic song. I also was lucky enough to be able to—what the hell, let's pretend that this is a dispassionate discussion and just be fans—I was lucky enough to do the video for 'Bad', and just assembling the video from a bunch of live buddies that I'd shot in a bunch of stages all over Europe was a fantastic thing. He's good at possession in that song, and it was a time when possession was the name of his game.

As mentioned in the introduction, Bono has in the past reflected on the issue of Irish identity. How important was the Dublin identity or the Irish identity? It has, after all, been suggested that U2 could have been an American band, could have been a British band; that there is not anything distinctively Irish about them. Was that something Devlin accepted?

> Well, it's only the British and the Americans who say that! I mean, Jonathan Ross was saying, mischievously, 'Why you Irish—some of you are English—couldn't you go back to being English? Wouldn't that be better?' and Adam had a very funny answer. Adam said, 'I think being Irish in the end was safer!' But funnily enough, I think that's a kind of a rhetorical question, because if you ask an American—or anyone in the world—where U2 are from, they know they're from Ireland, but they will also say they could only be from Ireland. There's a lyrical quality—there's something about how the music is put together—that I genuinely think is not borrowed from anyone. It doesn't borrow from Planxty or anything like that, but I think that it could only come from Dublin. Maybe I'm wrong. Maybe I'm being romantic about it.

To wind Fanning up, I mentioned an interview when Bono was asked about the identity question, and he did suggest that there was an Irishness to what U2 did, admitted he was not quite sure what it was, but then talked about the abandonment with which Larry played the drums, and Edge's melodies, and suggested that the way they performed them was intrinsically Irish.

Fanning responded:

> Oh gosh, that's going too far. I couldn't go that far. I did a pro-gramme once for *The South Bank Show*. It was called, 'Cool, Clear, Crystal Streams', and when I look back on it, it's really embarrass-ing—really bad—and it was Bob Geldof who was involved in the whole thing, and you had to talk to Van Morrison and Bono and all that, and it was the 'There's something inherently Irish about Irish artists that makes them so Irish that even if they wanted to avoid their Irishness, their Irishness comes through anyway' kind of thing. I know—a full hour on that stuff. Anyway, the point about it is, no, I'm not going to start going into Larry's drumming being Irish or Adam's faith being Irish—that is really a rung on that ladder too far. Oh, it's a different ladder!

Nonetheless, Devlin observed:

> I still do feel that there's something Irish about a track like 'Bad' or even 'Sometimes You Can't Make It On Your Own'. I mean, okay, there was this period in the middle when they became Stetson-wearing Americans and . . . but even then, 'Running to Stand Still' is off *The Joshua Tree* album, and for years I assumed it was about America, and in fact it's about Ballymun.

Fanning remembered this track for a different reason:

> Can I just say something fantastic? A very famous DJ, who shall remain nameless, played it, saying, 'A great track from U2—it's called "Running to a Standstill"!'

How influential have the politics been and Bono's quest to save the world and cancel the debt? Would Bono have been better off if he had just stuck to the music? Both responded in unison: 'Yes, big time—hugely'.

Fanning elaborated:

I mean, first of all, I'd like to ask Barry, 'How many Bonos are there?' Seriously—he's with Christy Turlington, giving her away at a wedding in the morning; he's in South Africa with Nelson Mandela in the afternoon; and he's in somewhere in Hanover Quay or in the Docks, having a drink at night. He seems to be everywhere, so the minute U2 aren't doing anything, he's out doing the Bono thing.

Devlin added:

I was going to use the word 'ubiquitous'. I have grave questions about that as well. I think that Bono may actually now have adopted the womble concept, where there is a Bono suit that various musicians are handed out and they can go off around the world and be Bono for a while, while he's at home or rehearsing with the band. Because it's true—he's just everywhere.

What does the future hold for a band whose members are still relatively young? Fanning suggested:

There's a couple of things about this. First of all, they're all about 42/43/44 at the moment, and there's so many things they shouldn't do, but they do, and that's just what amazes me. Number 1 is, they look cool, they are cool, they still look cool on stage. I mean, that Jonathan Ross thing you mentioned—a small little stage, as you say, in front of just a few people in the studio and Mr Cynical Ross there and they really pumped it out and did it exactly just as they did in Hanover Quay—brilliant sounds, and just as they do on stage anywhere around the world and all the rest of it. The other thing is, the big question could be the 'what ifs'—if it hadn't all come together, like the Rolling Stones, say, by about their thirteenth album, or whatever it was—*Emotional Rescue*. I know for a fact none of you can name one song off that album, but still, 26 albums later, they still tour, they're still huge but they're not critically lauded necessarily, and commercially, in terms of records, they don't necessarily sell. Twenty-five years of the career of U2, 12 or 13 albums later from the studio—the latest ones of which have sold 10 or 12 million copies, which is just ridiculous—but U2 continue to do all this and I don't quite get how 25 years later, commercially and critically, they are so absolutely hugely successful. And one last thing I want to say is about the current album which was released a few months back there in November [2004]. The point about it is, the industry was waiting for this as much as they wait for a new Spielberg movie in the cinema—it was just like, 'Great, it will get people back in the record shops; it'll get people back buying records' in the same way as a big Spielberg movie gets people back in the cinema. It's phenomenal for a band that's 25 years old. Why aren't people more worried about the fifth White Stripes album, the third Strokes album or the something else album, but we're all—'Great, U2 are going to bring out a new album.' It's their twelfth album in 25 years—that's almost a contradiction.

Devlin concluded:

U2 have two functions. Every time they bring out an album, they save the industry again, so all the guys in the industry are going—'Jesus Christ, please give us a new U2 album', but the new U2 album, with a very, very few exceptions, has always been the best album that year.

Chapter 19

What if Britain had imposed restrictions on Irish immigration in the 1950s?

From the early 1920s to the end of the twentieth century, roughly one and a half million people emigrated from the 26 counties of independent Ireland, while approximately half a million emigrated from Northern Ireland. It is tempting to assert that this continued exodus of mainly young men and women represented a damning indictment of economic and political failure, but it also served to make life somewhat more comfortable for those left behind, given the huge amounts of money sent home to Ireland by emigrants.

The reasons behind the decision to emigrate could sometimes be more complex than simple economic necessity. What emigration meant for the individual changed over time, and one of the most notable changes witnessed Great Britain replacing North America as the destination of the majority, and affordable air transport revolutionised travel. Some emigrants returned, but many did not. The 1950s are remembered as the decade of the vanishing Irish. Between 1951 and 1961, 500,000 people emigrated from the Republic of Ireland. Nearly 60,000 people left in the year 1957 alone. But what if it had been more difficult to emigrate? What if these thousands of emigrants had stayed in Ireland? How different would Ireland have been?

On a grey summer's morning in July 1954, the writer Anthony Cronin looked out his window and suggested, 'here, if ever was, is

a climate for the death wish'.[1] It was an observation that encap-
sulates the gloom of the decade, and historians were later apt to
mirror such semantics and sentiments—words such as 'doom',
'stagnation', 'crisis' and 'malaise' have frequently been employed to
describe the 1950s. These assessments have been revised in recent
years, notably by Brian Fallon, who disputed the idea of Ireland as
a cultural wasteland and pointed to the artistic vibrancy that was
evident.[2]

It is more difficult to challenge the notion of malaise when it
comes to the issue of emigration. The figures are stark and the
human cost immeasurable. One in three people under the age of
30 in 1946 had left the Republic by 1971. For an issue so pervasive
in Irish society, there was a curious reluctance to talk about it;
indeed, Fr Jerry Kivlehan, of the Camden Irish Centre, maintained
in 2002 that 'Ireland hasn't even begun the debate' in relation to the
subject of emigration.[3] It is also the case that a defensive reaction to
the idea of so many emigrating was to depict them as somewhat
feckless and easily led, which amounted to a tendency to blame the
emigrants themselves rather than the society they had left.

It would certainly be inaccurate to see all emigrants as victims;
Catriona Clear has made the point that women could be making
a very positive choice in deciding to leave. One woman told the
writer Seán O'Faoláin succinctly: 'I saw what my mother went
through—not for me thank you.'[4] Undoubtedly, some Irish
experienced discrimination and racism, but Catherine Dunne,
who wrote about the Irish in London in the 1960s, was also able to
identify a perception that the English were a very tolerant people.
Undoubtedly, the 10 shilling notes the Irish sent home regularly
were crucial; in 1961, they sent home an estimated £13.5 million; in
the same year, the Irish government spent £14 million on primary
and secondary education.[5]

The Irish government had made it clear in the 1950s and 1960s
that it was not going to intervene actively when it came to emigrant welfare. Seán Lemass rejected a plea to fund Irish centres in
Britain in 1965 as this 'would be unsound from the point of view
of state finances and would in practice be incapable of being kept
within fixed limits.'[6] This parsimonious attitude and abdication of

responsibility continued up to recent years; in the midst of the Celtic Tiger boom in 1999, the government was providing just under £1 million in support of emigrant welfare. A task force on policy regarding emigrants, established by the Department of Foreign Affairs, reported in 2002 and made 34 recommendations, including a 300 per cent increase in funding and, most crucially, an agency for the Irish abroad. According to an RTÉ *Prime Time* investigation by historian Paul Rouse in December 2003:

> In fact, immediately after the Task Force reported, Irish government funding for the voluntary organisations working with the marginalized in Britain was cut by 5%. This year the Irish government's contribution to the Dion fund, which has provided funding for voluntary groups working with the elderly and marginalised in Britain, was increased by approximately £3.5 million—far short of the £8 million that the Task Force deemed a basic need.[7]

As the RTÉ *Prime Time* programme also revealed, the conditions in which many emigrants were living were appalling; in 2000, the homeless organisation, Shelter, found that 11 per cent of people sleeping rough on the streets of Greater London were Irish, and highlighted the fact that Irishmen were the only migrant group whose mortality rate is higher in Britain than in their country of origin. The programme gained access to film in Arlington House, a 'wet' hostel in Camden, 'where up to 450 men live—more than a quarter are Irish. Of these, approximately twenty die each year. Once a thriving home to 1,200 men who poured onto the building sites every day, the hostel now houses men suffering from physical and mental illness, depression and chronic alcoholism.'[8]

This programme was an attempt to contribute to the beginning of the debate that Kivlehan identified as absent. The two guests were historian Pauric Travers, who in the past has looked closely at the issue of female emigration from Ireland, and Ultan Cowley, author of *The Men who Built Britain, A History of the Irish Navvy*. The idea for this programme was prompted by reading the tone of panic emanating from the Department of External Affairs and the Department of Industry and Commerce during the Second World War: it was all very well, it seemed, for Irish emigrants to be employed in London or Birmingham, but what if they returned to Ireland at the end of the war? Internal government correspondence referred to 100,000 men 'who no doubt will have imbibed a good deal of "leftism" in Britain, dumped back here', suggesting that their return needed to be 'staggered', so that the Irish government could cope with it 'by degrees'. It was also suggested that 'an efficient central organisation' was needed, to deal with the problem, as 'whatever the danger of social revolution in this country, it is certain to be in its maximum during the last year of the war and during the next year or two after it.'[9]

To open this programme an archival clip of interviews conducted by Paddy O'Gorman with Irish emigrants of the 1950s and 1960s was played, in which men talked about the trip down to the North Wall in Dublin, with their suitcases, in order to take the old cattle boats to England. For those who remained in England, in some cases for over 50 years, there was a feeling, to quote one of them, 'to go back now, you're like a stranger in your own country'. Of course, to paraphrase Christy Moore, they also brought their music to ease their lonely hearts—one song, sung by Tommy Maguire in Manchester, indicated the centrality of alcohol to many of their lives: 'in the pub they drank their sub . . . washed off mud with pints and quarts of beer.'

I questioned Travers about the attitude of the political establishment to these people. Is it fair to say that there was a lack of political and public discourse about emigration in the early years of independence, despite the fact that it was so central to the Irish experience?

> I think that's reasonable, or, if I could amend that slightly and say that the discourse in relation to emigration was encapsulated within the discourse about nationalism generally, and that the dominant interpretation of emigration in the early part of the state was that it was a product of colonisation—it was a product of British misrule—and it's not really until the 1940s and the 1950s, when a crisis engulfs the new Irish state, that people are forced to come to terms with what really is the root of emigration—who is to blame, what needs to be done about it, what can be done about it. There was a very painful re-assessment which takes place in the

late 1940s and in the early 1950s, and I think that results in a completely new appraisal of emigration and its role in Irish life.

Was part of that reassessment the decision to institute the Commission on Emigration, which sat between 1948 and 1954?

Yes, the Commission on Emigration, I think, does form part of a realistic appraisal of what the causes of emigration actually are. Okay, it took six years; it met 115 times—it sounds like a classic tribunal! It didn't produce any miracle cure for emigration; it confirmed that emigration is largely economic but it also arises from an interplay of social, psychological and political decisions. But above all, I think the importance of the Commission is that it represented a significant national debate about emigration and its causes, and I think thereafter the discussion about emigration is much more realistic and much more pragmatic.

The reaction to the report within government circles was relatively muted—was it the case that it let the government off the hook to a certain extent by stressing that it was very much a personal decision to emigrate?

I'm not sure that it did. I think it forced all parties, not just the government, to consider the issue, and of course the government changes repeatedly from 1948 to 1957, and that political instability is a product of the social pressure arising from large-scale emigration, among other things. All the political parties are forced to re-assess some of the sacred cows, and above all to re-assess economic policy in terms of the opening up of the economy, the promotion of foreign investment, and so on. The big change that comes in 1958 with *Economic Development* and subsequently with the *Programmes for Economic Expansion*—those are a product of a very painful experience from 1948 to 1958, during which a half a million people emigrated from the Irish Free State.

An archival clip was played of Noel Hartnett, a member of Clann na Poblachta, in which he excoriated the government regarding emigration. In the election campaign of 1948, Hartnett and others made much of the failures of Fianna Fáil, suggesting, according to this clip, that Fianna Fáil was 'completely indifferent to an evil without parallel in Ireland's long, agonised history. Emigration threatens us with total extinction. To this terrible evil the government remains cold and indifferent.'

I asked Travers to assess the political fall-out and reaction to emigration in this context, in terms of the degree to which it could ever be seen as a party political issue, given that all political parties were obviously 'against' emigration.

> Yes, but the issue in 1948, when Fianna Fáil had been in power for 16 years, was that they were being asked by Clann na Poblachta to account for their stewardship, and then the inter-party government had a go from 1948 to 1951. I'm not sure whether Clann na Poblachta had any miracle cure for emigration. In a sense, what they were doing was facing Fianna Fáil with their original policies. Clann na Poblachta was a revival of the original Sinn Féin agenda rather than a dramatic new recipe for dealing with emigration, but through-out the 1950s there is an intense debate and it results in a reversal of economic policy—a reversal of economic direction. The tragedy it seems to me is that that reversal of direction only comes after 15 years of huge emigration and what you have therefore are a lost generation, the generation that Ultan has written so well about.

If these people had not been able to emigrate, would the government have been forced to come up with new economic policies at an earlier stage, perhaps in the early 1950s?

> I think there would have been that political pressure because the social pressure would have been such. I mean, one would have expected a polarisation, left and right, in the 1950s, if there were large numbers of unemployed people. There is a decline, there is a loss of industrial employment in Ireland in the 1950s and that's what leads to a surge of emigration, so the government would have had to deal with that and it's very hard to see what way they could have responded other than what eventually happens in 1958. The tragedy is, as I say, that most commentators by the early 1950s had come around to the inevitability of a sea-change in Irish economic policy and that is delayed for a full decade and the victims of that delay are the people that Ultan has written eloquently about.

When politicians did decide to speak about the issue, it sometimes backfired, as when Eamon de Valera in 1951 highlighted a report that had been carried out by the Young Christian Workers Association, which referred to the experiences of Irish emigrants in Birmingham. Many of the Irish in Birmingham were furious about the irony of de Valera highlighting poor conditions for the Irish abroad. There were other perceived political gaffes at a later stage, including Brian Lenihan's famous comment in 1987 about the island of Ireland not being big enough—that emigration was inevitable. Was this simply an issue that politicians chose to avoid or were resigned about? Did they feel ultimately helpless?

Travers observed:

> There was a helplessness which comes in the late 1940s and late 1950s. De Valera in 1948 is forced to declare, when he's berated for not doing something about this, 'Well, you can't corral the people in, you can't pass a law that says you can't emigrate', and I think that was an acceptance that there is a helplessness within the existing parameters and what was necessary was a change of economic direction in the 1950s. It reminds me a little of an anecdote about Peadar O'Donnell [veteran republican socialist and writer] who berated de Valera about the half million people who emigrated in this period, and de Valera reputedly said to Peadar O'Donnell, 'But if you had been in power, they would still have had to emigrate'—and Peadar O'Donnell supposedly replied, 'Yes, but it would have been a different half million!'

But whatever about election campaigns, political rhetoric and government-sponsored reports, what of the actual people who emigrated—what was Cowley attempting to document in his own researches?

> My concern has been predominantly the consequences of emigration and particularly the human cost, and that's enormous and almost unquantifiable. An Irish psychiatric nurse working on the condition of the older Irish in Britain today has summed it up by saying, 'We're finding deep wells of sadness in ordinary human lives', and, you know, that's something that people took over with them and have had to live with for maybe half a century as a consequence. It strikes me with reference to what Pauric has said

there, that the realistic assessment of the nature of emigration and an attempt to grasp the causes came very late in the day, the damage having been done, as I would see it, with the enshrinement of the uneconomic small family farm as the central unit of society—you know, the cosy homesteads and the frugal comfort. But even that, which we today would consider in an age when we aspire to sustainability and treading lightly on the earth—noble as it is as an aspiration —was very far from what was being delivered by the Irish state in the early decades following independence. I often wondered about the enormous volume of remittances that came back here—often, I would say, under duress—a kind of emotional blackmail, as in, 'Goodbye Johnny Dear, but send me all you can'. My research came up with a figure of £2.5 billion between 1939 and 1969—in the form of cheques and money-orders—not cash, which couldn't be done.

Was there any official acknowledgment of the scale of this injection into the Irish economy? Travers observed:

It's very interesting that even as early as the late 1920s, the Department of Finance was expressing some concern because emigration seemed to be declining in the late 1920s, and was expressing concern precisely about the emigrant remittances—the hidden earnings that came from remittances. That is one of the 'what ifs'—if emigration had not taken place, one of the ways that the state would have suffered would have been that there would not have been the emigrant remittances, and I think they made not just a personal, but a significant economic, impact in the Irish state from the 1920s onwards.

On that very point, particularly in terms of the climate that existed in Ireland in the 1950s in relation to unemployment, could there potentially have been a socially explosive situation, if there had been restrictions for example on emigration to Britain? It was clear, after all, especially in Dublin, that groups like the Dublin Unemployed Association and the Unemployed Protest Committee were attempting to mobilise people in order to force governments to react. According to Travers,

It depends on the particular context, but certainly in the 1950s, emigration acts as a safety valve and, by definition, if that safety valve isn't open, if people are forced to remain at home and if there are, as there are in the 1950s, rising expectations, people aren't willing to accept the platitudes in relation to frugal sufficiency—if they are looking at economic recovery elsewhere in Europe and worldwide, they are likely to become restless and, as it is, the 1950s is one of the more unstable decades. One of the great features of Ireland in the twentieth century is that it is a relatively stable society. We tend not to think of it that way, but it is a remarkably stable society and the only exceptions to that are brought about, particularly in the 1950s, by the return of large-scale emigration. And, just going back for a second to the remittances, I think there's quite an interesting development in the late 1940s. During the war, emigration is restricted—there's some limited licensed emigration to work in essential war industries in Britain. Towards the end of the war, the Department of Finance again becomes concerned with what happens if these emigrants come back and start looking for jobs.

With left-wing ideas, perhaps?

Well, that was a matter of concern also to a great many churchmen, who were rather worried that if these emigrants who had experience of a rather different kind of society came back with expectations of Ireland in the post-war period, that that was going to pose a very significant challenge, so one of the paradoxes is that what worried a great many Irish policy-makers more than emigration was the prospect that emigrants might return or mightn't leave, and I certainly think that it is one of the great 'what ifs'—if there was no emigration, there certainly would be large-scale instability in Ireland, particularly in the 1950s.

Of course, to earn that amount of money and to send home that amount of money, these navvies that Cowley wrote about were working very hard. How did that impact on their own lives?

They were working very, very long hours in very poor conditions and going without, depriving themselves in many cases, although it has to be said that people's expectations coming from this society were almost incredibly low from, let's say, an English urban proletarian point of view. England in the 1920s and 1930s was very impoverished—the economy was in dire straits—but by the 1950s they were on the up, relative to ourselves, and people would put up

with a great deal, and were encouraged in many cases to do so. One
Irish 'subbie' talked to me about men living in the attics of terraces
of houses in Manchester, knocking through the walls from one end
to the next and poking little holes in the slates to let the smoke out
from cooking on primus stoves and so on—unbelievable conditions.

Were all their experiences negative?

No, I wouldn't say so. I would think in many cases they were young
men freed from the scrutiny of priests and parents and they had
escaped from the monochrome, dull, drab de Valera dispensation
here to unbelievable freedom, not the least aspect of which was just
the sheer handling of cash. It had been the case in rural Ireland
that a young man getting work with the Council would see his
father arrive on a Friday evening to take his wages from the
ganger-man, and he might throw him a shilling!

In terms of their social life and experience, how dominant a role
did alcohol play?

Well, the pub was and is, in the construction industry, the labour
exchange—that's where a man finds out word of work; that's
where the ganger-man takes him on; that's where he buys the
ganger-man pints at the end of the day so that he'll be taken on the
next day—it's what you would call an occupational hazard, apart
from the unattractive accommodation aspects that encouraged
them to remain in the pub with their mates.

A clip from the archives was played, recounting the experiences of
Irish emigrant Joe McGarry, in which he talked very powerfully
and emotionally about the impact of drink. It was recorded by
Cowley in the course of his research and included the observation
that, 'I was very dependent on other people's information, a very
dependent person.' He recalled his feeling one Christmas:

Do I really want to be down this hole on a Christmas evening,
waiting on the whim of some ganger-man to say, 'It's okay, now, it's
Christmas, you can go off' . . . what the fuck am I doing this for?
Because I never felt that I fitted in. I took drink to make me fit in,
to make me feel that I belonged. Who I belonged with was other

Irish people living in the same shit-holes and there was a cama-
raderie of pain there, of knowing another man's pain . . . a recog-
nition of pain amongst us—homeless in a park with a cider bottle.

Cowley had a vivid memory of the circumstances of that recording:

The conditions were difficult. It was in Arlington House in
Camden Town where a lot of older Irish men, many of them
alcoholic, live now, sadly. I think it's perfectly understandable.
Drink numbs the pain, very simply.

Alcohol was only one issue that concerned those attempting to
improve the welfare of Irish emigrants. They were also expressing
reservations about the conditions in which emigrants were living,
especially in the larger cities, and also fearful that the emigrant
experience would give rise to loss of faith, and were particularly
preoccupied with the number of young women who were
arriving. Cowley observed:

The Catholic Church was the only, shall we say, official body,
ironically enough under John Charles McQuaid, who took an
interest in, and acknowledged some responsibility for the plight of,
the Irish in Britain, when the Irish government consistently refused
to do so. The Irish bishops set up the Chaplaincy Scheme which
metamorphosed into the Episcopal Commission for Emigrants,
which is still extant.

On a related subject, I asked Travers about the tendency to depict
emigration as a male phenomenon, particularly with regard to the
male world of the construction labourer and the macho culture of
drinking. But wasn't it the case that, in the immediate post-war
period, there were more Irish women leaving than Irish men?

That's one of the great misconceptions about emigration. It's seen
as a predominantly male experience—the young restless male
seeking fame and fortune or whatever because he had a negative
profile, in Britain or in the United States. In so far as his female
counterpart is considered at all, it's as a secondary mover, somebody who emigrates later to join her sweetheart or her husband or
her parents, whereas in fact one of the remarkable features of Irish

emigration in the twentieth century is that more females than males emigrated, and in six out of ten decades, from 1871 to 1971, the number of female emigrants outweighed the number of male emigrants. I think there's probably a rough and ready parity between male and female if you exclude the inheriting male—in other words, the son who stays at home to inherit the farm—if you exclude that, then you get a parity, but even that is remarkable in European terms. Irish women are unusual in European terms in emigrating in such large numbers, and it's important to realise that they are on average younger than their male counterparts. A great many in the 15 to 20-year-old category, in the earlier part of the period, emigrating to work in domestic service, and then in the post-Second World War period, when domestic service had gone out of fashion, to work in factories, to work as nurses, to work anywhere they can find employment which is not on a small Irish farm in the west of Ireland. There is another factor that bears on the number of Irish women which is that Irish women were less inclined to return. And, notwithstanding the stereotype about the woman who emigrates to earn her dowry and then comes back, Irish men were more likely to return to Ireland than women (though admittedly they return in small numbers), for whatever reason, and I think it does relate to their decision to emigrate—why it is that they decide they're going to leave rural Ireland.

Cowley elaborated on this: 'I think the women are more pragmatic about the realities of their situation and therefore more inclined to make the best of their situation', to which Travers responded, 'That's right and they're also more likely, as you'd expect, to integrate. Irish women are more likely to marry outside the Irish ethnic group than are Irish men.'

When it came to the reaction of the church authorities to this female emigration, is it the case that there was a tendency on the part of some clerics to depict these women as effectively seeking husbands rather than work; the idea that they were dazzled by the bright lights that they saw in the cinema, believing that foreign streets were paved with gold and men?

Travers suggested:

Well, there was certainly a tendency on the part of the church to worry about the implications of their being attracted by the bright lights and they probably overstated that. I certainly agreed with the statement that Ultan made earlier in relation to emigrant welfare. The only organisations that worked on behalf of emigrants in the period we're talking about were established by the churches, and, interestingly, then it was suggested by the Commission on Emigration that if so many people are going to emigrate, then there should be preparation for emigration. People should receive education for emigration. It was too hot a potato—you couldn't admit that you were raising children to emigrate, although the reality for vast numbers—particularly in the period 1946 to 1951—was that that's what they were being raised for—for emigration.

To what extent did Cowley believe anti-Irish prejudice existed in the 1950s and the 1960s in Britain? Has it been exaggerated in the collective folk memory?

Well, the old cliché—'No blacks, no dogs, no Irish'—was not a myth, and I remember seeing those signs myself, even though historians today debate their existence, in shop windows in North London in the early 1960s. It really reflects, I think, in large part, the insularity of the English prior to the new Commonwealth immigration. But then, if you concede that the construction industry is the largest employer of Irish males, you get a con-centration, as you always did, in fact, in these boarding houses, of young Irish males—students today wouldn't be much different. As I said, they were away from home for the first time with money in their pockets, in an industry where drink is endemic, coming home with a fair fill of pints at the end of the night, sometimes sleeping two to a bed—there's going to be a lot of what they know in the industry as 'damping the bed' going on, and how many mattresses can you expect a landlady to replace before she changes her letting policy? In fact, Dónall Mac Amhlaigh describes a very interesting experience where he was put up at short notice in a boarding house in London by a woman who said, 'Go in there and you'll be grand', and he jumps into the bed and finds a Cork man inside it and the two of them were there, naked, in the bed, total strangers, and the Cork man starts giving out the rosary, and Mac Amhlaigh says, 'It's the first time I ever said the rosary naked in a bed with another man!' But they were very moral, all of those Irish of that era and prior to it. That's been remarked on in studies done on

the hydro damns up in Scotland in the 1950s where a young sociolo-
gist went to work in that industry and several others for comparative
purposes, and remarked on the prevalence of holy pictures on the
Irishmen's lockers, and the fact that they would kneel at the side of
their beds and say their prayers before going to bed at night.

In the midst of the economic boom of the late twentieth century,
there were many suggestions that there was an onus on Irish
governments to be more pro-active in facilitating the return home
of those who wished to spend their remaining life in Ireland. Did
Cowley think that there was an onus on a rich society and
government to facilitate that?

> I think there is a moral obligation on the Irish people, never mind
> the government. There is no point in passing the buck to the
> government and saying, 'Let them deal with it'—it's a bit like
> saying, 'Let the police enforce civic order in our housing estate or
> on my road or on my next-door neighbour's children.' The *Task
> Force on Emigration Report* last year was rapidly shelved, but I hope
> it will at some point see the light of day, even if it's only to produce
> the kind of modest assistance that the older Irish in Britain called
> for, which is free travel.

Travers suggested that if many emigrants had not returned home,
the Celtic Tiger might not have been as successful:

> I have no doubt that the Celtic Tiger owes something to the
> expertise of returning emigrants, people who went to Britain, the
> United States and Australia, and then came back and brought their
> expertise with them, and I think that emphasises or underlines the
> extent to which not all emigration is bad. Emigration is a positive
> thing as long as it's not a forced economic emigration, but there
> are benefits. I was tempted, although it may be a little bit flippant,
> to say in relation to 'what ifs', that if there had been no emigration,
> well then John F. Kennedy would have been the President of
> Ireland, while Boy George would have played hurling for
> Tipperary, and, above all, having driven across through Dublin
> traffic, and bearing in mind Ultan's work, we'd have a proper
> underground system because we have developed such expertise
> and skills all over the world in providing underground systems.

Chapter 20

What if Noël Browne had not been involved in Irish politics?

Noël Browne's was a remarkable life, personally and politically, during which he always polarised opinion, frequently enraged, often enthralled and rarely bored.

The impression given by his most recent biographer, John Horgan, is that Browne had an exceptional capacity to alienate, and found great satisfaction 'in identifying and denouncing enemies, even if this obstructed his journey towards a desired objective'. Horgan suggests that this was a reflection of youth, inexperience, and passion, but ultimately innocence of the reality of power politics, following his appointment as Minister for Health, in 1948, on his first day in the Dáil, as a TD for Clann na Poblachta. His failure to introduce the Mother and Child Scheme successfully in 1951 has been well documented: a tale of shifting loyalties, mistaken decisions, powerful friendships and enmities, incompetence in government and the extent to which class snobbery lay at the heart of much of the opposition to health reform and the attempts to introduce a public health scheme to improve the services available to pregnant women and young children.

The opening of the voluminous archives of Archbishop John Charles McQuaid has revealed that Browne gave undertakings to McQuaid that question the credibility of the reasons he gave for his own resignation, and document the contradictions that seemed to permeate Browne. Horgan suggests he was 'dismissive and supine by turns' in his dealings with the hierarchy. The question of Clann na Poblachta's relationship with the Catholic Church had to be seriously revised with the opening of the archive. In the words of John Bowman, his party leader, Seán MacBride, sent extraordinarily 'unctuous and fawning' letters to McQuaid, as well as, in a telegram to the Pope, expressing the party's desire 'to repose at the feet of your holiness'. McQuaid's papers contain an account (and, of course, we must be conscious of how McQuaid wanted the records of these events to damage Browne and enhance his own reputation) of a meeting in which McQuaid notes that Browne 'asked me to believe he wanted to be only a good Catholic and to accept fully church's teaching'. Another bishop, Bishop James Staunton, also recorded Browne's wish to apologise to the hierarchy.[1]

Browne was a man who hated Christmas but shared a domestic bliss with his remarkably loving wife and children, over 29 changes of address; he was an independent crusader who still managed to hold high office in four political parties during 35 years of political activism. He was far-sighted in recognising the value of the media, aided by Aodh de Blacam and Frank Gallagher, perhaps the first of the modern Irish spin-doctors.

Given his political restlessness, it was perhaps just as well that Browne was so adept at public relations skills, particularly given his capacity to bite the hands that nourished him, 'sometimes right up to the elbow'. But how was he able to command the support of such a remarkable range of people, notably of women, even though, according to Labour's David Thornley, he 'has changed his mind so often that he baffles even me who has known him for 25 years'? Baffling perhaps, but also charismatic, commendably anti-materialistic, often genuinely and originally independent, though unfortunately capable of outrageous spleen and personal bitterness. Horgan contends that although Browne could be self-obsessed, his at times considerable power came from his ability 'to project undeniable human needs as a basis for legitimate, positive and creative public emotion'. It was also an ability which underlined the injustices that surrounded him.[2]

Browne's own version of his life, *Against the Tide*, was published in 1986 and was a huge success. The public response to it seemed to confirm that there was a remarkable admiration for him and a sense of empathy with someone perceived as having paid a price for refusing to renege on his principles. The book covered not only his political life, but also the devastating impact that tuberculosis had on his own family. The book also angered many, particularly because of his attacks on former colleagues and his vicious portraits of people like the Wicklow minister, James Everett; the Bishop of Galway, Michael Browne; and Browne's contemporaries, David Thornley and Justin Keating.

In his memoirs published in 2000, former Labour Party Minister Barry Desmond strongly criticised Browne, in a chapter titled 'An Icon Revisited'. His portrait of Browne depicted an embittered man with a persecution complex, who was 'quite incapable of consistent loyalty to the democratically elected executive of any of the parties he joined'; whose economic analysis of capitalism was 'repetitive and ill-defined', and a man who 'craved political love and acclaim'.[3]

Which of these assessments is true? Could Browne have been a more effective politician? What if he had stayed outside politics and stuck with medicine? Or would things have been different if he had stayed with one political party? His career raises many intriguing 'what ifs', some of which were debated by the two guests on this programme—Ruth Barrington, author of *Health, Medicine and Politics in Ireland, 1900–1979*, and David Neligan, a dentist and close political ally of Browne. Neligan was one of the 'Liaison of the Left' group within the Labour Party that left in 1977 with Browne to form the new Socialist Labour Party, having clashed with the party leadership. One thing was abundantly clear from the programme—his loyalists are not for turning, despite any attempt at revising him into anything less than an icon.

This programme opened with an archival clip of the voice of Nuala O'Faolain, who gave her assessment of the importance and the appeal of Noël Browne:

> When I first came across him at the end of the 1950s, he was at the height of his political popularity with the people. There wasn't anywhere in Ireland where he wouldn't have been immediately elected and that was because the people believed that he had

fought back against TB . . . and I don't know how they believed it, before television, that he had done it with a personal passion unknown elsewhere in modern Irish politics. I worked for him in a by-election and he wasn't an organised politician in any way; he didn't have an inner cabinet, he didn't have an organisation—he just had followers, many of them former TB patients. You could say he was a failure as a practical politician and he was—compared to what a lawyer like Mary Robinson, let's say, was able to do for women—he wasn't able to actually deliver much. But there's more to politics than what you actually get out of the system and he was very important in the whole political culture, because for decades he was the only example of a man of emotions, a man that everybody in the whole country believed wasn't in politics for himself, but for the underprivileged. He opposed the macho glad handling, wink, stroke stuff, no matter what party he was in and no matter how ineffectual he was. Everybody knew that, and he was the only politician, of course, ever to have put his skin on the line for women, which he did in the Mother and Child Scheme.

I began by asking Ruth Barrington about the context in which he was appointed Minister for Health, and the debate that surrounded health and welfare reforms and proposals at that stage. She suggested:

It was extraordinary that Noël Browne ever became Minister for Health at all. He was made Minister for Health on his first day in the Dáil and the reason he was in the Dáil was because for the first time ever, health was a major issue in the 1948 election. It seems strange to us now, but during the 1940s, even though the health of the nation by our standards was deplorable, it didn't really impinge on public policy, not until about the middle of the 1940s. But by about 1948, people were really angry about the state of the health services and, in particular, about the neglect of TB—about 4,000 people a year were dying from TB, about twice as many as in other comparable countries, and there just didn't seem to be a political will to do anything about it. What Browne was able to do, as a member of the new party, Clann na Poblachta, was to mobilise public opinion and to make TB an issue in an election, to get elected on that ticket and then, fortuitously, to be made Minister for Health on his first day in the Dáil.

Is it the case that he should be remembered more for the fight against TB than for the Mother and Child Scheme?

Well, I think his great achievement was to mobilise people to fight TB. A lot of policy decisions had actually been taken about how to tackle the epidemic of TB, because that's what it was, and it was fortunate that a lot of the groundwork had been done when he became Minister for Health. But what hadn't been done was to really reach out to people and persuade them that TB was something that could be overcome and treated. I think the parallel today is with South Africa and the status of AIDS, when you see Nelson Mandela coming out and saying publicly that his own son has died from AIDS—to overcome that reluctance to accept the nature of the epidemic. People in Ireland covered it up—they denied it, they didn't want to face it—so what Browne was able to do, having suffered from TB himself, being so articulate, standing on a public platform, putting his neck on the line for TB, he was able to persuade people to come forward and be treated, and the resources were then put into the beds, the surgeons and, of course, fortunately, the drugs were coming on the market to treat TB much more effectively.

I wondered was this the reason why David Neligan had become involved with politics and Noël Browne: that sense of wanting to be associated with someone who was championing the vulnerable?

Well, Noël's greatest association is with TB and I think that's what he should be most remembered for. I think a lot of people think that it is the Mother and Child Scheme he should be remembered for, but they were both pretty fundamental moments in Irish life. The Mother and Child Scheme and his battle with the Catholic Church who thought that giving free medical care to mothers and children was against Catholic teaching, and the mistake they made then—when they won the battle and lost the war so to speak—the mistake they made then has changed the face of Irish politics forever I think. I grew up in comfortable circumstances in Dublin; my own twin sister had TB and I had known of Noël when working in London (I'm a dentist and I was working in the health services in London) and I came back to Ireland in the 1960s and I thought that Noël Browne was the greatest thing since fried bread and I still think it. He did wonders for this country, and the fact that we're here talking 57 years later about what he did or didn't do says it all; I mean, how many people are remembered for 57 years having been three years as a minister?

But what about the issue of Browne as a 'practical politician'? Had he been more practical, or assumed ministerial office when he had more experience, could he have been a more effective politician? Could he have pushed the Mother and Child Scheme through (in the way that Fianna Fáil effectively did in 1953)? Was Nuala O'Faolain correct in her assertion that he wasn't really able to deliver much?

Neligan was utterly dismissive of any such argument:

> I profoundly disagree with Nuala O'Faolain. I think she's a wonderful lady but I think she's wrong. I do not think Noël Browne was a failed politician. I think he achieved more in three years than most politicians can dream about. What he achieved in terms of TB was a sensation; in five years, in Dublin, from 1948 to '53, statistically, there was an 83 per cent drop in the number of children who died from TB in the city—that was a hell of an achievement. He was lucky—there were plans there to build hospitals and so on and there was the Mother and Child Bill proposed by James Ryan [Fianna Fáil's Minister for Health], but the difference between having a bill on paper and pushing it through and getting agreement about it is significantly different. Noël Browne was a man of action, a very practical politician; I've never seen the likes of him.

This was not a view that the doctors seemed to share. An archival clip from 1950 introduced the voice of Browne emphasising the importance of cherishing all Irish children equally, the importance of the family 'and the necessity of preserving that unit unbroken', but also stressing that any reorganisation of the health services 'should not interfere with the existing relationship between the doctor and patient. There will be no compulsion either on the parents or on the members of the medical profession to take part in the scheme. The main difference in this very important doctor–parent relationship will be that many patients will have a wider choice of doctor. The doctor–patient relationship as it exists at present being wholly, completely unaltered.'

There was no mention here, of course, of the church, and indeed, the label 'church–state' clash, to describe what happened in the early 1950s, is in many ways a crude and inaccurate simplification of what occurred. The really difficult nut to crack was to get the approval of the doctors. Was that an impossible task in 1950?

Barrington made the point:

> From the point of view of health policy, I think it's important to remember that the Mother and Child Scheme was one of the steps that had been proposed, initially by the Fianna Fáil government, and then taken up by the inter-party government. It was the first of the steps towards a universal health service on the model of the National Health Service that was being implemented in Britain and Northern Ireland, so it wasn't a stand-alone service, despite how it is depicted in retrospect. In fact, it was part of a much wider ambition to establish a first-class comprehensive health service for the whole population, in which the ability to pay was not the determining factor as to whether you got access to medical care or not, and the medical profession realised this early on and were determined to use whatever means at their disposal to fight this Mother and Child Scheme, not solely on the grounds of the Mother and Child Scheme, but really as the first step in this nationalised health service, or state-run health service, as they would have termed it. In one sense, Browne's lack of political experience or lack of judgement led him to make some very serious errors in trying to build up a coalition of interests that would carry that Mother and Child scheme. It became evident to the medical profession early on that the support at government level for this scheme wasn't particularly strong, and then there were some very clever medical politicians who were able to use some of the arguments of Catholic social policy to persuade the Catholic hierarchy that the Mother and Child Scheme, and then this NHS that was behind it, threatened Catholic moral and social teaching, so the groundwork was laid for a church–state clash.

The different accounts of Browne's relationship with the church and Archbishop McQuaid can be contested; and Browne published his own version of what happened, in his best-selling autobiography, *Against the Tide*, in which he makes no reference

material mentioned in the introduction and uncovered by
...an and others. But surely this sort of material would
prompt some kind of reassessment of Browne's perhaps self-
serving and selective account of the controversies in which he was
involved? Once again, Neligan was not for turning:

> Well, the church, I think, came very badly out of it, though they
> won the battle. McQuaid, who was leading the band for the
> church, and saying it was contrary to Catholic social teaching and
> so on, imposed a form of tyranny on the country, where the
> hierarchy was trying to dictate to an elected government. They
> were entitled to their say, but they were trying to dictate policy to
> an elected government; and this was an almost fascist set-up, in the
> sense that the government meant nothing. The writer Seán
> O'Faolain put it very succinctly in *The Bell*, when he said the
> Browne case showed that there were two parliaments in Ireland—
> one in Maynooth, and one in Dublin. 'Dublin proposes and
> Maynooth disposes' is what he said and then he said, when it comes
> to decision making, 'The Dáil has one right of decision, and that's
> the right to surrender.' That says it all, and I think historically, as
> Tom Garvin has pointed out in his recent book, *Preventing the
> Future*, Noël Browne was a man of vision, but I think historically
> the church came a ferocious cropper, and I think it was in a sense
> very good for the state and good for them too that we moved away
> into an arena where, instead of a lot of airy fairy thinking about
> what sort of a country we should have, we got down to practical
> thinking, and health care and medical care had become an issue
> for the first time. And where are we now, 57 years later? Medical
> care is a major problem and the doctors are at it again—going on
> strike next week because a British insurance company refuses to
> pay for them, and these paragons of the market want the state to
> pick up the tab.[4] So we still need strong leadership in the area of
> health; we need a Noël Browne again to deal with it, I think.

But was it necessary for Browne to be so vitriolic in *Against
the Tide*? Why did he pen such harsh portraits of his former
colleagues and adversaries? According to Neligan:

> They treated him like a dog when he was in there. I think that's
> part of the problem, and he spoke a lot of truth—it's not often you

see in print what does happen at cabinet meetings, because that cabinet, dominated by John A. Costello, the Fine Gael Taoiseach at the time, believed that secrecy was the way government should go, and what Noël Browne did for the first time in Irish politics was to destroy the secrecy when he gave to the *Irish Times* the entire correspondence going on between the Taoiseach and Archbishop McQuaid as to how they should fix up the health services and how they shouldn't fix up the health services, and, in effect, the Catholic hierarchy were trying to dominate government and be the government, and Browne broke this connection and that was a major watershed in Irish politics, and he should be remembered for that alone.

Did Barrington have a view on the importance of Browne's book? Was it a reliable source?

Well, it's a fascinating book; like all autobiographies one has to take it with a grain of salt because people are writing from their own personal perspective and, I suppose, sometimes the truth can be reflected in different ways. But in writing about that 'clash' between church and state over the Mother and Child scheme, my view is that there was a clash coming—you couldn't have had personalities like McQuaid and Browne, the Bishop of Galway, who had very great ambitions for the church in Ireland and really to turn Ireland into a Catholic society—it seems to me that's what they were trying to do—so there was going to be a clash with government over some issue and the circumstances dictated that it would be over health care, but what was different of course, was that if that clash had come with a Fianna Fáil government, and to some extent it did come with a Fianna Fáil government in 1953 over the revised Mother and Child Scheme, it would have been done behind closed doors, and nobody would have claimed victory one way or the other. Interestingly, the Fianna Fáil government never claimed victory over the church in the 1953 Health Acts, which, in fact, went much further than the Mother and Child Scheme, but what Browne did was provoke this by publishing those letters—he really did lay it open to the whole population to see what was going on, and to that extent it is a landmark in the development of politics in Ireland. People, who up to then were very trusting of the church, very trusting of the government in many ways, suddenly saw what was going on, and political life was never the same again after it.

In the course of over 30 years, Browne was a member of not only Clann na Poblachta, but also Fianna Fáil, the National Progressive Democrats and the Labour Party. In an interview with John Bowman, from the archives, he talked about how important it was to be in the Dáil, primarily 'for propagandist reasons' and, at times, educational reasons, and he acknowledged that he was rarely a comfortable colleague, for example, in the Labour Party, adding, 'I don't think anyone could doubt that I've been a socialist all my life'. He maintained that what he and those who worked with him had done was simply to 'take up a socialist position and maintain it', and that as a result he never had disagreements with people he worked with for 30 years—Jack McQuillan, Matt Merrigan and Johnny Byrne, to mention a few. He had joined the Labour Party with McQuillan in 1963, and Merrigan and Byrne were also involved in the 'Liaison of the Left' group within the Labour Party, who broke ranks in 1977. Would Browne have been better off sticking with one party; would he have been more effective? Or was it a case that personal loyalty to him was more important than any party loyalty? Once again, the redoubtable Neligan took umbrage at any suggestion that he should have done things any differently:

Why should he have stuck to one of them? Some of them are the greatest collection of dossers ever to hit this earth! I've been in some of them myself, and I'm not in any of them now, let me hasten to add! Noël Browne was a man of action; he had one messianic view of life which was to help the poor, the old, the sick and the suffering. Medicine is there to alleviate suffering and he believed in it and he wanted to do the job and, if he couldn't get what he wanted in one party, then he went to another party. And so what? The whole business of party politics has shot its bolt in Western Europe; it's in very poor shape—all you have to do is canvass on the doorsteps and hear the response, 'Why should I vote for him? They're all the same!' Even in 1977, when we were more or less forced out of the Labour Party, and I became his director of elections over in Artane, we had an hilarious campaign when hundreds and hundreds of young people turned out, including the young Roddy Doyle and people like that, and he ran in Charlie Haughey's constituency, and he ran Charlie close to the top of the poll, and the Labour Party, who had more or less thrown us out, ended up without a single seat on the northside. From Tallaght all the way to Howth, they were decimated—at that stage, they still hadn't recognised what had happened to them in the 1977 election which was a very important election.

Whatever about the politicians and their view of Browne, how does Barrington feel he is now regarded in the world of medicine —would there still be a lingering resentment?

Certainly they give him enormous credit for the way he mobilised resources and opinion to fight TB—I don't think anybody would have anything but praise for what he did there. Opinion would be divided in relation to his handling of the Mother and Child controversy. In the medical profession, if you believe in private practice, you would feel that it was an important victory that he wasn't able to get his way. If, on the other hand, you believe in a more egalitarian approach to health and improved health care for people, irrespective of their ability to pay, well then there would be people who would feel it was a setback—not irreversible, but it certainly was a setback and definitely has influenced the outcome of current-day health policy. You only have to compare the different approach to health care in the two parts of this island to see the legacy of the battles that were fought in the late 1940s and early 1950s. This passionate commitment that Browne had to improving the lot of the poor—perhaps the other side of that was this difficulty in coping with authority of any sort. I think John Horgan brings it out in his biography—even in his school days. It may be something to do with the really tragic circumstances in which he grew up, but he had great difficulty accepting party discipline or cabinet discipline or the basic rules that go with being a part of a collective that's working together to achieve something, and I think you can see that pattern throughout his life and it's just a pity—he perhaps could have achieved more if his ability to work with people had been a bit more highly developed.

Unsurprisingly, Neligan would not accept that assessment:

I don't accept that. I think he would have been subsumed into the system. I think if he hadn't clashed with Costello as Taoiseach at that time, we'd probably still have secret government going on, and we'd still have the Catholic Church in control. I think it was sad that it happened, and I suppose in some senses it would have helped if he had managed to get something more through, but it went through eventually anyway. But I think his place in history is secure.

And what of the personality of this history-maker? Was he introverted? Was it the case that he really did not like public life?

Well, Noël Browne was very poor on television in a television age and a lot of people may have got the wrong idea from that. He was a highly entertaining and very witty individual. I saw, in a review of John Horgan's book, a headline in one paper that said he was 'a tortured soul'. Noël Browne was not a tortured soul! He was one of the most relaxed people I've ever met; he was a hilarious character. To the day he died, he was interested in politics and interested in change, and helping the poor and the sick, and I think there's a lesson there to be learned by politicians. What he didn't do was promise things he couldn't deliver. He delivered every single thing he promised. He promised 2,000 beds to alleviate TB in 1948, and he delivered them two years later—that was against the whole background of people like de Valera, who promised to end partition and restore the language and made promises he couldn't keep, and James Dillon [Fine Gael Minister for Agriculture in the 1950s] said he was going to throw every rock in Connemara into the sea!

Finally and, again, at a personal level, how could anyone possibly have endured moving house 29 times in one lifetime? Neligan acknowledged:

Yes, it's astonishing, but he was out of a job—when he was dismissed as Minister, he was unemployed for a year, and he had to retrain as a psychiatrist. The medical profession, as it is with a lot of the professions, are pretty vicious when you step outside the pale, and they gutted him for a long time. He got a job eventually in the public service, having retrained as a psychiatrist, and he had very little money for a very long time. Ministers were very poorly paid at that time because it was a part-time job—even to this day there's a bit of a hangover from that in that the hours of the Dáil are based on the idea of turning up in the law library and earning your income down there and then strolling down to the Dáil and getting another job down there as part-time, which is what the John A. Costellos of this world were at—they were immensely rich people dabbling in politics. Noël Browne was a full-time politician and always was and never accepted anything except a salary from the state. He never had a private patient in his life.

Notes

Introduction (PAGES XI–XVI)

1. Niall Ferguson (ed), *Virtual History: Alternatives and Counterfactuals* (London: Picador, 1997).
2. Ibid., pp 2–19.
3. *History Ireland*, Vol. 1, no. 3, winter 1993.
4. Tom Garvin, 'The Rising and Irish Democracy' in Máirín Ní Dhonnchadha and Theo Dorgan (eds), *Revising the Rising* (Derry: Field Day, 1991), pp 21–9.
5. Ferguson, *Virtual History*, p. 227.
6. Margaret MacCurtain, 'Women, the vote and revolution' in Margaret MacCurtain and Donncha Ó Corráin (eds), *Women in Irish Society: The Historical Dimension* (Dublin: Arlen House, 1978), p. 16.
7. *History Ireland*, Vol. 8, no. 1, spring 2000.
8. See below, chapter on the Pro-Life Amendment.

Chapter 1. What if there had been no *Late Late Show*? (PAGES 1–13)

1. *Irish Times*, 1 January 1962.
2. Fergal Tobin, *The Best of Decades: Ireland in the 1960s* (Dublin: Gill & Macmillan, 1984), p. 63.
3. *Gaybo*, a two-part profile of Gay Byrne, broadcast on RTÉ television on 13 and 20 September 2005.
4. Ibid.
5. Colm Tóibín, 'Gay Byrne: Irish Life as Cabaret', *Crane Bag*, Vol. 8, no. 2, 1984, pp 165–70.
6. Ronan Sheehan, 'The Press and the People in Dublin Central', *Crane Bag*, Vol. 8, no. 2, pp 44–51.
7. *Gaybo*, RTÉ, 20 September 2005.
8. Gay Byrne, *To Whom It Concerns: Ten Years of the Late Late Show* (Dublin: Torc Books, 1972), p. 43.
9. *Gaybo*, RTÉ, 20 September 2005.

Chapter 2. What if there had been no pro-life amendment referendum in 1983? (PAGES 14–26)

1. *Irish Times*, 3 September 2003.
2. Thomas Henry Hesketh, *The Second Partitioning of Ireland? The Abortion Referendum of 1983* (Dublin: Brandsma Books, 1990).
3. Nell McCafferty, *The Best of Nell* (Dublin: Attic Press, 1984), pp 58–63.
4. Sandra McAvoy, 'Before Cadden: Abortion in mid-twentieth-century Ireland' in Dermot Keogh, Finbarr O'Shea and Carmel Quinlan (eds), *The Lost Decade:*

Ireland in the 1950s (Cork: Mercier Press, 2004), pp 147–64, and Ray Kavanagh, *Mamie Cadden, Backstreet Abortionist* (Cork: Mercier Press, 2005), pp 87–101.

5. Kavanagh, *Mamie Cadden*, pp 157–200.
6. Jennifer Spreng, *Abortion and Divorce Law in Ireland* (Jefferson, NC: McFarland, 2004). Introduction.
7. Irish Family Planning Association, *The Irish Journey: Women's Stories of Abortion* (Dublin, 2000). Introduction by Medb Ruane.

Chapter 3. What if there had been no *Magill* magazine? (pages 27–39)

1. *Magill*, September 1997, p. 3.
2. John Waters, *Jiving at the Crossroads* (Belfast: Blackstaff, 1991), pp 111–19.
3. *Magill*, September 1997, p. 3.
4. *Village*, 2–7 April 2005, p. 7.
5. Garret FitzGerald, *All in a Life: An Autobiography* (Dublin: Gill & Macmillan, 1991), p. 625.

Chapter 4. What if John Charles McQuaid had not been appointed Archbishop of Dublin in 1940? (pages 40–51)

1. John Banville, 'The Ireland of De Valera and O'Faolain', *Irish Review*, nos. 17–18, winter 1995, pp 142–53.
2. Deirdre McMahon, 'John Charles McQuaid: Archbishop of Dublin, 1940–1972' in James Kelly and Daire Keogh (eds), *History of the Catholic Diocese of Dublin* (Dublin: Four Courts Press, 2000), pp 331–44.
3. Ibid.
4. Dermot Keogh, *Ireland and the Vatican: The Diplomacy of Church–State Relations 1922–60* (Cork: Cork University Press, 1995), pp 145–6.
5. McMahon, *John Charles McQuaid*.

Chapter 5. What if Ben Dunne had not gone on a golfing trip to Florida in 1992? (PAGES 52–64)

1. Fintan O'Toole, *The Irish Times Book of the Century* (Dublin: Gill & Macmillan, 2000), p. 313.
2. *Magill*, September 1997, p. 29.
3. *Irish Times*, 25 July 1998.
4. Dick Walsh's weekly politics column, *Irish Times*, 13 February 1999 and 6 March 1999.
5. Eunan O'Halpin, '"Ah, they've given us a good bit of stuff": Tribunals and Irish political life at the turn of the century' in *Irish Political Studies*, no. 15, 2000, pp 183–92.
6. Joe Lee, *Ireland 1912–85: Politics and Society* (Cambridge: Cambridge University Press, 1989), p. 297.
7. Quoted in O'Halpin, 'Tribunals and Irish political life'.
8. Paul Cullen, *With a Little Help from My Friends: Planning Corruption in Ireland* (Dublin: Gill & Macmillan, 2002), p. 81.

Chapter 6. What if Bishop Eamon Casey's secret had not been discovered?
(PAGES 65–75)

1. Louise Fuller, *Irish Catholicism since 1950: The Undoing of a Culture* (Dublin: Gill & Macmillan, 2003), pp 251–3.
2. Bernard J. Canning, *Bishops of Ireland 1870–1987* (Donegal: Donegal Democrat, 1987), pp 270–71.
3. See chapter on emigration.
4. Canning, *Bishops of Ireland*, p. 354.
5. Ibid.
6. Annie Murphy with Peter de Rosa, *Forbidden Fruit: The True Story of My Secret Love Affair with Ireland's Most Powerful Bishop* (London: Little Brown & Company, 1993), p. 46.
7. See chapter on the *Late Late Show*.

Chapter 7. What if there had been no 1916 Rising? (PAGES 76–89)

1. *Studia Hibernica*, no. 7, 1967, pp 105–7, and Diarmaid Ferriter, 'The Bureau of Military History', *Dublin Review*, no. 5, winter 2001–2, pp 5–15.
2. Annie Ryan, *Witnesses: Inside the Easter Rising* (Dublin: Liberties Press, 2005), pp 23–9.
3. Ibid., pp 104–13.
4. Ibid.
5. Joe Lee, *The Modernisation of Irish Society 1848–1918* (Dublin: Gill & Macmillan, 1973), pp 155–6.
6. Charles Townshend, *Easter 1916: The Irish Rebellion* (London: Penguin, 2005), p. 400.
7. Ibid, p. 19.

Chapter 8. What if the Treaty ports had not been returned in 1938? (PAGES 90–103)

1. See chapter on the Blueshirts.
2. Maurice Moynihan, *Statements and Speeches of Eamon de Valera, 1917–1973* (Dublin: Gill & Macmillan, 1980), p. 416.
3. Michael Kennedy (ed), *Documents on Irish Foreign Policy: Volume IV, 1932–1936* (Dublin: Royal Irish Academy, 2004), and *Sunday Independent*, 7 November 2004.
4. Kennedy (ed), *Documents*, p. 126 ff.
5. Eunan O'Halpin (ed), *MI5 and Ireland, 1939–45: The Official History* (Dublin: Irish Academic Press, 2003), p. xiii.
6. Joe Lee, 'Imagine if Winston Churchill had invaded', *Sunday Tribune*, 10 December 2000.

Chapter 9. What if the Blueshirts had attempted a coup in 1933? (PAGES 104–116)

1. Dermot Keogh, *Twentieth-Century Ireland: Nation and State* (Dublin: Gill & Macmillan, 1994), p. 82.
2. Mike Cronin, *The Blueshirts and Irish Politics* (Dublin: Four Courts Press, 1997), pp 193–9.

3. Ibid, p. 135 ff.
4. Fearghal McGarry, *Eoin O'Duffy, A Self-Made Hero* (Oxford: Oxford University Press, 2005).

Chapter 10. What if de Valera had stood down as leader of Fianna Fáil in 1948 instead of 1959? (PAGES 117–130)

1. Gabriel Byrne, *Pictures in My Head* (Dublin: Wolfhound Press, 1994), p. 40.
2. Fintan O'Toole, *The Irish Times Book of the Century* (Dublin: Gill & Macmillan, 2000), p. 205.
3. Tim Pat Coogan, *Eamon de Valera: Long Fellow, Long Shadow* (London: Hutchinson, 1993), p. 630.
4. J. R. Hill (ed), *A New History of Ireland VII: Ireland 1921–84* (Oxford: Oxford University Press, 2003), p. 294 ff.
5. Tom Garvin, *Preventing the Future: Why was Ireland so poor for so long?* (Dublin: Gill & Macmillan, 2004), p. 169.

Chapter 11. What if Donogh O'Malley had not introduced free secondary education in 1967? (PAGES 131–143)

1. National Archives of Ireland, Department of the Taoiseach, 96/6/356, 'Education: Developments, 1966–67'.
2. John Horgan, *Seán Lemass: The Enigmatic Patriot* (Dublin: Gill & Macmillan, 1997), pp 298–9.
3. J. R. Hill (ed), *A New History of Ireland VII: Ireland 1921–84* (Oxford: Oxford University Press, 2003), p. 732.
4. *Irish Times*, 18 December 2004.
5. An Irishman's Diary, *Irish Times*, 26 September 2005.
6. Seán O'Connor, *A Troubled Sky: Reflections on the Irish Education Scene 1957–1968* (Dublin: Educational Research Centre, 1986).
7. NAI, DT 96/6/356 'Education: Developments, 1966–67', 14 September 1966.

Chapter 12. What if the *Irish Press* had not closed down in 1995? (PAGES 144–158)

1. Ray Burke, *Press Delete: The Decline and Fall of the Irish Press* (Dublin: Currach Press, 2005).
2. J. R. Hill (ed), *A New History of Ireland VII: Ireland 1921–84* (Oxford: Oxford University Press, 2003), p. 682.
3. Mark O'Brien, *De Valera, Fianna Fáil and the Irish Press: The Truth in the News* (Dublin: Irish Academic Press, 2003), p. 85.
4. Noël Browne, *Against the Tide* (Dublin: Gill & Macmillan, 1986), p. 234.
5. O'Brien, *De Valera*, pp 102–12.
6. Weekend Review, *Irish Times*, 4 June 2005.

Chapter 13. What if James Joyce and Samuel Beckett had stayed in Ireland? (PAGES 159–172)

1. Brian Fallon, *An Age of Innocence: Irish Culture 1930–1960* (Dublin: Gill & Macmillan, 1998), pp 59–60.

2. Declan Kiberd, *Inventing Ireland: The Literature of the Modern Nation* (London: Jonathan Cape, 1995), p. 533 ff.
3. See James Knowlson and John Haynes, *Images of Beckett* (Cambridge: Cambridge University Press, 2003) and James Knowlson, *Damned to Fame* (London: Bloomsbury, 1996).

Chapter 14. What if Frank Duff had not established the Legion of Mary in 1921? (PAGES 173–185)

1. Finola Kennedy, *John Henry Newman and Frank Duff* (Dublin: Praedicanda, 1982). See also León Ó Broin, *Frank Duff* (Dublin: Gill & Macmillan, 1982).
2. In a letter to the author, 20 January 2004.
3. Peter Somerville Large, *Irish Voices: 50 Years of Irish Life, 1916–1966* (London: Chatto & Windus, 1999), p. 259. See also John Cooney, *John Charles McQuaid: Ruler of Catholic Ireland* (Dublin: O'Brien Press, 1999).
4. Eamon Dunn, 'Action and Reaction: Catholic Lay Organisations in Dublin in the 1920s and 1930s' in *Archivium Hibernicum*, Vol. XLVIII, 1994, pp 107–18.
5. Diarmaid Ferriter, *The Transformation of Ireland* (London: Profile Books, 2004), p. 397.

Chapter 15. What if the Jim Duffy tape had not been released during the 1990 presidential election? (PAGES 186–199)

1. John M. Kelly, *The Irish Constitution* (2nd edition, Dublin: Jurist, 1984), pp 53–69.
2. *Magill*, June 1983.
3. John Waters, *Jiving at the Crossroads* (Belfast: Blackstaff, 1991), pp 1–21.
4. Emily O'Reilly, *Candidate: The Truth Behind the Presidential Campaign* (Dublin: Attic Press, 1991), p. 125.
5. *Magill*, September 1997, p. 11.

Chapter 16. What if Proportional Representation had been abolished in 1959 or 1968? (PAGES 200–211)

1. Tom Garvin, *Preventing the Future: Why was Ireland so poor for so long?* (Dublin: Gill & Macmillan, 2004), pp 22–3 and pp 82–3.
2. J. R. Hill (ed), *A New History of Ireland VII: Ireland 1921–84* (Oxford: Oxford University Press, 2003), pp 302–3.
3. Joe Lee, *Ireland 1912–85: Politics and Society* (Cambridge: Cambridge University Press, 1989), pp 84–8.
4. Garret FitzGerald, *All in a Life: An Autobiography* (Dublin: Gill & Macmillan, 1991), pp 78–9.
5. Barry Desmond, *Finally and in Conclusion* (Dublin: New Island Books, 2000), pp 170–71.

Chapter 17. What if T. K. Whitaker had not been appointed Secretary of the Department of Finance in 1956? (PAGES 212–225)

1. Ronan Fanning, *The Irish Department of Finance* (Dublin: Institute of Public Administration, 1978), p. 504.
2. Ibid., p. 509.

3. National Archives of Ireland, Department of the Taoiseach, S16066A, 12 December 1957.
4. Joe Lee, *Ireland 1912–85: Politics and Society* (Cambridge: Cambridge University Press, 1989), p. 359 ff.
5. John Horgan, *Seán Lemass: The Enigmatic Patriot* (Dublin: Gill & Macmillan, 1997), p. 175 ff.

Chapter 18. What if the members of U2 had gone to different schools in the 1970s? (PAGES 226–238)

1. *Magill*, December 2004/January 2005, p. 44.
2. Eamon Dunphy, *Unforgettable Fire: The Story of U2* (London: Viking, 1987), p. viii.
3. *In Dublin*, 15 May 1986.
4. *Sunday Times*, 7 November 2004.

Chapter 19. What if Britain had imposed restrictions on Irish immigration in the 1950s? (PAGES 239–252)

1. Anthony Cronin, 'This Time, This Place', *The Bell*, Vol. xix, no. 8, July 1954, pp 5–7.
2. Brian Fallon, *An Age of Innocence: Irish Culture 1930–1960* (Dublin: Gill & Macmillan, 1998).
3. *Prime Time Investigates: Ireland's Forgotten Generation*, press release, December 2003.
4. Catriona Clear, 'Too Fond of Going: Female Emigration and Change for Women in Ireland, 1946–1961' in Dermot Keogh, Finbarr O'Shea and Carmel Quinlan (eds), *The Lost Decade: Ireland in the 1950s* (Cork: Mercier Press, 2004), pp 135–47.
5. Catherine Dunne, *Unconsidered People: The Irish in London* (Dublin: New Island Books, 2003).
6. Enda Delaney, *Demography, State and Society: Irish Migration to Britain, 1921–1971* (Liverpool: Liverpool University Press, 2000), p. 259.
7. *Prime Time Investigates: Ireland's Forgotten Generation*, press release, December 2003.
8. Ibid. and *Irish Times*, 22 April 2003.
9. National Archives of Ireland, Department of Taoiseach, S 11582A 'Irish Labour Emigration', 18 May 1942.

Chapter 20. What if Noël Browne had not been involved in Irish politics? (PAGES 253–265)

1. John Bowman, 'At the disposal of the Archbishop', *Irish Times*, 6 November 1999 and 13 November 1999.
2. John Horgan, *Noël Browne: Passionate Outsider* (Dublin: Gill & Macmillan, 2000), pp 292–5.
3. Barry Desmond, *Finally and in Conclusion* (Dublin: New Island Books, 2000), pp 114–35.

4. In March 2005, hospital consultants were threatening to strike when the British-based Medical Defence Union ceased to continue their cover; the consultants claimed that the Irish Department of Health was placing the profession in financial jeopardy over disagreements about medical indemnity.

Bibliography

Primary Sources
National Archives of Ireland: Files of the Department of the Taoiseach (DT)
RTÉ Radio and Television Archives

Newspapers, magazines and periodicals
Archivium Hibernicum
The Bell
Crane Bag
Dublin Review
History Ireland
Irish Political Studies
Irish Review
Irish Times
Magill
Studia Hibernica
Sunday Independent
Sunday Times
Sunday Tribune
Village

Books
— Browne, Noël, *Against the Tide* (Dublin: Gill & Macmillan, 1986).
— Burke, Ray, *Press Delete: The Decline and Fall of the Irish Press* (Dublin: Currach Press, 2005).
— Byrne, Gabriel, *Pictures in My Head* (Dublin: Wolfhound Press, 1994).
— Byrne, Gay, *To Whom It Concerns: Ten Years of the Late Late Show* (Dublin: Torc Books, 1972).
— Canning, Bernard J., *Bishops of Ireland 1870–1987* (Donegal: Donegal Democrat, 1987).
— Coogan, Tim Pat, *Eamon de Valera: Long Fellow, Long Shadow* (London: Hutchinson, 1993).
— Cooney, John, *John Charles McQuaid: Ruler of Catholic Ireland* (Dublin: O'Brien Press, 1999).
— Cronin, Mike, *The Blueshirts and Irish Politics* (Dublin: Four Courts Press, 1997).
— Cullen, Paul, *With a Little Help from My Friends: Planning Corruption in Ireland* (Dublin: Gill & Macmillan, 2002).
— Delaney, Enda, *Demography, State and Society: Irish Migration to Britain, 1921–1971* (Liverpool: Liverpool University Press, 2000).

— Desmond, Barry, *Finally and in Conclusion* (Dublin: New Island Books, 2000).

— Dunne, Catherine, *Unconsidered People: The Irish in London* (Dublin: New Island Books, 2003).

— Dunphy, Eamon, *Unforgettable Fire: The Story of U2* (London: Viking, 1987).

— Fallon, Brian, *An Age of Innocence: Irish Culture 1930–1960* (Dublin: Gill & Macmillan, 1998).

— Fanning, Ronan, *The Irish Department of Finance* (Dublin: Institute of Public Administration, 1978).

— Ferguson, Niall (ed), *Virtual History: Alternatives and Counterfactuals* (London: Picador, 1997).

— Ferriter, Diarmaid, *The Transformation of Ireland* (London: Profile Books, 2004).

— FitzGerald, Garret, *All in a Life: An Autobiography* (Dublin: Gill & Macmillan, 1991).

— Fuller, Louise, *Irish Catholicism since 1950: The Undoing of a Culture* (Dublin: Gill & Macmillan, 2003).

— Garvin, Tom, *Preventing the Future: Why was Ireland so poor for so long?* (Dublin: Gill & Macmillan, 2004).

— Hanley, Brian, *The IRA 1926–36* (Dublin: Four Courts Press, 2002).

— Hesketh, Thomas Henry, *The Second Partitioning of Ireland? The Abortion Referendum of 1983* (Dublin: Brandsma Books, 1990).

— Hill, J. R., (ed), *A New History of Ireland VII: Ireland 1921–84* (Oxford: Oxford University Press, 2003).

— Horgan, John, *Noël Browne: Passionate Outsider* (Dublin: Gill & Macmillan, 2000).

— Horgan, John, *Seán Lemass: The Enigmatic Patriot* (Dublin: Gill & Macmillan, 1997).

— Irish Family Planning Association, *The Irish Journey: Women's Stories of Abortion* (Dublin, 2000).

— Kavanagh, Ray, *Mamie Cadden, Backstreet Abortionist* (Cork: Mercier Press, 2005).

— Kelly, James and Keogh, Daire (eds), *History of the Catholic Diocese of Dublin* (Dublin: Four Courts Press, 2000).

— Kelly, John M., *The Irish Constitution* (2nd edition, Dublin: Jurist, 1984).

— Kennedy, Finola, *John Henry Newman and Frank Duff* (Dublin: Praedicanda, 1982).

— Kennedy, Michael (ed), *Documents on Irish Foreign Policy: Volume IV, 1932–1936* (Dublin: Royal Irish Academy, 2004).

— Keogh, Dermot, *Ireland and the Vatican: The Diplomacy of Church–State Relations 1922–60* (Cork: Cork University Press, 1995).

— Keogh, Dermot, *Twentieth-Century Ireland: Nation and State* (Dublin: Gill & Macmillan, 1994).

— Keogh, Dermot, O'Shea, Finbarr, and Quinlan, Carmel (eds), *The Lost Decade: Ireland in the 1950s* (Cork: Mercier Press, 2004).

— Kiberd, Declan, *Inventing Ireland: The Literature of the Modern Nation* (London: Jonathan Cape, 1995).

— Knowlson, James, *Damned to Fame* (London: Bloomsbury, 1996).

— Knowlson, James and Haynes, John, *Images of Beckett* (Cambridge: Cambridge University Press, 2003).

— Lee, Joe, *Ireland 1912–85: Politics and Society* (Cambridge: Cambridge University Press, 1989).

— Lee, Joe, *The Modernisation of Irish Society 1848–1918* (Dublin: Gill & Macmillan, 1973).

— McCafferty, Nell, *The Best of Nell* (Dublin: Attic Press, 1984).

— MacCurtain, Margaret and Ó Corráin, Donncha (eds), *Women in Irish Society: The Historical Dimension* (Dublin: Arlen House, 1978).

— McGarry, Fearghal, *Eoin O'Duffy, A Self-Made Hero* (Oxford: Oxford University Press, 2005).

— Manning, Maurice, *The Blueshirts* (2nd edition, Dublin: Gill & Macmillan, 1987).

— Moynihan, Maurice, *Statements and Speeches of Eamon de Valera, 1917–1973* (Dublin: Gill & Macmillan, 1980).

— Murphy, Annie with de Rosa, Peter, *Forbidden Fruit: The True Story of My Secret Love Affair with Ireland's Most Powerful Bishop* (London: Little Brown & Company, 1993).

— Ní Dhonnchadha, Máirín and Dorgan, Theo (eds), *Revising the Rising* (Derry: Field Day, 1991).

— O'Brien, Mark, *De Valera, Fianna Fáil and the Irish Press: The Truth in the News* (Dublin: Irish Academic Press, 2003).

— Ó Broin, León, *Frank Duff* (Dublin: Gill & Macmillan, 1982).

— O'Connor, Seán, *A Troubled Sky: Reflections on the Irish Education Scene 1957–1968* (Dublin: Educational Research Centre, 1986).

— O'Halpin, Eunan (ed), *MI5 and Ireland, 1939–45: The Official History* (Dublin: Irish Academic Press, 2003).

— O'Reilly, Emily, *Candidate: The Truth Behind the Presidential Campaign* (Dublin: Attic Press, 1991).

— O'Toole, Fintan, *The Irish Times Book of the Century* (Dublin: Gill & Macmillan, 2000).

— Ryan, Annie, *Witnesses: Inside the Easter Rising* (Dublin: Liberties Press, 2005).

— Smyth, Sam, *Thanks a Million Big Fella* (Dublin: Blackwater, 1997).

— Somerville Large, Peter, *Irish Voices: 50 Years of Irish Life, 1916–1966* (London: Chatto & Windus, 1999).

— Spreng, Jennifer, *Abortion and Divorce Law in Ireland* (Jefferson, NC: McFarland, 2004).

— Tobin, Fergal, *The Best of Decades: Ireland in the 1960s* (Dublin: Gill & Macmillan, 1984).

— Townshend, Charles, *Easter 1916: The Irish Rebellion* (London: Penguin, 2005).

— Waters, John, *Jiving at the Crossroads* (Belfast: Blackstaff, 1991).

Index